W9-BEF-871

BICYCLE!

A Repair & Maintenance

MANIFESTO

2nd Edition

Sam Tracy

Bicycle! A Repair & Maintenance Manifesto, 2nd Edition
by Sam Tracy © 2013 Sam Tracy

This edition copyright © 2013 PM Press All Rights Reserved

ISBN: 978-1-60486-640-7
LCCN: 2012913627

Cover by Peter Davidson
Layout by Jonathan Rowland

PM Press
PO Box 23912
Oakland, CA 94623
www.pmpress.org

10 9 8 7 6 5 4 3 2 1

Printed on recycled paper by the Employee Owners of Thomson-Shore in Dexter, Michigan.
www.thomsonshore.com

CONTENTS

Introduction   1

I. **Tools**   3

II. **Frames**   17
  A. Frame Damage   19
  B. Creaks   21
  C. Forks   23

III. **Headsets**   27
  A. Threaded   28
  B. Threadless   30
  C. Overhauls   32

IV. **Stems**   37
  A. Quill   39
  B. Threadless   40
  C. Adjustable   41

V. **Wheels**   43
  A. Tubes   43
  B. Rim Strips   45
  C. Tube Sealants   46
  D. Tires   47
  E. Truing Wheels   48

VI. **Seats and Posts**   57

VII. **Handlebars**   63
  A. Mountain   64
  B. Road   67

VIII. **Control Cables**   71

IX. **Brakes**   83
  A. Sidepulls   87
  B. Centerpulls   90
  C. Cantilevers   92
  D. Linear Pull   97
  E. Disc   101

    F.   Leverage   103
    G.   Hydraulic   105

X.   **Drivetrains**   109
    A.   Friction   110
    B.   Indexing   115
        1.   Rear Derailleurs   116
        2.   Front Derailleurs   118
        3.   Cable Adjustments   122
    C.   Shift Levers   123
    D.   Planetary Gearing   131
    E.   Chains   134
    F.   Pedals   142
    G.   Cranks   148
    H.   Bottom Brackets   157
        1.   One-Piece   158
        2.   Sealed-Cartridge   158
        3.   Three-Piece   162

XI.   **Hubs**   165
    A.   Freewheel   167
    B.   Cassette   169
    C.   Overhauls   171

XII.   **Boxing Bikes**   175

XIII.   **Winter Riding**   179

XIV.   **On-the-Road Repairs**   185

XV.   **Scavenging, Rust, and Security**   193

XVI.   **Building Your Own Wheels**   203

XVII.   **Singlespeeds**   219

XVIII. **Recumbents**   223

XIX.   **Fixed Gears**   231

        Resources   241

        Index   243

Acknowledgments

I would first like to thank Seng Chen, Peter Davidson, Sara Lindstrom, Dan Osterud, Joey Paxman, Kerri Spindler-Ranta, and Nancy Tracy for providing the graphic balance this book relies upon. I would also like to thank the good folks at the Hub in Minneapolis for the chance to catch up on things, and everyone at PM Press for the opportunity to put it to words. Finally, the success of this book owes much to Mohamed O. Hmeida, Mohamed O. Amar, Ramatas, Hawa Diaz, Dahane, Ahmed O. Jiyid, and of course my lovely wife Kerri.

Go: get on your bike, slip out into the yawning morning traffic, find your groove, and get there. It's the start of a new day for so many of us, all around the world—in forward-thinking cities like Amsterdam, bicycles already account for 35 percent of all trips taken. In Groningen, a Swedish city of 180,000, it's 60 percent. The vitality that comes with riding intoxicates— as the Dutch NGO Interface for Cycling Expertise puts it, "Cycling in reality may be less difficult, less dangerous, faster and more practical than many people suspect." Even in China, nascent star-child for the automotive industry, cyclists still outnumber drivers by more than fifty to one.

Even the most casual glance confirms that distinct bikes are lately available to suit just about any useful ambition, at points all up and down the quality spectrum, but in the end we ride what we have, and that fairly describes the scope of this book. Whatever you paid for your bike, however cool it happens to look, it will eventually need some work. The trials of our passage can cost more than we might like to think, in terms of wear and tear, and one day the bill will surely come due. That day need not overwhelm! Bike repair begins with at least two advantages: an injured bicycle is a hell of a lot cheaper to fix than certain other forms of transportation, and the mechanical principles in play are also much more accessible—no gas, no explosions. Given some insight and a few tools, the odds are good you can do it yourself.

The original *Manifesto* came together in 2005, when I worked as a mechanic at a high-end bike shop in San Francisco. This new edition began in the Islamic Republic of Mauritania, where my wife Kerri and I served as Peace Corps Volunteers. As might be imagined, the distance between the two places left an impression. There was no carbon fiber to be seen over there, let alone titanium; just plenty of chromed steel rims and old cottered cranks. Those dusty old garage relics, donated to groups like Re-Cycle or Bikes Not Bombs? From all we saw, people end up making very good use of them.

Our spotty internet made it possible to follow technical developments in the cycling world—as a longtime mechanic,

Introduction

it might be more correct to say that these were difficult to ignore. Yet, from such a vantage, the latest and greatest also became less relevant. Bikes in the RIM (République Islamique de Mauritanie) are taken for their last possible miles, literally ridden to ground, drawing the focus back to the opposite end of the spectrum. This edition will duly consider the new math, in all its ultra-light glory, but my heart remains with the older and more proven technology, much of which is still in use all around the world. Ultimately I am most interested in making the most of what is available, whatever that happens to be, with the goal of providing the fundamentals for as many cyclists as possible.

There is nothing sacrosanct about fixing bikes. More so than anywhere else I've lived, life in the RIM confirms that "mechanical aptitude" is merely a distinct pursuit, not unlike any other. Circumstance might lead any of us to have more or less exposure to mechanical concepts and applications, and with this the opportunity to develop fluency, but really that's about it. Success with bike repair follows from experience more than anything else, which to a significant extent grounds it squarely in the public domain.

The soundtrack to the second edition includes Seun Kuti, Faith & the Muse, Off!, Yo Majesty, Awesome Snakes, Black Angels, Cheater Slicks, Brunt of It, Best Friends Forever, Career Suicide, Frontside Five, Agent Orange, Cut Chemist, Fleet Foxes, Rudimentary Peni, Sisters of Mercy, Joy Division, New Order, Flux of Pink Indians, Bats in the Belfry and Radio Ninja on WMBR, MKEPunk.com, KUSF In Exile, Dark Dark Dark, and the muezzin.

Like other trades, bicycle repair is in most respects a specialty. Some of the skills and tools acquired elsewhere in life may become useful, as we'll see, and others will not. The use of force necessarily becomes much more judicious, to take one example—a fairly obvious point, given the scale of many of the parts involved. Our accelerating tendency to rush is best left at the day job, as well: it is possible to wreck just about anything, done fast enough.

In the ideal, it's best to have one place in particular to fix those bikes in your care—somewhere dry, well-lit, and reasonably calm, if you're especially lucky. A truly exceptional workshop will feature a sturdy bench or table as well, mounted with a vise. There will of course come times when we don't have any of these things—a topic further explored in *Roadside Bicycle Repair: A Pocket Manifesto*—but given the luxury of planning, it is well worth the time to set things up right in the first place.

The **BICYCLE REPAIR STAND** is very useful to the craft, though it is not strictly necessary. The improved vantage stands provide makes it much easier to see and interact with a bike's nether regions; over the course of a tune-up this makes for a lot less squatting, bending over, and peering beneath. The stands also accomplish the useful trick of removing the wheels from the ground, which greatly simplifies our work on the brakes and the drivetrain.

A number of companies produce bike repair stands. Those made by Park Tool of St. Paul, MN, as used in most North American bike shops, are perhaps the most visible examples. I have plenty of experience with Park's heavy-duty shop stands, but I rely upon one of their lighter consumer models at home, and things work out fine there as well. The central distinction across their range of stands is in the clamp—basic models employ simple spring-mounted jaws; better ones incorporate adjustable clamps. This detail becomes important with lightweight aluminum and carbon fiber frames, the tubes of which may respond poorly to excesses of compression. In truth, we're really not supposed to be clamping anything around any of that at all—much as cats instinctively carry their young by the scruff of the

I. Tools

neck, bike repair stands should strive to clamp the bikes by their seatposts. (Carbon fiber seatposts, available in only a few common sizes, can be temporarily replaced with dummy posts of the same dimensions.)

You may need to raise the post a bit more out of its frame, in order to successfully clamp it. Before doing so, mark its original position with a ring of electrical tape. And if there really is no alternative—as with some of the recumbents, which trade our bar stools for lounge chairs—slip a rag beneath the clamp's jaws, before biting down. Note that stickers and frame decals fare poorly under such pressure. so clamp elsewhere if possible.

This is all a little simpler if you're not working on anything too fancy—a sturdy

EZ Grip ratcheting clamp.

old steel frame, perhaps, without much paint left to worry about. If the situation does appear negotiable, go ahead and clamp down on the frame's seat tube, just beneath its top tube. Clamping in such a position makes it easier to move the bike around as needed.

Park repair stands, among others, feature detachable clamps for distinct purposes. Park's 100-4X Extreme Range Clamp is wide enough to grasp many of the fat-tubed recumbent frames, but some short wheelbase 'bents such as the Bacchetta will respond better to one of the traditional Park clamp jaws, wrapped tightly around the neutral side chainstay. Moreover, this very same feature allows us to clamp on to the bike first, before lifting the whole package up into the stand—a very useful option to have with some of the tandems and trikes.

Got any old toe straps kicking around? Wrap one of the straps around the stand's base. We'll occasionally need to keep a bike's fork from dropping out of its frame, as when replacing threadless stems, and the toe straps are ideal for such purposes.

Absent the stand, you might want to set up a **BIKE SLING**: two lengths of rope, strung down from above about two meters apart, long enough to suspend a bike's saddle and stem at useful elevations. I found myself setting up one of these upon arriving to our new home in Atar, Mauritania, and all things considered it proved useful enough. It is only with some of the more

Bike sling in action.

torque-intensive tasks—tightening pedals, cranks, or bottom bracket cups—that I need to pull an old-fashioned, flipping the bike upside down to rest upon its seat and handlebars.

WHEEL TRUING STANDS are also key. Here again, my own experience favors those produced by Park Tool. Their TS-2 shop version is pretty much the only one you'll see in U.S. bike shops, and it's all you'd ever need. I haven't yet played with their less expensive TS-8, but the design looks promising in that it appears sturdy. It wouldn't operate quite as fluidly as the business version. Nor would its stout construction allow the wheel to flex around, and this is the critical point—the better your wheel is able to sit still, the easier it is to true the thing. Avoid any "truing stands" with plastic arms. It's also a good idea to bolt your stand to something solid—the bench, for example. (You may secure it in a vise, alternately.)

With regards to hand tools, the choice of what you'll need depends a lot on what

you find yourself riding. It'd be good to start out with quality screwdrivers and metric box wrenches, regardless. It is also likely that you'll find use for a hammer, metal and woodworking files, box and needle-nose pliers, and a magnet. Beyond that, it is more a function of your bike's vintage than its brand. Cannondale is pretty famous for doing their own thing, and some of the recumbent manufacturers necessarily have been as well, but to a large extent at least everyone start out contemplating the same pools of technology, which grow a bit deeper with the passage of time. Darker and cloudier as well, one might argue. Your favorite local bike shop should be able to provide any bike tools you might need.

Pliers useful with bike repair.

Pick up some metric **ALLEN WRENCHES**, if you haven't already. The standard metric set includes 1.5, 2, 2.5, 3, 4, 6, 8, and 10 mm keys, any of which might become useful when working on bikes. The better

Allen wrenches.

Allen wrenches are ball drivers, which is to say that the longer ends are beveled, allowing us to adjust Allen bolts from slight angles, which can be a very nice option to have. The shorter ends, meant more for delivering torque, can become rounded with extended use; you would need to face them against a grinder wheel to sharpen things up again.

Campagnolo made use of an odd 7 mm Allen wrench for some of its crank bolts years ago, but the standard set should cover just about anything else that might come up. Note that the threading used with most modern bicycle framesets and components is also on the metric scale—you may find yourself tightening the water bottle cage's M5 mounting bolt with your 4 mm Allen key, for example, or the brake's M6 bolt with your 5 mm key. The only confusion possible arrives with the description, fortunately; in practice it should be quite obvious whether or not something fits. You should not need to apply force to start the threads—not with anything that is meant to be, at least.

With the notable exceptions of the broad cups and locknuts found on threaded headsets, which can range in size from 30 to 40 mm, as well as certain features associated with various ancient bottom bracket sets, just about all the wrench flats we see on bikes will be sized between 8 and 17 mm. Adjustable wrenches of the traditional variety are generally not as useful, in that their adjustments tend to require enforcement, lest they slip and strip things out. That said, my space-age Craftsman adjustable wrench, a gift from my brother, does not seem to share this problem—its spring-loaded claw seems to know exactly where to land, when applied to nuts and bolts up to a certain size.

I do keep a big old crescent wrench in my box, for the sake of the torque it

Big old crescent wrench.

provides—a nice attribute to have, when dealing with the threaded headsets. Some older threaded headsets also employ adjustable nuts faced with knurled surfaces, which may be met with a big pair of channel-lock pliers. With luck, you should not have much use for vice-grip pliers at all. Their forceful embrace can only suggest that diplomacy has been somehow allowed to fail.

As for the screwdrivers, you'll want at least four, to start: the #2 and #1 Phillips, a 3 mm flathead and another maybe twice that size. The longer their handles, the more leverage you will earn. The Phillips work well for many derailleur and brake adjustment screws, as well as those usually found on handlebar-mounted accessories. And despite our best intentions, the smaller flathead screwdriver might be most often misused, as a sort of miniature pry bar. Park once made an odd-looking wide-nosed T-handle screwdriver, meant for use with the brake levers found on older bikes. It was uniquely useful for such purposes, but it seems to have gone extinct.

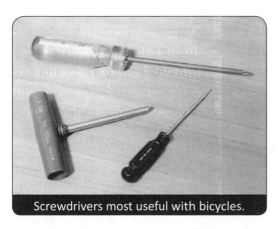
Screwdrivers most useful with bicycles.

One can find quality sidecutters strong enough to slice through bike cables, but for such purposes your cash would be better dispatched on a pair of dedicated **CABLE CUTTERS**, which enlist a hardened pair of wicked half-moons to sever cables and cable housing alike with predictable ease.

Bicycle cables are tightly wrapped braids of zinc or stainless wire, which is to say they're not easily defeated. Lower-quality sidecutters, the greater number of those available, will not be able to do the trick—the cutting angle is less than ideal, and the cheap jaws' steel is far too soft. Tools of good quality should be hard enough to reliably govern their more malleable subjects—this is why it's so difficult to drill holes in the wrench—but everything has its limits. Even the bicycle cable cutters' mighty jaws will lose the match, for example, when set against the stainless steel struts found on full fender sets. It's all about picking your battles, right? With extended use they'd be more inclined to loosen than wear out. The arms pivot on a short and stout screw, which passes through the one side and threads into the other, before being sealed with a nut: this last would need to loosen, before the bolt could be tightened. You'd want to end up with the jaws just barely loose enough to pivot freely, with the nut tightened down nice and solid.

Your new cable cutters are very much bicycle-specific; they will only coincide with the outside world at their leisure. Following on the heels of this opening is the amazing **FOURTH HAND CABLE TOOL**, an odd pliers with which we're able to counter the strong springs used with cable-driven brakes. The fourth hand

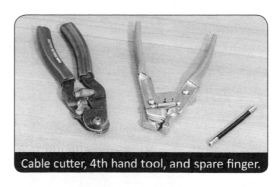
Cable cutter, 4th hand tool, and spare finger.

makes it much easier to hold a cable in a particular position while tightening a brake's binder bolt, basically, greatly simplifying our work. (The tool earns its name by replacing something called the third hand, itself a bent-up strip of metal bearing the profile of a teacup, meant to hold the brake pads in place against the rim. Don't let the sequence throw you; this middle step was nothing special.)

There will arrive occasions when there's just not the space to fit a fourth hand into any good position—racks or other fixed accessories might get in the way, for example—and in such cases it may be useful to introduce a small accessory. Cut yourself a few short centimeters of brake cable housing, as described on page 75, and fit each end of this with a housing cap. Slide this down the cable you're working on: the fourth hand tool will now be able to lever itself off this extension, rather than the component. In keeping with our theme, I propose we call these **SPARE FINGERS**.

As will be seen, work with the cable housing also requires a small sharp stick, in order to reopen the thin plastic liner within the housing, which collapses when the housing is cut. You can go out and buy one of these, needless to say, but it's cheaper to simply sharpen up a dead spoke. Hold one against somebody's bench grinder and rotate, slowly; it takes all of a minute. While the soldered ends of new cables are not nearly sharp enough to poke openings in the plastic cable liners, cables that have been already been cut down will only fray apart, when pressed to such duties. As simple a tool as it is, a sharpened spoke (or a similar implement) ends up being really useful with the cables. Something between a safety pin and a nail.

You might also want to score some **SPANNERS**—maybe, if your bike is old enough, or cheap enough. Park's green SPA-1 is meant for the older three-piece bottom bracket adjustable cups; the HCW-11 wrench (or the older yellow-handled spanner, if you can find one) addresses the same on the larger American-style bottom bracket cups. These are relatively light and even wispy creatures, all but bereft of persuasive techniques; component manufacturers have long since moved on to more reliable arrangements.

Headset and bottom bracket wrenches.

Where the spanners end, the **LOCKRING TOOLS** soon begin. Their functions are roughly parallel, but the lockrings only surround more central elements; their minders thus approach from the sides.

Your track hubs, bottom brackets, and a tiny group of ancient headsets may require their services.

Traditional threaded headsets—those bearing wrench flats across their foreheads—are adjusted with the curiously broad and flat **HEADSET WRENCHES**. A bearing cup is counter-tightened against its locknut to achieve the proper adjustment; there is no room to fit a big old crescent wrench in both positions at once. The flats range in size from 30 to 40 mm, dependent upon their vintage. The most common are 32 and 36 mm. The top locknuts on all of these threaded headsets may be grappled with the big old crescent wrench.

The 36 mm headset wrench may also have another use. Look at the edges of the drive-side bottom bracket cup, just inside the chainrings: does it feature a pair of wrench flats? These will *almost* always measure 36 mm. There is a specific bottom bracket tool that fits it best, because it catches their rounded edges as well, but your 36 mm headset wrench can fill in if it needs to.

The pedals on some bikes can be installed and removed with a regular 15 mm box wrench. In recent years, most of the others have adapted 15 mm flats too narrow to accommodate our clumsy old box wrenches, favoring instead the embrace of a dedicated **PEDAL WRENCH**. The same tool will also provide for the smaller and narrower ⁹⁄₁₆″ pedals found on most children's bikes. But the wrench flats are losing favor as well, among some of the

newer clipless pedal sets, which replace them with stylish metric sockets carved into the axle bases. You would need an Allen wrench.

Crown race hammer.

The **CONE WRENCHES,** available in sizes 13–18 mm, are even thinner: so thin, in fact, that the 15 would *not* be able to fill in as a pedal wrench. Pedals thrive on torque, as we'll see, and the metals used to make their axles are more than hard enough to damage something so dainty as a cone wrench. They're meant to be used with the hub bearing cones. The odd-numbered sizes are most common, and it's best to have a pair of each.

The cone wrenches remind me to mention Park's **OFFSET BRAKE WRENCHES.**

These are of similar dimensions, but the wrench heads are offset 90 degrees. They're meant for use with the road bike caliper brakes; we find situations where nothing else will really work. They are ambidextrous as well, with distinct wrench flats at either end, in sizes from 10 to 14 mm, as well as an odd one which grapples with the caliper's spring directly.

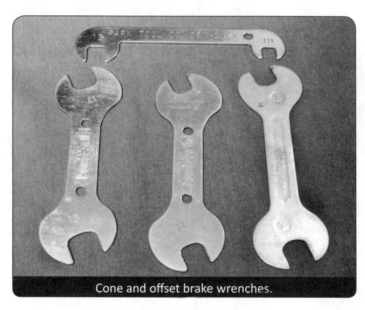

Cone and offset brake wrenches.

One other oddball you want to pick up is known as the **CRANK EXTRACTOR**. A minority of the higher-end crank sets spec'd on bikes around the turn of the century arrived with the clever self-extracting bolts, eliminating the need for this tool, and the more recent two-piece cranks employ a simpler recipe of their own, but it can still be said that the great majority of modern crank arms will only be removed with extractors.

The truly ancient steel cottered cranks, still widely used in places like Mauritania, are best removed with Park Tool's Cotter Press—which, like the cotter pins

themselves, is no longer manufactured. (An alternate method will be described in due course.) The removal of modern cotterless cranks relies upon threads carved into their interiors. Lacking such—as when these threads have been damaged, for example—the offending crank might only be removed with overbearing force: hammers, wonder-wheels, things like that. It is, unfortunately, all too easy to accidentally put yourself in just such a position; be sure to see page 155, on crank pulling, before beginning. Three-piece bottom brackets feature either the old tapered or the new splined spindles, to put it in a nutshell, and it is supremely important that you select the correct tool.

Crank extractors feature long flat handles, in their most common renditions. Professional versions are also available, replacing the handles with wrench flats. In either case, the central distinction is with the diameter of the extraction pin threaded into the tool's interior. The older and narrower tapered spindles found in most bottom brackets require the original sort of extractor (Park's CCP-22, with the *blue* handle). The wider and newer splined pipe-style spindles need the Octalin/ISIS Drive extractor instead, if they need one at all (Park's CCP-44, with the *black* handle). Note that older versions of Park's CCP-22 extractor featured a second, shorter stack of threads opposite the usual ones, which were meant for use with some older cranks made by Stronglight. A rare handful of older Campagnolo cranks makes use for a wholly distinct extractor with left-handed threads, and for the obvious reasons I would imagine these become less common each year.

Crank backer and tapered spindle crank extractor.

You should also grab a **CRANK BACKER**, Park's CNW-2. This is an odd little spanner used to hold the backs of the chainring bolts as you tighten them.

Prior to pulling your three-piece cranks, you must remove the bolts pinning them in place. If you have a really old bike and its ancient steel cranks feature obtuse nuts to their sides, you want to check out the rundown on cottered cranks; see page 149. More modern spindles are capped with sturdy nuts or bolts, either of which answer to 14 or 15 mm sockets, dependent on age and manufacturer. These are supposed to hide beneath dust caps, which might be threaded out or pried from the cranks, depending.

These crank bolts (or nuts) are only removed with sockets, such as those found on Park's CCW5C. The better and more recent a crankset is, the more likely its crank bolts will be surrendered to an Allen wrench instead. The size, depending upon circumstances, will be 5, 6, 7, 8, or 10 mm. You did get the full set, right? It would not have come with the 7, but it's not at all likely you'd need that one.

Also common are the three-way "Y" wrenches. Both the 2/2.5/3 mm and 4/5/6 mm Allen Y-wrenches and the 8/9/10 mm socket are pretty ubiquitous—they earn their keep quite well—but the larger 12/13/14 mm Y-wrench is not nearly as special. These larger sizes will generally require more torque than this relatively small tool can offer.

The **EXTRACTION TOOLS** are distinct from the crank extractors. They are more similar to the sockets, being small attachments used to grip and turn things, but the extraction tools feature various circles of splines or teeth. They're gripped in vises or wrenches, to remove specific components of matching dimensions. There exist maybe twenty such tools. The original varieties are meant to plug into freewheels, which are what we call the gear clusters found on cheaper or older bikes. The more modern extraction tools will remove cassettes—the more recent gear clusters—as well as newer bottom brackets and some crank parts.

You also need a **CHAIN TOOL**. Here again, I have to recommend Park. Every shop I've worked for has used their burly professional model, the CT-3. The smaller consumer CT-5 version is also good, in that its design is better informed than that deployed with lesser consumer tools. While the saddles used with inferior examples will break under the slightest misuse, those found in Park Compact Chain Tools are relatively thicker and less pronounced—sturdier. If you find yourself working on chains frequently, you really should get the business version. Whichever the case, don't forget to oil the threads now and again.

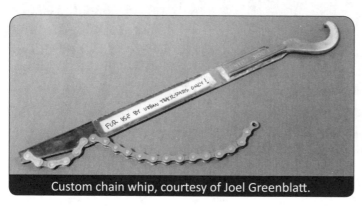

Custom chain whip, courtesy of Joel Greenblatt.

Following in the sequence is a **CHAIN WHIP**, such as Park's SR-1, whose focus narrows to better appreciate the gear clusters or the cog, with the track bikes. And you do have a floor pump, right? The smaller portable jobs get to be kind of stupid after a while.

In my haste I managed to omit the mighty **QUIK STIK** from this chapter in the previous edition. It is a very useful sort of **TIRE**

LEVER. An unfortunate oversight, alas only one of several corrected in this current edition, which benefits from the supreme luxury of more time to think. The tire levers' application is detailed more fully in the chapter on wheels, page 43; suffice it here to say it's best to have a few on hand.

You also want a patch kit. The glueless versions are worthless, in that they're made of stiffer and less flexible rubber. It'd be something akin to using a tarp as a blanket. I would encourage the reader to get a real one.

Speaking of the wheels, you will also need **SPOKE WRENCHES**. Park's red-handled SW-2 fits the spoke nipples used with most older and cheaper bikes. The smaller black-handled SW-0 *generally* fits those associated with newer and better equipment. I have never found use for their curiously sized blue and yellow spoke wrenches, and to my experience the medium-sized green SW-1 is only occasionally required. This simple list will coincide with the vast majority of wheels any of us might encounter, but surely not all of them; the high-end/low spoke-count racing wheels will require special spoke wrenches of their own.

If you do make a practice of repairing bikes, your work may be declared all the more precise with the introduction of certain reliable assistants. The **TENSIOMETER**

Files, magnet, and spoke wrenches.

We had these awesome hybrid-hammers at one of the last shops I worked at, with steel at one end and hard rubber at the other—the option is a nice one to have. I just have some rusty old claw hammer at home; I have not gotten around to picking up a rubber mallet. The dedicated spoke

provides exacting readings of a wheel's spoke tension, lending our corrections unrivaled precision. Their particulars are described on page 215.

More central to our diverse repair tasks is the **TORQUE WRENCH**. It is a long thin metal wishbone, joined by a socket fitting. One digit forms a sturdy handle, augmented with a short ruler-like gauge, while the other sprouts from the base: the very tip of this beanpole traces a course across the gauge as we press the handle, measuring the torque in either foot-pounds of pressure or Newton meters of force. Bicycle component manufacturers tend to suggest specific torque ranges, with regards to the installation and adjustment of their wares, and the only way we're able to actually report back on our findings is to use the torque wrench. When it is here suggested that a given part is tightened to greater or lesser degrees, the reader should understand this fulfills only the most general of descriptions. If a given component manual cannot be tracked down, solutions might be pursued through the manufacturer's website.

rulers simplify our measurements, by providing openings to accept the spoke heads, but they are not strictly necessary to the process. Conventional spokes are measured from the elbow bend to the end of the spoke threads, and all but the oldest are sold in metric lengths. It would make sense to get a **METRIC CALIPER** as well, if you're doing a lot of work.

A magnet is useful for collecting the hub bearings during overhauls, as Luke pointed out to me one afternoon up at Calhoun Cycle. You might also find use for a **JESUS BAR**—a hollow pipe of some kind, snipped from a dead bike frame for example, maybe a couple inches across on the inside, most of a yard long. It would fit around the handle of a smaller wrench, when extra leverage was needed.

It should go without saying that your tools will greatly prefer a dry climate. Maybe you can score a dehumidifier for your basement, or, failing that, some oily rags.

Our discussion to this point puts the various **MULTI-TOOLS** in a useful context. These are the compact amalgamations of those tools most often called upon, meant for portable roadside repairs. The trade-off comes in leverage and maneuverability—you can generally get down to business, from a svelte package no less, but everything will probably take longer. Asking one of these devices to fill in for the chores of regular bike tools on any consistent basis gets to be annoying.

Torx wrenches.

Bike chains are best fed with an **OIL DROPPER**—you don't get the after-spray all over the living room furniture; nobody gets in trouble. If the pressurized oil can is overbearing, superficial, and prone to unfortunate generalizations, the oil dropper would be more like a decent local public radio station. Gel lubes are displacing their Teflon forebears, just as the first dry lubes rendered the wet ones obsolete. I'm partial to the Rock "N" Roll brand myself.

Most bicycle chains never see nearly enough oil—their baleful and resigning squeaks ever fail to move us, somehow. Yet at the very same time, some especially fastidious riders seem more inclined to simply drown the chain with any available oil, as a balm against mechanical issues real or imagined—"the more, the better." The problem here is that a wet chain picks up more grit, and this makes for that nasty gunk all over your leg: the oil and grit conspire to form a sort of liquid sandpaper, which wears your drivetrain parts down to tortured nubs. Then you need new parts, which is really too bad, because after a point chain lubrication becomes entirely secondary to shifting performance. All the chain lube left in creation will not resolve maladjusted parts, nor ease the tortured travels of rusted-out cables. Balance is key: oil a rusty chain, or one that squeaks, and do your best to leave the rest alone.

The oil droppers can be refilled, incidentally. Is that cool or what? Grip the tip with your pliers and pull it out. Pop! This flattens out the hole therein; rotate the pliers and give it a little squeeze. Most worthy chain oils can be found in bulk quantities.

Always, always, always wipe the chain down when you finish with the oil, OK? The old-fashioned wet lube is best saved for the heavy winter, when they bust out the road salt, just before you take the drivetrain down for spring cleaning.

It would be easy to imagine that the spray cans will carry the oil into every crevice where it might be useful—I'm thinking of all the bikes I've ever seen with that conspicuous build-up of supplementary road grit right where we don't want it to be, up close to the bearing seals. But the dust caps sealing bearings from the outside world are designed to keep this very grit away; drawing it in with the oil is a bad idea. The sand gets in between the balls and the races, where it can do no good at all. You've heard about how pearls are made, when an oyster gets obsessed with a grain of sand? The hubs have not yet learned this trick.

Besides, bearings run on grease, not oil. Oil is thinner. It will break down and disperse the grease if it gets in. I use lightweight oil when overhauling bearing races, to clean any hardened old grease out of the way.

Grease guns and oil dropper bottles.

The thing we want for the hubs is a **GREASE GUN**. These you can find at the bike shops. The consumer versions are sold with tubes of the manufacturers' grease—you roll up the tube as you go, just as with toothpaste. (The grease tube does not stay rolled up, so you need to hold the end in some kind of binder clip.)

The refillable grease guns, such as the Dualco pictured here, can be fed with a tub of grease. One simply spoons it in. This takes more time, but it will prove to be a lot cheaper—a tub of worthy bike grease might cost all of five bones and will last a really long time.

The coolest thing about any of these is the pinpoint nozzle. It helps us become precise and disciplined in our work and not end up with slop all over the place. You could just paint in some grease right out of a tub, if you really needed to, but this would not be a good idea—grease tends to accumulate grit when it's left out in the open, and this is easily transferred down to the bearings. The same element will occasionally conspire to block up the grease gun's nozzle. Clear it with a pin, or blow it clean with an air gun.

We are lucky the grease has its guns, for it also has its enemies. At the far, opposite end of our elemental spectrum sit the thread-locking compounds, paint-like substances which introduce friction between threaded fittings, to counter the loosening encouraged by the infinite vibrations generated through the course of our travels.

The oldsters, preferring other purposes for their paints, adapted a strict mechanical approach to thread-locking. We still see versions of this approach today with most of our hubs, which counter-tighten bearing cones against locknuts to finalize adjustments. But not every situation is meant for such finality—the quick-release components, for example—so precious shades of grey have been duly introduced. Serrated washers inject friction betwixt a nut or bolthead and its endpoint, and the spring-loaded split washers do the same thing in reverse, by forcing the threads back a bit. Either approach may feature with toe clip hardware, to take another everyday example.

Liquid thread-locking compounds such as Loctite enlist chemistry in pursuit of their permanence. Threadlocking compounds of various strengths can be found, from Loctite's kind-of-stuck blue to its really-won't-budge green. Made more solid, the very same theory is reincarnated in **NYLOCK NUTS**. Spell it out with me: the nut is equipped with a nylon insert, which grips itself around the bolt's threads. The nuts holding your rack hardware together should be nylock, together with those fixtures capping all but the oldest quick-release skewers.

Suppose you want to do something truly heroic with your bike—save the day, start the revolution, score the very last point—more than anything else, it will be the frame that allows for this glory. A worthy frame will fit well, and it will be light enough to scale the mountains, rigid enough to avoid wasting your energies, but also supple enough to foster an appreciation of passing distance. Surely a treasure worth preserving.

Personal thoughts aside, a given frame's worthiness might best be measured as a function of both the materials used and the care taken during its construction. Both of these considerations can be glimpsed through the bike's **FRAME TUBING DECALS**. These are small and meticulous notes, usually found on the seat tube or the down tube, and perhaps a fork blade as well. Just as the acupuncturist can see so much from so little, so too can the mechanic read from a decal—they let us know how well a given bike has kept up with the news. Any old bike can be made to look like a superstar, fed enough fancy parts, but the frame tubing decal will always display its true colors.

Most bikes have always been built with steel frames— this may make it the element we've really learnt to trust or merely some kind of default setting, dependent on the point of view. The particular qualities associated with quality steel frames have earned its orthodoxy legions of zealous defenders, but bikes have also been made from aluminum alloys, carbon composites, titanium, bamboo, and various combinations thereof. As with the original approach, each adaptation offers its own unique attributes.

II. Frames

By default, I am most familiar with the majority option. With regards to steel frames, a decal advertising cromoly or *cro-mo* would be the first thing to look for—it would indicate that the frame's steel tubing had been alloyed with chromium and molybdenum, which is to say its strength has been enhanced. I am no materials scientist and, alas, cannot explain why this is so, but it is accepted as an article of faith in the wider cycling world. The same decal should also make reference to how the material was used. A decal advertising "cro-mo main tubes," for example, would suggest that regular old straight-gauge cromoly had managed to find its way into the frame's main triangle. A nice gesture, but nothing too special: we could assume that high-tensile steel had been used in the fork and rear triangle.

A quality steel frameset would begin with double- or triple-butted cromoly, in which cases the frame's individual tubes were machined to become slightly thinner through their midsections, in one or two gradients respectively. The effort makes the frame lighter, and by making the most of the steel's natural capacity for resilience it also provides for a more comfortable ride. It is only at their joints that the frames really need their strength; minimizing the middle dimensions does much to muffle the commotion imparted with distance.

Classic butted steel tubesets such as Reynolds 531 were designed to work with artful steel lugs. Advances in metallurgy have allowed their enlightened progeny, such as Reynolds 753, to eschew these braces. Aluminum, carbon, and steel lugs have also been used in the construction of aluminum, carbon, and bamboo frames—such creatures are glued together, essentially—but I have never seen them deployed with titanium.

Steel can rust, of course. Steel bikes that see a lot of rain, snow, or surf should be protected with the judicious application of grease on all their threaded fittings, as will be later described, as well as with the periodic application of Frame Saver spray to their tubes' interiors. Aluminum is lighter than steel and does not corrode as easily, but it is also stiffer. These characteristics make it an ideal material for many bicycle components, such as brakes and rims, but it also provides for certain complications when used to build frames. Aluminum bikes are more inclined to incorporate either carbon or suspension forks. Absent such intervention, the ride quality they provide would typically be much less forgiving than with the more resilient steel, translating every last jarring bump directly up through the handlebars.

The carbon is famously light and strong, but it is also curiously vulnerable to abrasions. Titanium remains a rarer element yet, with which I have little direct experience, but it is also supposed to be fairly ideal as a frame material, for somewhat different reasons. Bamboo strikes me as a fascinating prospect, but as yet I haven't found the opportunity to play with a thus constructed bike.

Nice old neutral side dropout.

require a specific chain tension, such as the singlespeeds or some planetary gears.

For quite a long time, the frame's **CHAINLINE** was charged with reconciling relatively small discrepancies in width—settling bottom bracket shells of 68, 70, or 73 mm within rear hub spacings ranging from 120 to 140 mm—but

In every case, the wheels attach to the frame and fork through the **DROPOUTS**, which will be designed to work with threaded or through axles. Those featuring up front are fairly straightforward, but the rear drops cater to distinct purposes. The **HORIZONTAL** dropouts are the most traditional—their elongated windows allow the rear wheel to be installed at a varying distance from the bottom bracket axis, which is sometimes necessary to a good chain tension. **VERTICAL** dropouts set the rear wheel in a fixed position in relation to the frame, allowing it to sit much closer to the bottom bracket axis, which contributes to a more agile and efficient riding experience. The **TRACK** dropouts, like the **BMX** dropouts, are entered from the rear—in either case, the solitary objective would be to facilitate the establishment of chain tension. Neither type makes any provision for derailleur hangers, as most of these others do. The **SLIDING** dropouts, which draw in the disc brake mounting tabs, are a more recent idea. They allow the discs to be used with wheels which

to a limited extent the so-called gravity bikes have really blown it all wide open. The acreage allotted to the rear wheel has been expanded not once but twice in compensation, to 150 and 165 mm, allowing the 8/9/10-speed cassette platform to become the star of a stronger (dish-less) rear wheel, which evidently becomes more important when plowing down the mountainside as fast as possible. This development, in turn, has called into being new bottom bracket shells of 83 and 100 mm width. This last size in particular may be somewhat counterintuitive, in that not everyone will find the 100 mm shell's bowlegged stance to be all that comfortable.

A. Frame Damage

All bike frames are vulnerable to damage, to one degree or another. It is only sometimes clear that anything has even happened. Problems with the bottom bracket threads are not unusual, for example—older bikes become more vulnerable to rust-related problems, as do those left to weather the elements too long, and any frame might be damaged if the bottom bracket is not installed correctly. It is best to get the threads re-tapped, in such circumstances. Most shops have the equipment to tap most bottom bracket shells, in the developed world at least.

Game over for the Lotus: crimped down tube.

The threads inside the rear derailleur hanger are also sometimes stripped. They may be brought back to health with a 10 mm tap, if we're lucky. Replacement thread inserts are available for use with many older bikes—the hanger only needs

to be wide enough to accept them—but newer non-steel bikes tend to use replaceable hangers instead.

Bad things are always happening to rear derailleur hangers. They become levers of sorts, if the bike dumps on the drive side, bending their hanger tabs in toward the frame. You can spot this problem pretty easily, looking down from the rear of the bike: pulling the derailleur's cage down by its rearmost pulley, the whole thing would be angled in toward the rear wheel.

Park and Campagnolo both make hanger alignment tools, meant to resolve this very dilemma. Each threads a relatively massive lever into the hanger tab, allowing us to bend it back in plane with the rear wheel. The handle is threaded into the derailleur hanger and then rotated back and forth around it, alternately pushed or pulled until the hanger's orientation aligns with that of the rear wheel. You may be able to do something roughly similar with your Allen key, if you're not thus equipped: slot its short end into the derailleur's mounting bolt, gripping the derailleur's body with your other hand, and see if you can gradually straighten things out. Do not yank! Move slowly. This is especially important with aluminum hangers.

Aluminum is more inclined to snap, shoved past a certain point, so the smarter alloy frames arrive with **REPLACEABLE DERAILLEUR HANGERS**. Cannondale was the first to popularize these, but at this point their mounting details vary from company to company, year by year. The derailleur tab itself needs to end up in its fixed position, but the bolt hole(s) and the mounting plate dimensions above it are more open to interpretation. There is not yet any standard replacement dropout, as far as I know. I'm not sure when we can expect to see one. In the meanwhile, a replacement derailleur hanger for any particular frame would be best obtained at a bike shop selling that brand.

Those riding alloy frames born before all this replaceable business would do well to pick up a Sinner derailleur supporter from Therapy Components, a sharp update on the clumsy old chrome derailleur guards.

It should go without saying that I cannot advise anyone to ride frames afflicted with crimps, buckles, or wayward bends. This is especially crucial with the head tube, the down tube, and the fork. It would be safest to abandon the project in question. Bikes ramming into fixed objects commonly stub their forks, for example. If you are left with any questions at all about a frame's integrity, take it to your friendly local bike shop.

FRAME ALIGNMENT is the larger issue here. Crashes are sometimes powerful enough to bend frames—these kinds of alignment issues are rarely obvious to the

eye, but a good shop will have the means to answer such questions definitively. Be sure to get the frame checked out if ever you're hit by a car, at the very least. Some clown up and cut me off in downtown Minneapolis a few years back, and the crash crimped the down tube on this nice old Lotus I was riding. A bummer of an afternoon, for sure, but a solid repair estimate got me $1,400 for the frame in small claims court. (The outcome was twice as judicious, in fact: it was the driver's slimy insurance agent who had originally sought damages against me, for denting the van's door. No kidding. So I had to ask the judge, "Your honor, am I suicidal?")

B. Creaks

It may be possible, in the course of your travels, that your bike will pick up a **CREAK.** This may or may not mean anything in itself—we'd need to track it down and see what was up, basically—but even the more innocuous sorts of groaning can pass a kind of judgment. Their mad echo proudly announces to the world that your bike is afflicted with some kind of loud and annoying problem.

The creaks exist to mock us. There might be other, more immediate considerations involved—these annoying ghosts must find reasons to haunt us—but their patient subversion invariably claims the last word. You may be all up there claiming you know the score, or whatever the hell it is, but it sure won't sound like it.

The creak is not going to sit down and have a drink with you. Nor will its unfathomable requests be salved by the passage of time. Odds are better it convinces its creepy friends to merrily croak along instead.

It is in the creaks' nature to be mysterious, and it is this very tendency that allows for their stubborn persistence. I have to stop short of calling them clever; their motives suggest more of a raw cunning. Their ultimate resolution tends to involve a good deal of careful hunting—for hours at a time, as the case may be—and this requires a disciplined approach. You first need to isolate the sound as best you can, and then attend to every possible remedy to the situation, testing the results of each.

Creaks are born within the intersections of metals and other materials, where one thing is faced against anything else at all. The bicycles, straining beneath, allow for a splendid range of opportunities. I have known water bottle mounts to squeak, straining against their wispy cages, or even the slightest flex arriving through their frame tubes. The solution, once a creak is found, is to smother it in grease.

Such treatment can only help the metal frames, in their endless and epic campaigns against the rust. It may or may not be a good idea to apply grease to carbon fiber, depending who you ask. For quite a long time, the consensus was that we should never apply any grease to carbon frames or parts, for fear of weakening or damaging the material. As a petroleum byproduct, a given piece of carbon fiber might be vulnerable to a fatal corruption, when salved with its kindred elements. Yet in recent years, this prescription has come under challenge. Anecdotes about seized carbon seatposts are not hard to find; reputable sources have suggested grease as a remedy in such cases. Bicycle repair sometimes comes to approximate history itself, in that it can become a series of unresolved controversies. I'd still be inclined to avoid greasing carbon fiber unless it seemed necessary—if a post was becoming hard to adjust, for example.

In any case, when hunting down a creak the first thing you need to do is locate

Bike used in Atar, Mauritania: bent fork, no brakes, DIY rack.

your target. Does the creak arrive when pedaling or coasting? Sitting or standing? Clutching tightly to the handlebars? With your hands resting atop the brake hoods? When stomping on the pedals?

The handlebars' midsections inevitably become somewhat wider, to better greet the stems which anticipate them. In the olden days the original aluminum drop bars incorporated sleeves for such purposes, which are famous for their creaking, so we're all lucky the drops enlist wider bugle sections instead these days. Regardless, it is generally assumed that there should always be a little grease between the stem's clamp and the bar. (Here again, use your discretion with carbon parts.) The brake lever clamps can creak as well; they can get the same treatment. Which could mean unwrapping your handlebar tape, depending. More of a hassle. Lather yet more grease inside or around the steerer tube, for threaded or threadless stems respectively, as will shortly be described. But the headset cups can creak as well, which is why we want to make sure they are installed into fields of grease. Even some of the actual headsets will manage to creak, in the final analysis, and might themselves need replacement to solve the problem.

Creaks haunting the bottom bracket can be just as entertaining. The unit itself will need to enjoy grease both inside and outside its cups, on the bolts, and perhaps the spindle as well, as per the manufacturer's recommendations.

But the chainring bolts will also need to be greased and tightened, together with the pedal axles, and maybe even the screws holding the pedal cages. Then we do the water bottle screws, front derailleur clamp and bolt, and any suspension pivot points.

Did that get it? What about the seat? Grease all the bolts you find there— the pinch, the mounting hardware, anything—and also get the rails, right around where they are clamped in the post.

Creaks crafty enough to survive such an assault might suggest structural damage, but this is truly rare, and it's well worth your time to consider the situation first.

C. Forks

The **FORKS** are designed for use with certain frames in particular. Differences in wheel size, steerer tube dimensions, and braking options will typically preclude their mixing and matching, though as we'll see some exceptions can be made.

Front axle spacing is the easiest detail to keep track of. An especially rugged handful of the new downhill mountain bikes have been showing up with dropouts meant to accommodate 20 x 110 mm or 15 x 100 mm through axles, and some folding bikes are born with 70 mm forks to match their own diminutive front wheels, but all the others can be expected to share the standard 9 x 100 mm axle spacing. The hub might fit a little snug into the dropouts—or, with cheaper and less trustworthy forks, things might be just a shade wide—but you should not need any contortions to make things work.

The through axle systems tend to be heavier, but they provide for at least one crucial advantage, in that they're immune to an issue that has come to haunt all those forks bearing both quick-release axles and disc brakes. The disc brake mounting platform, long a standardized pattern, was suddenly found to have the effect of gradually encouraging the front skewer to loosen, causing the front wheel to drop out of its fork. Very strange, but true. It is a function of how the force generated by the front disc brake intersects with the front wheel skewer's position, apparently. If your front disc brake does rely upon a quick-release skewer for wheel retention, in other words, it is up to you to make sure it stays tight: I would recommend checking before every ride. (One gets a sense of how sudden this revelation was, looking over contemporary technical literature; a lot of people were taken quite by surprise. The problem was first highlighted by James Annan, a Scottish mountain biking enthusiast working in Japan. He published his findings at http://www.ne.jp/asahi/julesandjames/home/disk_and_quick_release/.)

The **FORK RAKE** is a measure of its trail, which is to say how far back the fork's steerer tube sits in relation to the front axle. The effect is meant to complement a given frame's geometry; it will further accent what is already there. More rake is associated with older touring bikes; less rake is found with the younger racing bikes.

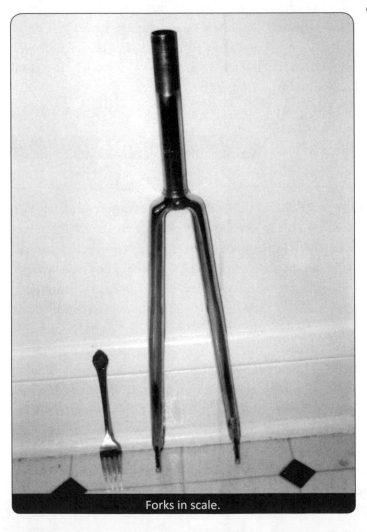

Forks in scale.

Just about every fork has rake, but some are slyer about it. The angle may rest inconspicuously within the fork's crown, and its legs would otherwise appear to be straight—a runaway trend, with the modern road bikes.

An appreciation of a fork's rake can help us determine how straight it is, following a crash: the contours of each leg should always precisely match the other, looking from the sides. The presence of a wheel can mute or disguise any difference between the two; take it out before you check. Forks that are only slightly bent might be realigned, using the combination of either a Jesus bar or Park's FFS-2 to impress, and the FFG-2 to verify. Sorely bent forks cannot be safely straightened. It's impossible to be more specific than this, from the present vantage; suffice it to say that anything questionable should definitely get checked out at a shop.

A new fork needs to fit with a given frame's wheel, brake and headset. We need to make sure the **STEERER TUBE** is of the correct dimensions, before doing anything else: it needs to be tall enough, and just wide enough, and its top section may or may not be threaded.

The curious old 1 ¼" steerers have been steadily fading from view, not unlike their contemporary rock ballads, though we still see them now and again. The proprietary systems such as Cannondale's Headshok are about as rare. Our world has largely settled upon the lighter 1" and 1 ⅛" steerer tubes.

The steerer tube's height may simply be copied from the original, but it can also be deduced by means of a simple formula. For threaded headsets, we add the head tube's total length to the headset's **STACK HEIGHT**, which is the sum of its exposed pieces. We can assume for a 35 mm stack for 1" forks, or 40 mm for 1 ⅛". With the threadless headsets, the steerer must also pass through the stem and any spacers, to stop 5 mm short of the top: add the collective heights of these other features to the head tube and stack height, then subtract 5 mm. This formula would provide for the most exacting measurement, but really the threadless headsets are able to work with longer steerer tubes as well, given enough head tube spacers.

Some shops still have the tools required to extend fork threads down a steerer tube, if it needs to be cut, but this is becoming an outmoded operation. Threadlessness pretty well renders its forebears obsolete. Thread-cutting tools are relatively expensive and maintenance-intensive themselves, considering how little they are required these days, and any excess of threading diminishes a fork's versatility. The quill-style stems used with threaded headsets need to anchor themselves below the threaded section; any extra threads will limit your options in safely raising the stem. Wholesalers still offer a smattering of basic steel threaded forks for use with older bikes, but any fork with an aluminum or carbon steerer will have already made plans for threadlessness.

Were hierarchy imposed upon the bicycle's parts, the **HEADSETS** might stand out as the executives. They are charged with uniquely strenuous responsibilities, negotiating from frame to fork, yet their very position insulates them from most harm—outlying components will take a hit far sooner. And, as with the other bearing systems, even the simplest headsets are in many respects built to last. Chains and brake pads are regularly replaced; headsets tend to stay put until upgraded. Their missions are very clearly defined, and it is only the sloppiest among them that run into trouble.

As with enlightened leadership more generally, we don't necessarily want to be aware of the headset's presence. Together with the bars and stem, it should merely translate our steering impulses, without exception or hesitation. When problems do arise, those few headsets not amenable to improved adjustments are replaced as compete systems. In such cases, you'll need another one matching both the outgoing headset's dimensions and its style—threaded or threadless, or perhaps internal or integrated.

Most bikes on the road today were born with threaded headsets. In recent years, the superior design manifest in threadless headsets has left all of them somewhat more obsolete, in the strictest reading at least. Taken to its logical extreme, this viewpoint vanishes up the noses of the fanciest frames to become **INTEGRATED HEADSETS**: suddenly, everything is just *perfect*. The bearing cups are done away with entirely; hollows carved from the head tube itself are made to host the bearing cartridges. Alas, the arrangement has also proven controversial: the headset cups help assure a meticulous fit for the bearings, and their presence spares the head tube some damage, with the aluminum frames in particular. The worry is that the bearing cartridges might gradually widen out their hollows, under diverse loads: while a headset could simply be replaced in such circumstances, not much could be done for an integrated frameset.

Thus arrive the **INTERNAL HEADSETS**, which pull the same kind of trick, but with bearing cups as well. A handful of high-end manufacturers such as Colnago have

III. Headsets

further begun to produce bikes with **ASYMMETRIC HEAD TUBES**, which in their case match a smaller 1.125″ upper bearing to a slightly wider 1.25″ lower, as means to harvest the evident improvements in steering such a profile may provide. Sounds like a good idea, but as with these others it is still pretty much off on its own expensive little planet.

The 1″, 1 ⅛″, and 1 ¼″ headsets have each been available in both threaded and threadless versions. The 1″ threaded headsets were the norm for a very long time, but the consensus has largely shifted toward 1 ⅛″, for the threaded and threadless styles both. The former are still used extensively across a broad range of more basic bikes, and the latter became something like a standard for better quality. It still is, in many respects, but we also see increasing numbers of integrated and internal headsets, all of which use cartridge bearings, in arrangements mimicking the threadless format. Integrated and internal headsets both track right off the usual map, in terms of their specifications. (That's another cool thing about inventing your own standards: it's a great way to get into selling proprietary parts.) Such details aside, both approaches align with the same essential threadless headset design, and will be amenable to similar sorts of adjustments.

One thing to understand about any of these is that they're meant to work as cohesive systems. The mere fact that disparate headset cups, bearings, or races are meant for use with the same sized head tube does not necessarily suggest that they'd work together as individual pieces—some bearing retainers are slightly shorter or wider, for example, while others are taller and narrower. We replace them as complete packages. I ended up compiling a respectable collection of headset debris working at bike shops over the years, but in all that time I think I pieced together all of one complete set.

The loose headset is easy to spot. When you lift the handlebars and drop, the bike rattles. It is an annoying, obvious problem. Things rarely become too tight up there, but this too is hard to ignore—you'd *really* be able to feel the bearings, holding the frame and turning the bars, as if they are almost ratcheting into position. The worst cases develop to become a sort of indexed steering: the bearings wear slight hollows in their races, from which they only move reluctantly.

Threaded and threadless headset adjustments are described in the following paragraphs. In either case, loose headsets are best identified and resolved with the bike on the ground, while overly tight headsets are easier noticed and dealt with when the bike is in the stand.

A. Threaded

The threaded and threadless headsets look at least vaguely similar, but the originals wear more exciting collars. There are almost always at least two distinct layers to these turtlenecks, each of which may be turned, and *this* is our cue, in distinguishing the **THREADED HEADSETS**. There are always wrench flats, or at least a knurled surface to turn, to suggest threads around the exterior of the fork's steerer tube. Only rarely, as with the curious Stronglight X-15 headset, are these elements hidden.

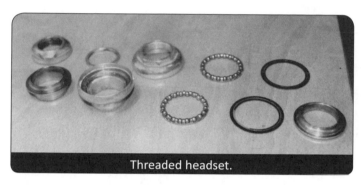
Threaded headset.

The headset's bearing cup and locknut are counter-tightened against each other, to set the appropriate bearing adjustment. The locknut flats measure 30, 31, 32, 36, or 40 mm. The 30 and 31 are very old and fading fast; the 40 is in nearly as precarious a position. The 32 and 36 both still enjoy active use, for 1″ and 1 ⅛″ headsets respectively.

The bearing cup beneath this lockring also features 32 or 36 mm flats, if we're lucky. Here again, 40 mm is less and less common, and neither the 30 nor 31 mm were used in this application. But we may instead find basic knurled collars, with very old 1″ stacks. These are lame! They were the first draft; the gaps between these oldsters and their bearing cups are sometimes wide enough to almost see the bearings. So grit gets in

there, where it does no good at all. Nor will the limited purchase offered by this old-fashioned knurling business lend itself well to tightening—squeeze tightly with your channel-locks; it's about all you can do.

There should always be a washer between the locknut and the bearing cone, to ease their friction. These are most often "keyed," which is to say their interiors feature small nubs—or flat spots, depending—to correspond with matching features carved to the rear of the steerer tube. Any spacers or cable guides that may be required also need to fit in this same place, between the cone and locknut. Cable guides used with threaded headsets should be appropriately keyed as well.

We can find locknuts with supplementary thread-locking features, if a headset is having trouble retaining its adjustments, but I'd first be curious about what else may be going on. The final adjustment probably is not being made tight enough. We don't want the bearing cup and locknut to be all crushing down on the bearings, but they must be tightly pressed against *each other*.

Mismatched parts, poorly aligned bearing races, or missing bearings may also impact upon a headset's staying power. Such problems might leave a headset too loose at some angles but too tight in others. You also want to make sure you don't install the headset seals upside down, or pinch them at odd angles between the other parts. Ultimately the frame's head tube itself may need to be faced, if nothing else works. Metal cutting dies are brought against either end of the head tube in precisely parallel positions; any discrepancies they encounter are literally shaved away. Your friendly local bike shop should have the exotic metal-cutting equipment this task would require.

The preferred headset adjustment will hover evenly in the middle distance, without binding or rattling, and its adjustable parts will be left supremely tight against each other. It is best if you can arrange to complete your adjustment by clasping your hands over the two wrenches, to tighten them together. This makes for better leverage—more power to you, basically. Stand just in front of the handlebars and brace the front wheel between your feet, while finishing this adjustment; this will allow you to determine whether the cup or the locknut is being turned.

We should also lay to rest the remnants of an old dispute, so long as we're here, about the precise meaning of this "one inch." Everything was sorted out prior to the arrival of threadless headsets, fortunately, so this old confusion only really haunts their threaded peers. The larger sizes are totally safe—they're truly standardized—but this only follows on the protracted slaughter of little "one inch."

A few headsets bearing slightly different measurements have each adapted this moniker, essentially. Japanese Industrial Standard (JIS) features a fork crown race with an inner diameter of 27.0 mm, and we see it used with low-quality department store bikes. The 1″ threaded headsets found on better and more recent bikes enlist 26.4 mm for the inner crown race diameter. The wrong race will simply slip loosely into position, in other words, or else it will not fit at all.

We find ways around either of these situations, by milling the head tube's base or knurling its surface, but either of these will involve even more shop tools. The dispute extends forward from there, actually—the vast majority of 1″ forks will accept stems bearing 22.2 mm stalks, but a goofy 21.5 mm stem will occasionally show up on older department store bikes. The BMX "one inch," finally, features frame cups that are almost 3 mm wider than all the others.

B. Threadless

THREADLESS HEADSETS represent a better design. Everything is more straightforward, and usually lighter as well. The threadless fork's steerer tube extends up well past the top of the threadless headset, because the threadless stem clamps in place around it.

An M6 bolt with a 5 mm head shoots through a big fat washer, which caps both the stem and the steerer tube.

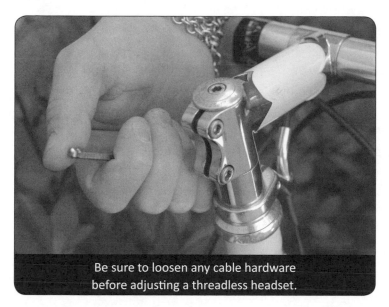

Be sure to loosen any cable hardware before adjusting a threadless headset.

cases, the front) of the stem, and this is what secures the threadless stem to its steerer tube. Note that these bolt(s) will need to be loosened before adjusting the preload bolt, as would any other bolts securing cable hangers around the steerer tube.

We call the fork's fitting the **STAR NUT**. The old threaded headset's dramatic mission is miniaturized, with the threadless—where old school tightens its external parts against the fork's crown fork race, the threadless system merely tightens its diminutive bolt into the star nut. The

This **PRELOAD BOLT** threads into a fitting, which itself rests suspended in the middle of the fork's steerer tube: tightening the bolt squeezes the frame and fork together. A further bolt (or two) is laid horizontally across the back (or in some

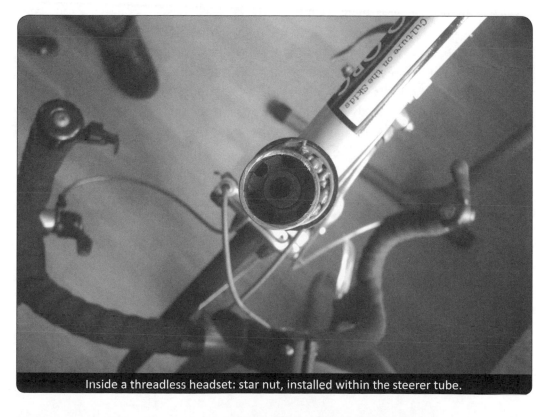

Inside a threadless headset: star nut, installed within the steerer tube.

threadless headsets' crowning features are the hats they wear, which we call the **ADJUSTING CAPS**. Threadless headsets are required to wear caps, at least as wide as the steerer tubes they cover, and these are meant to lay perfectly flat.

Quill stems will sometimes wear headgear as well, but it'd always be distinctly smaller, and the quill stem caps are usually set back at an angle. The style of a threadless headset's cap can tell us how old it is, or even its pedigree—where the older, simpler sorts favor basic black plastic hats, their replacements sport sharp aluminum berets instead. It was a little too easy to over-tighten the preload and press the bolt right through the plastic adjustment caps, so this makes for a happening trend indeed.

The adjustment we're looking for mimics that sought with the old threaded headsets, at midpoints between binding and rattling. Be sure to bounce the threadless bike's front wheel on the ground a few times before finalizing a given adjustment, because its parts will take a little more convincing to settle into position.

C. Overhauls

The threaded and threadless headsets each rely on two sets of bearings, one upstairs and one downstairs. These are usually held in nice circles by means of thin metal retainer cages. We will occasionally find needle bearings, which suspend their diminutive rollers within resin bases instead. Loose bearing headsets, once the only approach, are all but extinct, outside the still-considerable realm of fairly old bikes. Most high-end manufacturers have long since skipped right over the caged bearings to settle upon the headset's final format, which enlists sealed bearing cartridges. If these are not moving fast enough, they are simply replaced. Things are different now; that's just how it is.

Loose bearing headsets have always been especially easy to clean. Use your headset wrench to remove the locknut and upper bearing cup. Note how many bearings feature upstairs and downstairs—it may be two different numbers—and then collect them all on a rag, and roll them around in some thin oil. Apply the very same oily rag to the smooth surfaces featuring upon the headset's bearing cones and races and you're done. The loose bearing headset's successful reassembly presumes for a grease gun, or at least an artful hand. Lay a nice fat donut of grease in each bearing cup, and then put all the little balls right back where you found them.

Caged or needle bearings would be better soaked in undiluted bicycle-specific citrus solvent. (I've had less luck with the generic hardware store degreasers.) Where soaking removes the grit-laden grease trapped up inside the bearing cages, the oily rag only glosses things over. Can you let them soak overnight, or a couple nights even? Cool. The citrus rinses off with water. Be sure that everything is dry before reassembling the headset.

Cartridge bearings should be covered with a thin film of grease prior to being installed. This will minimize their creaks, if not vanquish every last one. I have heard of people prying up the cartridges' bearing seals in order to refresh the grease therein, but when this procedure is even possible, such seals are easily bent out of shape, so proceed at your own risk.

As mentioned, the cups and cones can be cleaned up with an oily rag. With the truly old 'n' crusty headsets, you may first need to dispose of some hardened grease: douse this crap with lightweight oil to break it down. Polish the bearing surfaces as best you're able. This will also highlight any scars etched to their faces—the less you rely on a pitted headset, the smarter your bike will become.

The lower headset bearings rest atop a **CROWN RACE**, which itself is hammered into place around the slightly wider base of the fork's steerer tube, right where it meets the fork crown—the fork's fat lip. We pound them down with stout sections of pipe known as crown race hammers. A blessedly simple tool, available in each of our three sizes.

We use a hammer and punch to remove crown races from their forks. There should be a nice slice of the race's bottom hanging over the front and rear of the fork crown; we pound on these spots to knock it off. Many suspension forks are built around fat aluminum fork crowns, which will extend well past

the aforementioned ledges—the punch won't have anywhere to go, all of a sudden—but that's fine, as my colleague Jon Londres observes, because the J.A. Stein company makes a tool meant for just such situations.

You also want to keep an eye out for any bearing seals, which will generally seat right around the edge of the crown race—tightening these at angles will probably destroy them, or at least leave them warped beyond use. It would be better to press the fork up into the frame from beneath when reassembling, with everything sitting just where you like it to be. Spin the fork a little, to be sure. Hold it just like that, with the one hand, while you tighten down the upper deck with your free hand. Your headset should have a similar seal protecting the top bearings. Take the same cautions with this one as well.

Older or cheaper headsets often lack such amenities, but we can help them out all the same. Go find a dead mountain inner tube, and chop it into sections: 1″ donuts. You and all your friends now have a lifetime supply of retrofit headset seals! Y'all do have to remove the fork to fit them, of course. There should be an overlap onto the fork. It will dampen the steering some, but not to any extent that will impact the ride; you would only want to account for such an improvement when dialing in the headset adjustment.

The threadless headsets are somewhat easier to work with. The seals charge up

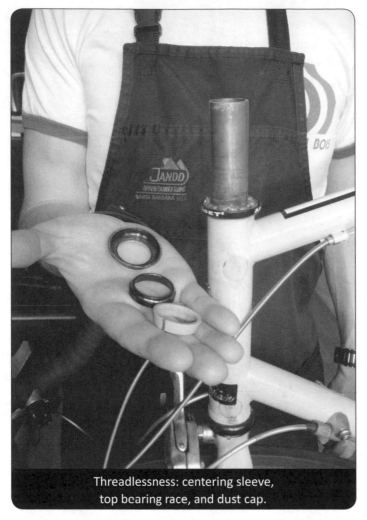

Threadlessness: centering sleeve, top bearing race, and dust cap.

Headsets are somewhat further removed from the ever-present road grit, comparing to the bearings in the hubs and the bottom bracket, so they can generally survive on less maintenance. The biggest risk to just letting things go might be the stem seizing in place. This is why we grease them before they're installed.

If you are **REPLACING A HEADSET**, it is best accomplished using the appropriate tools. The bearing cups need to be press-fit into the head tube, and it is important that the two become precisely parallel to each other. The **HEADSET PRESS** we use at the shop for this procedure is a long threaded rod, equipped with curiously stepped fittings, which press the cups into the frame. The steps coincide with each of our three common headset sizes. You would have yourself a hell of a jigsaw puzzle trying to piece one of these together at the hardware store.

and over their bearings, filling the gap from bearing cup to handlebar stem; the upper bearing surfaces are incorporated directly to their undersides. Just above or immediately below these threadless seals, we find a peculiar wedge-shaped washer known as the **CENTERING SLEEVE**. Its outer face slopes down to correspond with an equally steep slope on the top bearing race's interior, underneath. This sleeve complements the preload bolt, transmitting its narrow imperatives out to the wider steerer tube, and the threadless headset would fare poorly in its absence.

It is also possible the head tube would need to be faced, whereby specialized metal-cutting kit is enlisted to ensure the head tube's opposing ends are made fully parallel. Something as simple as a build-up of paint can throw off the headset's adjustment. But the tools here are ridiculously expensive; it's unlikely that anyone would just go and loan them out. We had a boxed Campagnolo frame tool set at the shop I worked for in Milwaukee; those of us allowed to peer within had our names noted on the lid.

Secure front wheel with toe strap, before removing threadless stem.

Rounding off the proud roster of our official headset installation tools is the **CROWN RACE HAMMER.** It is a sturdy piece of pipe, maybe 6″ tall. You set the race on top of the fork's crown and pound it into place. The impacts will start to sound a little different once the race touches down and goes flat. I'll go and pound it a few more times, just to make sure. You may even pick one of these up, if you find yourself doing this much. They're not so expensive. It is the other tools that would break you.

Lacking a headset press, the only alternative I'm aware of for getting the cups in is the sketchy procedure described in my first book—the two cups are installed individually, using a hammer and a wooden block. Careful! And for fuck's sake, don't even pretend to hammer on carbon fiber anything. This would not be worth trying on any worthy metal frames either, actually, because it may begin to flare out the head tube. This flared effect can happen to steel racing bikes as well, if they really get worked. But this is rare; I've seen it all of twice in my life. And you do not want the head tube to flare out, because the cups will lose any interest in staying put. The headset will just keep coming loose.

I did fix a flared head tube on an old RB1 once, by adding some brass to the tube's interior with a torch. It was necessary to mill and face the head tube, to clean up the excess, but things firmed right the hell up. It is far more likely that your bearing cups are stuck in there pretty well. The inner edges of the headset cups provide for dramatically thin ledges, which we need to pound upon to knock the cups out. We shop rats have yet another unusual tool for this—I want to tell you about it, but it really defies easy description—you can do about as well with a section of steel tubing, something with a good edge to it.

Considering our place in the story so far, it seems like a fine time to get into the **STEMS**. They are the graceful acrobats, spanning the distance from fork to handlebar. Where other parts of the bicycle require reinforcements in their work, the stems demonstrate the focus to concentrate their strength within a solitary beam.

Tightening any stem: brace the front wheel between the feet.

Theirs is a pointedly ambitious pursuit, and it would be fairest to say that some pull it off far better than others. A good stem prevents the handlebars from flexing, when you stand up and jam on the pedals, and this makes the bike more efficient. An even better one will do so within the confines of lightweight construction.

Stems are described by their length, from the center of the steerer tube to the center of the handlebars, and by their angles of inclination. As with the headsets, we must consider the steerer tube size and headset type, but a stem must also account for the handlebar's clamp diameter. A stem will be meant to work with either threaded or threadless headsets, which are themselves designed around 1″, 1 ⅛″, or 1 ¼″ steerer tubes. At the same time, the far end will feature a clamp of 25.0, 25.4, 26.0, 26.4, 28.6, 31.7, or 31.8 mm for the handlebars. This may already be more freedom than we really find useful, but that's how it is. Love it or leave it.

This fledgling constitution already requires a number of amendments, actually—older BMX stems, some integrated systems, a few oddballs from Cannondale. But the bikes form a democracy, and their great majority has agreed to follow these simple rules with the stems.

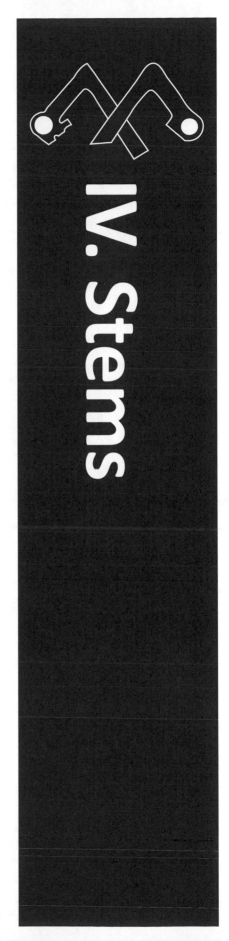

IV. Stems

The steerer tube size is easy enough to keep track of, as are the headset details. The clamp diameter is less obvious to the naked eye, but we can figure it out. The fit should be nice and snug. The bar should not be able to wriggle around, when the stem's clamp bolt is released. There is some leeway possible with the steel stems. Their clamps can be safely pried or squeezed past small discrepancies—when fitting 26.4 mm Cinelli bars in a 26.0 mm road stem for example—but this is not a good idea at all with the aluminum stems.

Clamp diameter.

are typically too square to even allow the drops to pass. The drops' graceful curves require half-moons cut out of the stem clamp, in order to snake through; these have always been more of an alloy thing.

Our world has witnessed the rise of the **TOP-LOADING STEMS**, more recently, and these careful diplomats are able to resolve many of the old schisms. Their firm but transient facemasks are simply bolted and unbolted, to accept different handlebars. None of the grips or control levers need to be removed, in other words, and the bars can curve as they damn well like.

A drop handlebar's navigation through its stem might be expedited by means of the stem clamp penny trick, as outlined by Brad Quartuccio in *Urban Velo*. Thread the stem's binder bolt out, slip a penny up between the stem clamp's jaws, and then thread the bolt back in from the *opposite* direction, so that it comes to press the penny against the far side of the clamp, thereby widening the stem's ravine.

The old alloy stems can be pretty nice. They only need the right handlebars. The drop bars are often a good match with the old aluminum stems, and not just for the clamp diameters. Their steel kin

Some of the new high-end road bars fully require top load stems, as their flattened wing sections will not fly through any pedestrian circular clamps. Top-loaders may also forgive small discrepancies in size more easily, between 25.4 and 26.0 for example. I cannot necessarily recommend this kind of mere estimation, for the expected sorts of reasons, but the aforementioned substitution has always done me fine. This said, I do ride fairly pedestrian sorts of bars and stems—used or free, for the most part—I really couldn't encourage any mismatching on high-end ultralight parts, where this will likely become a more crucial consideration.

A. Quill

Stems meant for the threaded headsets, which we call the **QUILL STEMS**, reach back and slip their straws down inside the fork's head tube. The threaded headsets only happen to surround this exchange; they are not immediately involved.

The gap between the quill stem and its steerer tube must be lined with grease, lest things seize in place—this has happened plenty of times before, and it secretly wants to happen again. An **EXPANDER BOLT** shoots down from the quill's crown, to thread into an offset nut in its base: tightening this down will brace the stem against the steerer tube. The nut will either wedge against the bottom of the stem, or it will draw up between a slit or two to expand the stem itself.

The expander bolt always needs to become very tight. Under no circumstance should the stem allow the bars to move independently of the fork. If you're having troubles here, slop some grease on the bolt's threads and under its head as well.

We also need to keep an eye out for the maximum height lines, with the quill stems. These notices, etched at midpoints across their stalks, warn us

against raising a stem high enough to allow its expander bolt to press against the upper threaded section of the steerer tube, which is weaker. I've seen steerers bend and crack for just such reasons. Leaving aside the fascinating yet comfortable realm of recumbents and semi-recumbents, high-rise stems and handlebar options have been made available to fit just about any upright bike. Every last

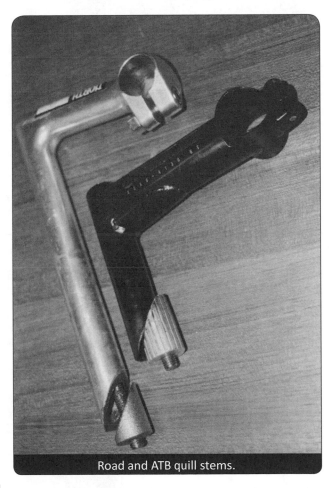

Road and ATB quill stems.

high-rise quill stem is also marked with the very same maximum height line, because it really is that important. Raising the bars has become an increasingly popular pursuit. Safety merely demands that we set things up right.

B. Threadless

The **THREADLESS STEM** is also found in each of our major steerer sizes, but this is where the similarity ends. They wrap

Threadless stem.

around the fork's steerer, rather than plumbing its depths. This may be the single best way to recognize threadless stems, at this point; they'll always be wide enough to slide down around the fork's steerer tube. Their tail sections will be about as wide as the frame's head tube, in other words. They're most often clamped in place by means of two bolts strapped across their backsides, but this has not always been the case: there may only be one, and it may be hiding under a button, in *front* of the steerer tube.

Threadless stems are found in a variety of lengths, rising to a range of different heights. Circumstance also provides them with a further trick: they can be flipped, to provide more or less rise to the bars. You may not need a whole new

stem, in other words; maybe the old one only needs to be made right side up. It's easy enough to check, with the aid of a removable face plate.

Spacers mounted around the steerer tube above or below the stem allow further discretion, with regards to the handlebar position. The steerer tubes of threadless forks aren't always cut to size, actually, with spacers filling out the distance above or below the stem. Trimming the steerer spares us a few tedious little grams, of course, but leaving it long allows for versatility, which at the very least can make a big difference in resale situations.

Most headset spacers are alloy. Fancier examples are minted from carbon fiber. My Sycip is equipped with one of these last, and it hasn't failed me yet. In a pinch? That black plastic reflector bracket around your seatpost might do the trick—strange, but true. The bike I ended up with in Mauritania was short a 10 mm spacer, and its reflector bracket emerged as the closest available match. Nothing I'd want to take off a loading dock or anything, but around town at least it held up just fine.

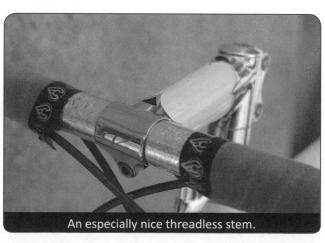

An especially nice threadless stem.

C. Adjustable

Threadlessness more generally is a blazingly efficient program, outlining the leading edge of all we know so far. Unfortunately, the marketing team has in the years since presented us with a long series of recurring mistakes, known collectively as the **ADJUSTABLE STEMS**.

I like to imagine that the industry's more righteous engineers would have called them on this crap a decade or two ago, but the precious new whiz kids sheltering beneath the major manufacturers evidently lent their acquiescence instead. The project has subsequently sprawled forward to the point that adjustable stems are an expected feature. This does not make them normal.

The adjustable stem was first noticed in the late 1990s; it has since come to afflict threaded and threadless stems alike. The adjustables usually sport the smart new face plates, but only because they had the fortune to show up at a convenient time. The gesture falls well short of any adequate compensation. A small number of higher-end adjustable stems may sidestep the issues outlined here, but the vast majority cannot.

People tend to develop specific inclinations about their preferred handlebar positions—stretched-out for speed and stability, or more upright for comfort. The adjustable stems strive to make bikes more ambidextrous in this respect, as if we somehow cannot make up our minds. Yet so much else would need to change, moving from a truly performance-oriented profile to a more leisurely platform—assuming, that is, that we are persuaded by the balance of the industry's advertising.

Under load, even a correctly installed adjustable stem begins to feel disconcertingly flexible. What strain the stem might encounter becomes concentrated on a solitary bolt, shot through the stem's upper and lower extremities, and this bolt needs to be made supremely tight: its positioning leaves it particularly vulnerable to loosening, and to my experience this is exactly what happens after a while.

Improvised threadless headset spacer. Worked just fine.

Most such bolts seem to have been greased back at the factory, but this doesn't seem to help. I really don't think a thread-locking compound would be of use in this particular situation; it'd also be a bit counterintuitive. The wrench fittings we find tend to be surprisingly shallow, given the bolt's size and purpose: de-

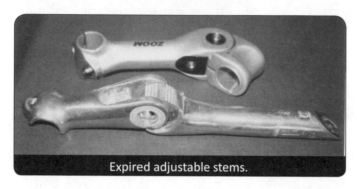

Expired adjustable stems.

signed more to present a svelte appearance, rather than for functionality. Their heads strip out fairly easily, after which point you are no longer able to tighten them. There starts the terminal phase:

the bolt loosens further, the stem begins to rock around, the gaps between its major parts are widened. The problem compounds itself and becomes permanent—after it has succeeded in widening itself out, there is no good way to convince such a slab of aluminum to reform itself.

The adjustment itself, accomplished with sets of facing splines and a further bolt on the stem's underside, generally proceeds without undue complication, alas this is not enough. The adjustable stems look kind of overbuilt, which is unfortunate, but neither does this help their case. The problem is that these things were let out into the world in the first place. Fortunately—owing to the removable face plates—the adjustable stems are easily replaced.

A. Tubes

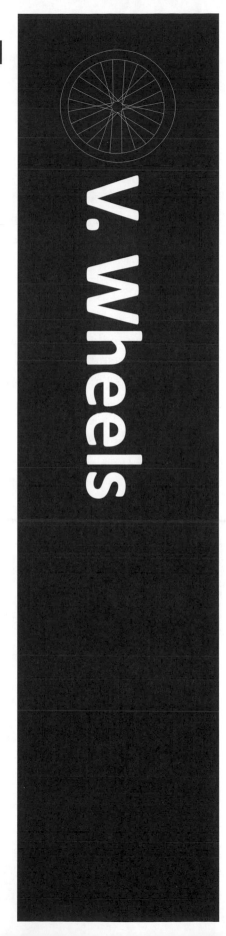

It is tempting to imagine that there exists an organized conspiracy to pop your **INNER TUBES**. Flat tires may implicate divine forces beyond our ken, amusing themselves for diabolic and untoward reasons we dare not speculate upon, but our villains in truth are only opportunistic—they spy an opening, and they go for it. We may have called them entrepreneurs, in another setting.

I would like to see the staples given a more prominent position in the tragic pantheon of puncture folklore, myself. The wire is just thin and sharp enough to make it the perfect unassuming nemesis. It is good to avoid running over debris to any extent that this becomes possible, but there's no way we can spot every last piece of it; the tire's characteristics will inevitably become relevant. Those thorns lurking

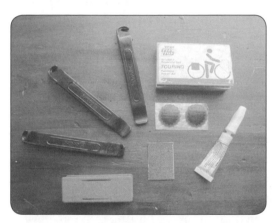

to the garden path's shadowed periphery may well indeed have scores to settle with your inner tubes, but something has to let them in first.

Our tires are removed with the **TIRE LEVERS**, which travel best in triples. We only need two, for the act itself: their hooks are slipped under the tire's bead on one side, a couple inches apart, and both are pulled back in an arc, simultaneously, so that their portion of the tire's bead is dragged out into public view. The far end of one lever is then hooked under a spoke, to better hold its position, while its mate is dragged up the length of the rim, prying the bead free as it goes.

The operation becomes arduous enough to occasionally snap the plastic levers, with smaller high-pressure tires especially, which is why the levers' sedan typically makes room for an alternate as well. This is not at all an issue for the brilliant black and yellow **QUIK STIK**, the proud iconoclast among the tire levers, which is burly enough to go it alone. You jab it into place, peel back, and pull. The original was evidently carved from wood by a cyclist stranded without tire levers.

It is best to carry a spare tube in your travels, and the easiest way to build up a stock of these is to repair the old ones. Just hang them in a corner somewhere. You'll eventually be able to patch a whole loop of tubes at once, and the exercise will suddenly become eminently practical and efficient, not unlike the industrial revolution itself. The On-the-Road treatment (page 185) outlines practices for more spontaneous situations.

Once you do have a few tubes to patch, grab your floor pump and see how many can be inflated up to maybe two or three times their natural size, nice and fat. (This will be possible, most of the time, as the holes tend to be pretty tiny—otherwise, you'd be able to see or hear the hole pretty easily.) Take each tube in turn and run it past your ear. You may hear the air rushing out of its hole, or feel its tiny breath on your cheek. You would need to go and do the dunking-underwater thing, otherwise, but even that would be worth the time. What do new tubes cost these days, $5 apiece?

Regular felt-tipped markers are useful for keeping track of the holes you find: unless the tube is still wet, in which case I would recommend using a safety pin instead. Seriously—the marker would need a dry surface, just as the glue will, and you're already in the process, right?

Anything you can fit a patch over can be fixed. You want like a ¼″ overlap to each side. Tubes can and do last for decades; long blow-out gashes or holes right up by the valve stem are the only things that really kill them dead. Patch kits are typically born with one or two larger patches, which I find myself cutting into halves or thirds for smaller projects most of the time. All you really need to do is make sure the tube is nice and clean, and the glue is really dry. Most patching maneuvers that do fail trace back to one of these two points.

The patch kits feel obliged to present us with a little square of sandpaper, to scuff the tube. It is a nice

Find that hole quickly: line up the valve with the tire label.

gesture, but I cannot even remember the last time I actually used one of these. The sandpaper hangs over from the crazy old days, before they got the other elements figured out.

Dose a good puddle of glue right over each hole, enough to surround the patch completely, and let it sit like that for a good long time. This dries the glue way the hell out, which is precisely what we want it to do. Peel the foil and lay the patches down, pressing firmly. I tend to press the patched sections in an EZ-Grip clamp, actually—you just line the patches up like pancakes and press. Leave them like that for a couple hours, if you can; this seems to do some good. Our final exam inflates them fully again, to see if they hold all their air overnight.

The **TUBELESS TIRES** explain away the inner tube, replacing it with an airy void of their own design. The tire's bead and the rim hook up in more meaningful ways. The spoke nipples are hidden from view by means of small plugs, which thread into place; everything stays nice and airtight. Be sure to treat these eyelets with threadlocker, before they go in.

Why? Tubelessness allows the tires to run at lowered air pressures. Where the stupid old inner tubes predictably succumb to pinch flats if you run them too low, these new space tires provide nothing to pinch, and the wider contact patch that results will take your bike places other tires would not.

B. Rim Strips

The spokes are sharp metal sticks, and the inner tubes are only bags of air; theirs is no likely combination. The spokes are already under great tension. The hopeful tube expands out to meet them, like it wants to be friends or whatever, and after a point they just pop the poor thing. But the danger is no less real on the more sophisticated double-walled rims, which secret the spokes' nipples up on a second floor. The tube will still try to crawl up and greet them, which would take its breath away just as surely.

Our prescient intermediary is the **RIM STRIP**, yet another patient and reasonable diplomat, which in this instance manages to quietly obscure the tube and spokes' divergent interests. Neither the composite wheels nor the new tubeless tires need to ask after rim strips, for the obvious reasons, but all the other wheels require such protection.

The wheels may favor one sort of rim strip or another, based upon their features. The simplest are the big black rubber bands. Different sizes are available, to perhaps include a choice on the width. The size may be marked somewhere, in ungainly white block lettering, listing the nominal wheel size in inches and the width in millimeters. Odd. But the rubber bands become brittle after a while, and even the freshest ones will threaten to snap. They were associated with the bottom-feeder bikes for a pretty long time, but some wretched loser eventually chanced upon an even cheesier approach, using strapping tape for the rim strips. The heavy plastic crap, like what we found around the newspaper bundles on the old paper routes? Where the basic rubber rim strips may be pulled aside to replace a spoke, or even reused on a wholly different wheel, we have no such luck with the plastic. You need to destroy it to change out a spoke nipple, and then we have to sell you a new rim strip.

The rubber version only costs a buck, but it would be better to just get one of the real ones instead. The rubber bands snap far too easily! Nor can we trust them at higher pressures, especially on the double-walled rims. Several manufacturers have produced useful updates on the old rubber bands, using thin plastics just strong and pliable enough to do the job, in the 26″ and 700 cm wheel sizes at least, but the **RIM TAPE** has always been the more traditional choice. The first variety you'll see is probably going to be the classic Velox tape, the face of which reads "Fond de Jante" over and over again. Nice and thick, about like cardstock, only cloth. It is usually sold in individual rolls, in one of three widths, each of which is long enough to cover a road-sized rim. You pare it down to fit the smaller-sized wheels, folding it to cut a tiny diamond-shaped valve hole with the very tip of the sidecutters.

C. Tube Sealants

The rim strips are helpful and good. I relish their discussion, in fact, because

our next topic already brings the fighting bile to the back of my palate . . . it is the **SLIME**. Together with similar substances, the slime is marketed as a "flat preventative," meant to be introduced to the tubes through their valve stems. Slime and kindred substances will sometimes infect the new bikes' inner tubes from the time of their birth, but it is also sold as an aftermarket item. No more flats! We ended up with a batch of thus equipped mountain bikes at the rental shop I used to manage, my last summer there. I soon lost track of how many slime-filled inner tubes I replaced, on these blunted pioneers. From all I've seen, the so-called flat preventatives don't even do what they're supposed to do. Quality tires are much more effective in preventing flats.

The tube sealants do add some weight to your wheels, however. There is also the chance it may spray you: the air compressor hose hits the valve, just like before, only this time a mess of green ooze spurts suddenly from the valve. Or maybe not— seems to be kind of random—but you never know, so you want to keep your face well back from the wheel whenever you air the damned tire. I did this all summer long, with every last Specialized Expedition comfort bike in the fleet. We were crazy busy all the while; it was just ridiculous.

The sealant may or may not clog up the tube's valve over time. You would know if it did, because you wouldn't be able to fill the tube anymore. But then, at least, you wouldn't get sprayed!

These things said, I have also met people who absolutely swear by the stuff. At the 2006 Bike! Bike! Conference in Milwaukee, a friend from Arizona recommended tube sealants as a final line of defense against the dreaded and remorseless goathead thorns, which have been known to defeat even the mighty Specialized Armadillo tires. Seen in this light, Slime might be the last realistic alternative before the heavy thud of solid rubber tires, which can also be found but aren't nearly as popular.

D. Tires

A tire's **SIZE** will be noted at some point on its sidewall. The measurement might be impressed in inches or millimeters, or even both, as the case may be. Dependent on the tire's vintage, this figure may refer to the tire's inside diameter, or perhaps its outside.

History has provided us with no less than eight distinct wheel sizes whose names begin "26-inch," to take one favorite example. Sutherlands' famous manual has dutifully kept track of their particulars. The metric measurements of 599, 597, 590, 585, 584, 571, 561, and 559 mm each refer to a distinct **BEAD DIAMETER**, which measures the wire that hooks into the rim. Yet the same eight sizes might just as easily be listed as 26 x 1.375, 26 x 1 ¼, 26 x 1 ⅜, 26 x 1 ½, 26 x 1 ¾, 26 x 2.25, and 26 x 2.0, each of which would more correctly describe a tire's outside diameter.

The smaller sizes have suffered as well, but not nearly as much. While "20-inch" may suggest a bead diameter of either 406 or 451, the "16-inch" may be either 305 or 349. I'm not aware of any outstanding disputes around the 12-inch tire size, but the hairs have split again up at 24-inch—the label typically refers to a kids' bike tire size, but a distinct high-pressure slick tire makes an occasional appearance, on my wife's Terry for example. Also available are 14-inch and 17-inch tires, but each is even less common. The same could be said for all the dozens of other different tire sizes the world has witnessed, the greater number of which has at last been laid to rest. The vast majority of bicycle wheels now answer to either the 559/26, or the 700c, which is our external-diameter shorthand for the ubiquitous 622-bead diameter.

The 29-inch tires are also becoming popular again. The term "29-inch" approximates the outer diameter of the ubiquitous 700c size; it is only the knobbier, wider big brother to the 700c hybrid tires we've known for many years. Nor is the concept especially new; Diamondback sold such a bike in the early '90s.

The nearly nostalgic 27-inch road size still finds its way in, now and again. Its ISO bead diameter is 630; a few basic tires are still broadly available. These bead diameter measurements are the only ones that really matter—we cannot fuck around with this; it really needs to be spot on. A tire also needs to be at least as wide as its rim, or just narrow enough to fit in the intended frame.

Knobby tires manage to convey a kind of rugged survivability. I have no idea how this is for the trucks, but it is no rule for the bikes. The small free-standing knobs on the mountain tires mushroom out and wriggle around, as they're pressed to the pavement, and this actually reduces their traction. Knobbies are also meant to run on an air pressure somewhat lower than that prescribed in other scenarios, and this makes for a wider contact patch hitting the ground, which really slows things down. Thus do we see road tires in mountain bike sizes. The smoother and thinner the tire, and the higher its pressure, the quicker you will become.

A tire's wear is most evident in terms of **DRY-ROT**. The sun and the water both have business with the soft rubber tires; their efforts will eventually affect small cracks. We can see these easily enough, with older and cheaper tires—you'll see them better yet, if you let the air out and squeeze the tire flat. The cracks tell us the material has become dry and brittle.

The best example of this phenomenon may be the decrepit gumwall tires on the dusty old basement bike, suddenly rescued after years of abandonment. The bike itself may have potential, but its tires are probably toasted. Their treads may even have retained their unblemished gumwall grin, all these long years, but it will not mean a thing.

"Gumwall" refers to the sidewalls, which are rendered in the same cheap compound used for the tread. The two areas may be different colors, but it will not make any difference. It's about the cheapest way to make a tire, and so we should not be surprised when the dumb gumwalls keep losing their little arguments with the glass.

More realistic tires have long since adopted distinct materials, for tread and sidewall both. This becomes a useful point of departure, in considering tire quality; its riding characteristics and durability are both functions of the materials used. Various types of basic armor plating have filtered down to the cheaper tires, but these simpler examples also tend to be heavier.

E. Truing Wheels

Pedestrian as it may seem, the ordinary bicycle wheel was an extraordinary invention. The very idea that one can both carry weight and transmit momentum through nothing more than tightly laced bits of wire—it must have been amazing.

When problems do arise, the wheel's straightforward construction allows us to replace only those parts we'd need to—it is delicate, but it is magnificent. There are better and worse things we'd like to see when appraising a wheel, and a lot of the time these are only separated by degrees. Our wheels are battered in an endless campaign of attrition; our skills in repairing them accrue in the opposite direction.

Our wheels are all of hubs, spokes, and rims. Each must remain worthy for their project to continue. The great majority of injured wheels I've come across are in fact repairable, but this is providence, not scripture.

Are you sure the hub is cool? Hub adjustments are discussed beginning on page 172. What about the spokes? Are they all present and accounted for? Their pattern should be the same, all the way around—no gaps, no blank spots—and their relative tension needs to be even. Spoke tension is crucial.

The truing process begins by squeezing the spokes together to make sure nothing is secretly busted. This is how it usually happens—the spokes break up by the hubs, but their lacing and the nipples hold the shattered wands in place. And they just hang out, like there's nothing going.

The rear spokes carry most of the rider's weight, and this makes them more vulnerable to failure, but more generally we should not resign ourselves to seeing any of our spokes break. It is not any natural condition. Spokes pop when the wheel takes a serious hit, or when they are asked to carry more than they are meant to handle. If a wheel is losing spokes on any kind of regular basis, something needs to change. The wheel may be usefully rebuilt with a stronger lacing pattern—three cross in place of radial, for example—but it's more likely that we would want to get more spokes involved in the first place, and that is a different wheel.

Those spokes that do snap tend to go one at a time, but not always. A poorly adjusted rear derailleur may allow the chain to hop off the last cog, massacring several spokes at once. The effect is not subtle; the spokes nearest the chain get all mangled. They may not fail right away, but the carved-up ones will be inclined to, so you should go ahead and replace them first.

This is what the **PIE PLATES** are for, incidentally; to prevent this kind of thing. Yet pie plates are not even remotely fashionable, outside the lower reaches of the bicycle hierarchy. They are the mechanic's training-wheels, out in full public view. Their presence has come to suggest some basic uncertainty with regards to the derailleur adjustments. But that does happen, sometimes, and the derailleur hangers get bent all the time, and so does the slaughter continue.

A rim's health can be harder to measure. We will certainly spot some of the more obvious casualties—the Pac Man, the potato chip—but others are less forthright. They may be able to suck it in just enough to pass, from a certain view at least.

It is sometimes possible to make a bent rim look straight, by playing with its spoke tension—you jack it all the way up on the one side, then loosen the others to some more noodling consistency—but this creates a weak spot, even if the wheel still appears to be true, and the slack generated therein saps away at the wheel's strength. You have accidentally thumped the apple, and so you expect to see a bad spot. The hub and spokes concerned may be reused, but a bent rim is toast. Go ahead and recycle it.

It is easy enough to take a wheel apart, once any gears are removed. (See pages 168, 171, and 233 for details on removing the old freewheels, the newer cassettes, or track cogs, respectively.) Dose a drop of oil atop each spoke nipple, to loosen things up. Spin the wheel a bit, to let the oil centrifuge down the spoke threads, grab your spoke wrench and start unraveling. The wheel's tension will gradually diminish, as you wind out each spoke in turn, at last revealing the full extent of the rim's troubles.

The relative size of a wheel's bad spot in itself is not necessarily indicative of anything, up to a point. What really matters is the spoke tension. It should even out as you true the wheel, resolving differences between the excessively tight and the way-too-loose.

Our discussion here really transpires along a continuum; the dead rim is only the final extension of a far more common problem. Were the rim bowing out to the right, for example, we would locate the center of the problem and see about tightening up the spokes on the left. But it is possible these were already as tight as we really like them to be—visiting their comrades across the left, to determine a rough average—in which case we would move to loosen up some of those over on the right. The two things might happen at once, in fact. In the best case scenario, the spoke(s) in need of tightening should already be a bit loose, and those

in need of loosening will be slightly tight. Tensioning levels on rear wheels are typically distinct to each side, for reasons soon to be explored, but in the ideal each side should become reasonably even all the way around. This balancing provides the wheel its lasting strength.

The more you work on wheels, the more you will come to appreciate the relevance of spoke tension. It is best measured with a tensiometer, as described in the wheel building section—see page 203—but we rarely whip one out for simple truing work. Newly built wheels are often usefully re-tensioned after their first 100 miles or so, but that's about it. Lacking a tensiometer, see if you can track down a quality hand-built wheel. Squeeze its spokes together, and translate the feeling over to your own wheel. Wheels do tend to loosen up as parts settle into place. A good level of tension will hold its own, but may need to be refreshed again later in life.

Any **BROKEN SPOKES** will need to be replaced, before the wheel is trued. A replacement spoke will mimic the pattern it finds in place on the wheel. Most wheels are laced in a three cross pattern, for example, and this will find the new spoke going over two others and under a third on its way home. This journey typically involves bending the spoke, which is fine, because steel is so damned resilient. Spokes bearing actual crimps are less ideal, but even these may be straightened with the box pliers if they need to be.

The hub gears will most likely need to be removed, to install the spoke. (Some smaller fixed cogs and BMX freewheels make for exemptions—the incoming spokes can shoot straight over their heads—but everything else will have to go.) You may or may not need to replace spoke nipples as well, which would involve removing both the tire and the rim strip.

Note that you would want to be careful replacing any nipples in deep-dish rims, lest they tip into the taller rim sections, where they would happily rattle away until you managed to shake them out. We have a special tool for this at work, but you can get what you need by threading the nipple onto a spare spoke, backward. This is then stuck up a spoke hole, where the intended spoke descends from its hub to meet the nipple's top. Holding the handy surrogate in place, twist its gift up and away to the wheel.

Any new spoke should be of precisely the same length as its predecessor. It would do no good for the spoke to shoot through the nipple and stab the inner tube, but it still needs to thread at least most of the way in. Lacking an exact match, it is sometimes possible to file down a spoke too long, until its end is made flush with the nipple. Double-walled rims are more forgiving in this respect as well. Spokes too short are occasionally made to work with taller spoke nipples.

WHEEL TRUING is a series of three steps, repeated in succession. You position the caliper, spin the rim slowly past, and make your adjustment. Each step shares in the responsibility for your results.

Positioning the caliper is not difficult at all, with the Park TS-2 stands. One dial moves it up and down in relation to the rim, while another opens and closes its jaws. Pretty slick. Whichever stand you're using, you want to proceed with the same basic sequence—spin the rim, in order to determine where the biggest problem is, and then adjust the caliper so it just *barely* grazes against this mountain's top. You will be starting with this largest discrepancy, before working your way down through any smaller ones.

The calipers may outline a broader bad spot, without any particular center. This is less common, the product usually of poor building skills. It is resolved in much the same way, only amplified; you turn three or four spokes instead of the one or two.

You may find a truing stand's calipers to be themselves slightly off-center. It is generally possible to fix this problem, but in the meanwhile it's easy enough to flip the wheel around in the truing stand so the opposite side faces against the more useful caliper. The wheel's orientation in the stand is not particularly relevant to the truing process; it is more important that you can see what you are doing.

Our adjustments on the spokes are made with the spoke wrenches. Park Tool's black SW-0, green SW-1, and red SW-2—for small, medium, and large spoke nipples—are the most ubiquitous in North America. The correct choice fits nice and snug around the nipple: it should not be able to wiggle around. A spoke wrench too large will eventually begin stripping the nipples, which is to say that their edges would wear down and eventually disappear. Good luck working with those!

The spoke nipples themselves should be relatively difficult to turn. The spokes are supposed to be treated with thread-

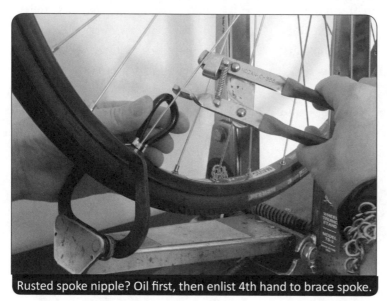

Rusted spoke nipple? Oil first, then enlist 4th hand to brace spoke.

ends to make the rim-mounted brakes squeak like hell.)

Alloy nipples? They are pretty, but they are also weak. They are indeed a bit lighter than the old-fashioned brass ones everyone else uses, but they are nowhere near as sturdy. My colleague Dan Ditty proposes a solution for their dilemmas, should they arise—first grip the spoke with your fourth hand tool, then try the adjustment. Set it up down low, just above the spoke wrench, at an angle such that only the tool's pinch is focused on the spoke.

Wheel truing adjustments are made in small increments, which grow smaller yet as the wheel becomes truer. We tighten spokes to pull the rim over toward their side, or loosen them to back it away. The loosest spokes might need to be tightened a few full turns, before their adjustments yield any visible changes, but it is more usual to begin with half-turns, measured a few at a time as the case may be.

locking compound, when first the wheels are built, but in practice many more end up getting a little rusty instead. The most recalcitrant examples will only move as one—the spoke would wind up and eventually snap, once its nipple was turned far enough. With the oldsters especially, it's always a good idea to start by dropping a bit of oil atop each of the spoke nipples. Hit the base of the nipple as well, while you're at it, right where it meets the rim. Then spin the wheel—the oil should work its way down the threads, as with a centrifuge. (Note that you will want to clean up any excess oil with degreaser or rubbing alcohol, once you finish, as it

Find what seems to be the most grievous problem, and make your adjustment. Then check your work: spin past the calipers again to see how you did. Finally, adjust the calipers as needed and repeat the process.

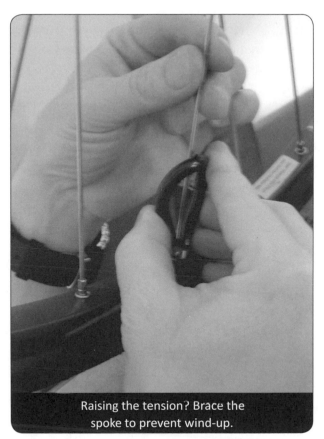
Raising the tension? Brace the spoke to prevent wind-up.

which in practice means that their spoke tension might be pretty random. The machines often know no better. For this reason, it is sometimes possible to save some time by starting out with a little shorthand, gauging the relative tension of the spokes on each side of a wheel and evening out their spoke tension. Limit this approach to the most glaring examples. Some spokes may be loose enough to rattle, while others are nearly too tight to even turn at first.

Other, smaller distortions will sometimes be made manifest, in the process of truing and tensioning a wheel. Fix these as they appear, but don't let their arrival throw you. Our progress toward the truth is often merely forward, rather than strictly linear. Adjustments on one spoke are translated out toward its peers, through their union at the hub; we will sometimes surf through a few ripples on the way home.

You want to get down to the point of making adjustments in quarter-turns, before finishing. But seriously, the only way you'll be getting there is by checking your work—consistently, methodically, every time you make adjustments. I don't want to sound like math class or anything, but that's just how it is. I've been truing wheels since 1993, and I still expect to do it this way, until the day I can true no more. You set and reset the caliper; you spin the wheel against it; you make your adjustment and you do it again, until the wheel is either made good or otherwise.

Recall our goal of equitable spoke tensioning, as you proceed. Most of the wheels in use today were built by machines,

The hops and flat spots, our peaks and valleys along the rim's topography, are somewhat less common than the lateral bends. Making imprudent leaps can earn your wheel a flat spot, but it's far easier to install them inadvertently, with the spoke wrenches. The hops, by nature, are always artificial.

The hops develop when a sequence of spokes is too loose. The flat spots appear when they're too tight, or when the wheel has suffered an especially rough landing. Any combination of the two would be roundly suspicious. A rim with a flat spot may still appear true from the lateral view. At the same time, issues with the spoke tension can cause a bad lateral bend to manifest as more of a flat spot.

Our treatment for the hops and flat spots works in much the same way, only sideways. All will be as it was before, with regards to the range of our adjustments—measured, patient, incremental—but the axis flips 90 degrees, from the horizontal to the vertical.

A rim's roundness and true are best corrected in tandem, with success in the one informing the other. As practice will reveal, this sounds a lot more complicated than it actually is.

The truing stand's calipers should allow some provision for measuring the wheel's overall roundness. We need to dispose of the tire to really check this out, if that hasn't happened already. The Park TS-2 calipers are especially good at this—the calipers are notched, allowing us to finish by checking the lateral true and roundness simultaneously. Travis showed me another nice trick for this, one day at the Freewheel: the calipers may also be positioned against the *top* of the rim, to better isolate the flat spots.

The last thing we need to consider is the **WHEEL DISH**—the wheel's centering, as it fits into the frame dropouts. This detail should have been resolved when first the

wheel was born, but any serious truing regimen may raise the point anew.

Where wheel truing valorizes the efforts of individual spokes, the dish is a fluid expression of their collective will—everybody works together, in equal measures, toward a common goal. This is most relevant out back, because the hub gears are generally wider than the spacers over on the neutral side. The two sides may be simply balanced against each other—the drive-side spokes are made a few turns tighter than their neutral kin—but it is more common to simply begin with slightly shorter spokes on the drive side, leaving the rim to sit off center in relation to the axle's end points.

You can check for wheel dish in the truing stand, by flipping the wheel back and forth, so that each side checks in with one arm of the caliper, but you may want to conduct the final exam in the frame itself. The wheel should appear correctly dished in either location, but the stand's calipers can fall out of adjustment, and both frames and forks may be knocked out of alignment. The frame test takes no effort at all. You sight down the top of the tire, using the hole in the frame's brake bridge or the fork crown as your reference point. Adjusting for wheel dish itself is simple enough: all the spokes on the one side get that very same tweak, be that with tightening or even a little loosening. We will do a half-turn or two apiece, typically.

The **FINAL TENSION** is the wheel's proof of enlightenment. As is further outlined in the wheel building chapter, 14/15/14 double-butted spokes used with most hand-built wheels should be tightened to an average 135 mm.

As your wheel approaches its fruition, the very last thing you want to do is stress the spokes. Grab them in pairs and squeeze hard, all the way around the wheel. You may also use the more thorough method, as described on page 214 of the wheel building section, for especially ambitious truing or re-tensioning projects. And then you check the true, one last time.

Our discussion to this point provides for a useful vantage on the space-age **COMPOSITE WHEELS**, which have rolled in more recently. They arrive here from some contrived and secondary dimension, where everything is simultaneously immortal and disposable. If you do manage to damage them, the odds are good they'd only be repaired back at the factory.

It is certainly possible to make stronger composite structures, but this would add weight, and the higher-end wheels just are not into that. The alloy hoops glued to many such wheels remain vulnerable to the problems any other wheel may encounter, such as denting.

The bicycle seats, known more formally as the saddles, can generate a conspicuous amount of controversy. People tend to develop distinct preferences regarding where they'd like to sit. My brother borrowed my old Bianchi Project 5 a few years ago, and he's made good use of it, since upgrading to a wider tractor-style seat. I asked him to save the bike's tattered San Marco Rolls—my old friend Tim had once recommended the Rolls as a fine saddle, back when we both rode downtown, and he was right.

The comfort sponges' ample padding soaks up a good measure of our pedaling energy; they're also a bit too wide to encourage any truly efficient transfer of power. The racing saddles are smaller and narrower, and usually quite a bit lighter. The merits of these are subjective, of course. We'll occasionally spy the poorly-fit profiles of retrofitted gel pads allegedly meant to make harder seats more comfortable, but in real life they tend to wriggle around in disconcerting ways, under use.

I'd never thought much of the simpler fabric seat covers until I went to live in Mauritania, where the relentless 120-degree sun bakes through plastic and rubber alike, tearing huge rips across targets so soft as our bicycle seats. We enlisted layers of duct tape to smooth out the edges, in the case of our Peace Corps bikes. I also ended up wrapping mine in tightly sewn rags. Goofy, but effective.

We also spy various saddles with curious splits right down the midsection. These were inspired by some doctor, who developed a concern that regular bicycle seats are potentially harmful to the male reproductive system. Specialized duly hired the guy to refine his gimmick, and it became a runaway success. The theme was found to resonate broadly! The good doctor's theories have since become more disputed—sometimes, maybe, but there never was any epidemic among cyclists. Some minute strata of hard-training racers may benefit from the innovation, perhaps, but there is no public health crisis.

Perhaps more usefully, a number of manufacturers have come to make women's saddles as well. The tail sections are

VI. Seats and Posts

wider, to better suit women's hips. Terry may have been the first to come out with one of these.

Replacing a saddle is easy enough. An ever-smaller fraction of truly ancient bikes use seats mounted on the old flat rails, and I've seen a goofy BMX saddle with only one big rail, but all the rest can be relied upon to sport ubiquitous pairs of round rails. Their width may vary, between 7 and 10 mm, but to the best of my knowledge they all subscribe to the usual sorts of seatpost clamps, which means that we're able to swap out just about any saddle for another.

The seatposts can be much more exacting than their charges, in terms of the size. The **SEATPOST SIZES** march in 0.2 mm increments from 25.0 up through at least 31.8 mm. Most sizes within this vast spread are very rarely called upon—they merely clutter up precious space at bike shops across North America, waiting patiently to meet one of those ever-rarer old bikes that could actually make use of them.

I would like to tell you that the posts file themselves into this nearly reasonable range of straightforward metric gradients, but as yet we're not quite so fortunate. The ⅞″ BMX seatposts are still fairly common; the long-obsolete steel stumps used with ancient Peugeot bikes still find occasional uses as well. And then we have the folding bikes, which have taken to exceptionally tall and wide posts. These disclaimers made, *nearly* all the other seatposts will coincide with

the aforementioned range. The numbers are carved to the front of the posts, just below the maximum height line, which itself is another important feature we'll soon arrive upon.

Some sizes—the 25.0, 25.4, 25.8, 26.2, 26.4, 26.8, 27.0, and 27.2—have really become more common. Their sustained popularity, in fact, renders the more obscure sizes fairly conspicuous. A 26.6 mm post may be the most useful thing ever, in Eastern Europe or Middle Earth or somewhere, but it'd be quite an odd creature to see in the Midwest. I would wonder if the 26.8 mm makes for a better match.

The very best scenario finds you pulling a properly sized post from its frame, noting the digits, and marching these down to your friendly local bike shop—as when upgrading from a curmudgeonly old steel post to a lighter aluminum one, for example. But seats are stolen all the time, with the posts as well, and it's even possible that a size too small may have been inadvertently installed.

The fit should be just snug enough. You should be able to adjust the post's position by hand, once its pinch bolt is released. A nearly seized post will move only grudgingly, until you get it out and paint some grease down in there—you may want to run it by the shop and have them hone the seat tube, first—but in no case should there be lateral play, across the seat post and its frame.

Sizing the post may theoretically be done with calipers, but the gradients are dispersed five-to-the-millimeter, so at the shop we use stepped metal gauges instead. The diminishing sizes are etched to the face of each successive step. We would need to root through the seatpost box, lacking such, to see which comes the closest—you may find your precise match, when the stars are shining brightly upon you, but this will probably follow upon the tedious process-of-elimination thing.

A post too wide won't fit. One of the correct dimensions may need a little help getting started down the frame's seat tube, but it will eventually be able to proceed, with enough grease. A post too loose, by contrast, will slide right down. But it wouldn't do any good to try and compensate by over-tightening the seat bolt, in such cases—this would only add an obtuse new crimp to the seat tube, with the steel frames. We would eventually expect to see cracks developing, with carbon or aluminum frames.

Steel frames can sometimes be tricked into working with posts a size too small—26.2 in place of 26.4, things like that—but this would still be four times as stupid, because the seat's pinch bolt would suddenly be charged with compressing a sturdy tube to dimensions smaller than those it was born with. The problem is obvious enough, if your frame is so afflicted: the gap behind the pinch bolt would be angled in toward the top, rather than parallel.

Remove the bolt and carefully lever things straight with the screwdriver, if

you come across this problem. Be careful not to flare the tube's ears out; they need to end up nice and round again.

So get the right post, and make sure you paint some grease down into the seat tube before installing it—unless, perhaps, you find yourself working with a carbon fiber frame or post. As previously noted, exercise your own discretion in such cases.

How to get the grease down there? We'll draft a piece of abandoned cable housing to make a wand, typically; a pencil would also work. Just get it in there and twirl. This is probably not going to be something you would spontaneously remember years down the road; you really want to do this when you first install the post. The danger—especially if the bike gets parked outside a lot—is that it may just rust in place. Happens all the time! Resolving such a dilemma, as we'll see, is a real mess.

The more we delve into the endless soup of bicycle repair, with all its contingencies and variables and odd old exceptions, the better one can appreciate the simplicity of such straightforward pronouncements. There are no two ways about it, once the tedious carbon exception has been duly dispatched; metal posts in metal frames should always get greased. Feels good, drawing little lines in the sand . . . So I'll tell you what—let it now be declared that all persons everywhere are forever forbidden from sailing their seatposts at any points above the ever-present **MAXIMUM HEIGHT LINE**.

Let this also be etched upon our precious consciousness.

As a rule, seatposts are not meant to sail at points above their self-inscribed maximum height lines. Trespassing upon this truth is only asking for trouble. The greater the transgression, the more likely something is going to bend or break. So they make this hard to do, by tracing a line around the base of the post. We would surely face the scorn and ridicule of our closest friends, reaching so far beyond our grasp. OK, people? Let's stick together.

The nearly viral ubiquity of stronger and lighter frame materials has allowed for more compact geometry, originally with the mountain bikes and hybrids, and more recently with the road frames as well, in the specialty market at least. We get a more generous stand-over clearance, and the bikes drop yet a bit more weight, so everything works out splendidly. The taller 300 or 350 mm seatposts are thereby more common these days, but the older and more doctrinaire roadsters stand as tall as they ever did; they still anticipate the shorter posts of days gone by. Whichever the case, the maximum height line should always be respected.

The original seat mounting hardware may be understood broadly enough to be considered intuitive: the seat rails are collected within the pieces of a contoured clamping assembly, the nostril of which slides down around the top of a seatpost. Nuts to either side tighten everything into place. Any tinkerer probably knows just what I'm talking about.

Said nuts are most often 14 mm across, and it is important to keep them supremely tight. The clamping assembly is built around splined adjustment surfaces, which can be expected to wear themselves down if they're able to grind against each other. This is precisely what happens, if one rides the seat loose. The hardware is routinely replaced, for this very reason. It is (almost always!) universal; any worthwhile bike shop has a set for you.

The clamp's business parts are meant to face the rear. Excluding the very occasional strange old bats, these clamp assemblies are expected to tighten around ⅞" poles. Older BMX bikes often use a straight ⅞" seatpost; others are drawn in to fit this dimension at the very top.

These original examples are known as the **STRAIGHT POSTS.** They are distinct from what we call the **LAPRADE POSTS,** which have no obtuse side-nuts to tighten. The more modern and reasonable Laprade posts rearrange the splined adjustment to a broader horizontal orientation, where it does somewhat better. The splines are more pronounced; their position is far more secure. Yet still they suffer the same ignoble fate, if they are not fully tightened. The mounting hardware is also made to be integral; you would have to replace the post itself if its hardware was allowed to deteriorate.

We may also come across a more curious beast calling itself **MICROADJUST** or similar, which updates and complicates our Laprade. A pair of nuts or bolts fore and aft see-saws the saddle to suitable angles. Seano at the Hub observes that microadjust posts can be a safer bet for performance and heavier riders alike, in that the single Laprade boltheads have been known to shear off under extreme pressure.

When it appears as a stock item on new bicycles, **SEATPOST SUSPENSION** tends to be heavy, non-adjustable, and poorly constructed. Cane Creek's aftermarket Thudbuster post presents improvements in every respect, though of course you'll pay for them.

Shock posts only arrive in a couple of general sizes, such as the 25.4 or 27.2 mm; their lazy manufacturers provide us with dubious **SEATPOST SHIMS** with which to accommodate the range of possible frame tubes. These bear fat lips up top, to keep the seat tubes from swallowing them whole.

The great majority of shock posts hide their springs beneath chintzy rubber boots. These things are disposable components in the truest sense. The prevailing design resists servicing just as surely as it denies adjustments; save perhaps for one—if a ridged ring appears around the base, hand-tightening it may lessen if not eliminate their unfortunate tendency toward lateral play, which can get to be pretty damned tedious. Said rings seem to loosen over and over again, over time, so keep an eye out.

The beleaguered OEM shock post becomes too wide to slide down the seat tube, so the most that might be said for the design is that it manages to encourage better fitting frames. A shorter person may be able to straddle an oversized bike, with the seatpost shoved all the way down, but she would most likely find the handlebars too far forward for comfort. By limiting the seat's descent, as we saw all the time at the rental shop, the suspension post showcases its only real utility—which, as it happens, could be matched by an insightfully positioned reflector bracket.

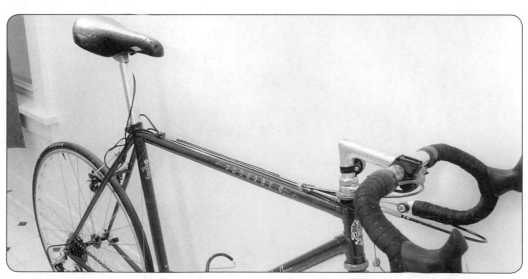

I f a bike's trajectory may be guessed through the tires, its personality might be glimpsed in the handlebars. The wide and flat mountain bike handlebar sets the hands farther out and apart, affording us the leverage we may need to navigate the trails. The shapely drop bar favors aerodynamics and speed, and it also thinks ahead, providing for a range of hand positions which may be keenly appreciated on longer rides. But these two standards are only the most basic examples; the handlebars have splayed and swooned in every direction over the years.

The **CLAMP DIAMETER**, measured across the handlebars' wider midsections, corresponds with distinct road and mountain stems. Older road stems might also be identified by the half-moons carved from their sides, meant to allow the passage of the curvaceous drop bars. (Newer road stems accomplish the same business with their removable face plates.)

Really old bars were sometimes born with a 25.0 mm clamp diameter. Soon thereafter, 25.4 became the standard, but only the mountain bars have stayed with it. Most, anyway; a bar and stem built around 28.6 mm was introduced more recently.

Road bars moved on to 26.0 and 26.4 clamps some time ago, but just lately a few have joined with some of the snootier mountain bars to regroup around a new 31.7/31.8 standard, meant to diminish the minimal flex associated with our simpler handlebars. But the old bar protocols have already done us fine for decades—this is only so much gold dust, sprinkled upon the precious fruits of Eden.

If the handlebar clamp sections have learnt to expand and try different things, their outer lengths have adopted no such courage. These regions have traditionally been the domain of the road and mountain **BRAKE LEVER DIAMETERS**, neither of which will easily be trifled with. These standards, set at 24 and 22.2 mm respectively, have each enjoyed an impressive mandate. Nearly all the hand control levers ever made have been meant to work with the one or the other; there would be no incentive to change a damned thing.

VII. Handlebars

It is often obvious enough if a given control lever is meant for the flat mountain or curved road bars, based on its profile. The cross or "in-line" levers found on many newer road bikes are more ambiguous in this respect, but we always have our simple litmus test: where it is not possible to fully tighten road levers around mountain bars, the mountain controls do not even fit on to the road bars.

There is one loophole. Mountain control levers built around steel clamps enjoy the flexibility needed to hop back and forth. This oversight allows for an arrangement I used to call "poor man's STI," which enlists a pair of steel-clamped mountain thumbshifters mounted just beneath the brake levers on drop bars to roughly approximate the advantages of Shimano's eponymous levers. Not unlike Suntour's brilliant Command Levers, which are even cooler but increasingly rare. Or, as I only discovered more recently, the Kelly Take Off Mounts, which basically accomplish the same business in a more legitimate way, mounting a down tube shift lever just inside the brake lever.

Anyway, poor man's STI sought to match the fine action of the classic old silver-capped Deore 7-speed levers with drop bars, but in truth any levers based on steel clamps will work.

A. Mountain

The majority of handlebars and control levers we are likely to come across will align with the narrower 22.2 mm **MOUNTAIN HANDLEBAR** lever diameter.

The oldest levers were built of steel, and thereby conspicuously heavy, from the wizened modern view at least. As with most other components, brake levers are mostly made from lighter aluminum these days, which also flexes less under braking pressure. Steel brake levers are still sometimes smuggled in aboard the department store bikes, hidden beneath plastic, but that's about it.

Shimano and SRAM have both produced various integrated brake and shift lever sets, but it's at least as common that these are attached as individual components. This may be preferable, actually—you wouldn't have to replace both if only one takes a shit.

That said, some of the individual brake and shift levers get along better than others. We see this most clearly with the **GRIP SHIFT LEVERS,** whose relative bulk can sometimes prevent older brake levers from being mounted flush next to them. But this has been getting sorted out as well; most new levers have made the requisite accommodations in their profiles. It only becomes relevant to the extent that it may impact upon the length of real estate along the handlebars. The combinations of levers, grips, and accessories only need to fit together on the same handlebar.

SRAM fixes their mountain brake and shift levers in place with metric screws, which answer to diminutive 2.5 or 3 mm hex wrenches. The handlebar controls are vulnerable to over-tightening; their selections here remind us to take it easy. Other lever fixing bolts feature sturdier 4 or 5 mm heads, but all of them usually thread into the aluminum clamp bodies. It's none too difficult to strip out the threads, given the wrong attitude. Each piece only needs to be tight enough to stay put.

Some SRAM mountain brake levers cannot be fully tightened to the bars. You tighten the screws all the way down; the clamp simply closes all the way around. I will guess that this was the intended effect—the brake levers are left fairly vulnerable in crashes, and leaving them just slightly loose like in this way might allow them to rotate out of harm's way.

When mounted on the hybrids and mountain bikes, our brake levers are traditionally set at about 45 degrees to level—their plane shoots right out over the top of the front wheel. The idea is that one shouldn't have to bend the wrists up to pull the brakes. The angle is somewhat steeper on cruiser bars, to better accommodate their more lateral hand positions, and the levers are best left horizontal or better on the 'bents for the very same reason.

Modern brake levers incorporate small set screws mounted to their insides, with which to adjust the lever's reach. They are dialed in, to better accommodate smaller hands. Note that you'll probably need to adjust the cable as well.

We would need to dispose of any hand grips, prior to rearranging anything installed to their interiors. Those poor bikes afflicted with foam grips are less of an issue for us here, because these can be slipped off fairly easily, if they haven't fallen apart already. You may have to pop off some plugs at their ends, depending. The more durable rubber and cork grips are installed and removed in the very same way, at every bike shop I've worked for. We use air compressors. The air gun's nozzle is slipped under the grip; squeeze the trigger and the grip pulls right off. Simple. We then spray the bar and the grip's interior with hairspray, prior to putting them back on, which provides for both a lubricant and a mild adhesive. The grips slip right back up the bars, and the air gun comes back in to dry them in place.

You don't want to use hairspray if you do not have an air compressor, precisely because it is so slick. The grips keep wriggling around; they threaten to shoot right off the ends. Don't be using oil for this, either; your grips get loose and stay that way. The home mechanic is better served to use something less synthetic. See if you can't do this with water. Mix in a bit of soap or degreaser if you need to.

The process becomes easier, if you're able to deploy the liquid from a spray bottle. Pry up the end of the grip with your small screwdriver, shoot your spray down into the opening, and twist the grip off and away. Rotating the grips on the bar makes for little channels underneath, allowing the water to get everywhere it needs to.

The operation simply reverses itself, putting the grips back on. Here as well, see if you can get by with water for lubrication, unless you do have an air gun.

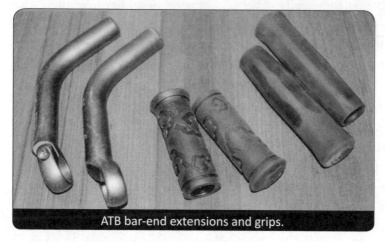

ATB bar-end extensions and grips.

The grips and control levers all move in just a bit, to make room for any **BAR-END EXTENSIONS**. With the exception of the triathlon bar kits, designed for use with the wider 24 mm road standard, the bar ends will be built around 22.2 mm mountain clamp diameters. Control Tech was swell enough to fit threaded brass inserts into the bases of their bar ends, but most others use mere aluminum throughout, meaning that they are left vulnerable to the union of torque and machismo as well, just like the control levers. They only need to become tight enough to stay put.

It is possible to bring bar ends back to life, if their threads do strip. Drill the bolt hole all the way through, before retapping its threaded section to M6. Or, if you have no taps, make plans to mount a nut opposite the bolt head.

We typically leave the bar ends sitting just better than level—in line with the stem, perhaps—but it is almost as common to find these pointed straight up, reaching for the sky. Such a posture may stand in for a high-rise stem, up to a point, but it leaves the new hand positions further removed from the control levers, which is really too bad if you need to grab the brakes in a hurry.

Whatever you do, it is best to avoid cutting the grips down. We never even think about doing it this way at the shop; everything on the bars is simply edged in toward the stem. The bar ends are meant to provide us with more hand positions; slicing the grips down diminishes upon the very same value. That said, reasons can be found to trim down the width of the handlebars themselves. The narrower the bars, the fewer distractions they'll confront slicing through the gridlock. I've known people to take this to logical extremes, but the loss in leverage must eventually crowd out any advantage.

With the mountain handlebars, we typically chop an inch or two from each side, using a pipe-cutter. Hacksaws make for sloppier results here, absent enlightened guidance—Park's SG-6 Threadless Saw Guide, for example. Even the pipe cutter will probably flare out the edges a bit; you may need to file down the results either way.

B. Road

Anything with the wider 24 mm lever diameter is considered to be a **ROAD HANDLEBAR.** The traditional drop-style bars are only the most obvious examples—the sympathetic and generous road standard is gracious enough to embrace the broad and ungainly spread of the triathlon bars, as well as timeless superstars like the sexy mustache handlebars.

The control levers on any handlebars need to become just tight enough. Excluding the SRAM mountain brake levers mentioned earlier, we tighten everything to the point that nothing is able to move around. With the drop bars, the brake lever positioning is meant to follow a simple formula: when a ruler is lined against the drop bar's lower extension, the tips of the brake levers should just reach its edge.

It does not take much to wrap **GRIP TAPE** on a handlebar, but there is an art to doing it right. This wasn't much a concern of mine, earlier in life, but a few years back my colleague Jon Londres finally cornered me and explained the professional approach.

Grip tape always starts at the handlebars' extremes, working its way in toward the center. We begin by leaving a good half inch of tape hanging all the way around the end of the bar, secured with a bit of electrical tape if need be. This remnant is bent forward and pushed in by the plugs, once you finish, providing them the purchase they need to stay put.

Once started, the tape needs to wrap in a particular direction. It should loop from the outsides over to the insides of the bar, so that when viewed from above the two sides' trailing edges form an arrow pointing forward. This affords us a solid foundation for the pattern up top, where the wrap's direction is more crucial.

Imagine the rolling motion the hands make on top of the bars, as you stand up and charge the hill: the grip tape can either be aligned with this force, or set against it. The hands either chafe against

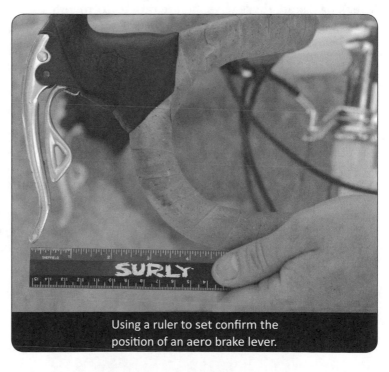

Using a ruler to set confirm the position of an aero brake lever.

the grip tapes' edges, encouraging them to unravel, or they seamlessly traverse across its surface. Where we wrap toward the bike across the lower reaches, we end up wrapping back toward the rider along the top, and this aligns the tape with our momentum.

The advancing angle should be slight and uniform, maybe 10 or 20 degrees from level, with each pass covering about half the previous layer. The brake levers will force a slight departure from this rhythm—the overlap narrows a bit up top, while expanding to a commensurate degree on the underside.

The levers' bases were traditionally wrapped in a figure-eight, to cover all the negative space, but advancements in lever hood design have really been rendering this obsolete. The tape is merely wrapped diagonally across the lever's backside, these days, before proceeding upstairs.

This detail becomes especially important with Campagnolo's dual control levers, which need a little more breathing room than their peers. The hoods on Ergopower levers feature small square hooks at their bases, which coincide with matching openings on the levers. These need to be free to connect, lest the hood interfere with the shifting action . . . But really, of course they do. There are so many arcane little rules with that company.

The cork tape is more comfortable, on the hot days especially; the vinyl is cheaper. Either will feature two additional smaller lengths, meant to wrap around that shadowy region just behind the brake levers, as well as a pair of plugs to fit into the handlebars. The classic cloth handlebar tape made more sense back home in Minneapolis, where the roads were, on average, smoother. It provides for no padding at all, but it lasts for years, if it is wrapped with due care, and it also carries the unique tendency to look even cooler as it ages. The fade goes to natural and gets a little shiny.

Whichever grip tape you choose, first secure any cables meant to burrow along underneath with electrical tape. Those trailing from the bar-end shifters and the aero brake levers will pass at least some distance beneath the grip tape. Really old brake lever hoods sometimes dry up and adhere to their levers, but the better ones remain pliable and good; you simply fold their rear sections forward, to install the grip tape beneath them. Go ahead and wrap that small piece of grip tape behind the brake levers, securing it with more a loop of electrical tape around the lever's body.

Pull fairly tight as you wrap, to avoid wrinkles. Take it easy as you go, because the grip tape can rip: unless, of course, it is the blessed cloth. You will want to conserve your resources, generally speaking, overlapping the tape only as much as needed. Women's handlebars and older drop bars tend to be a bit smaller; the overlap can be more generous.

Handlebar plugs come in a few sizes, for road and mountain bars. The classic chromed plugs are more ambidextrous in this respect, if you can find a pair, but more generally the plugs should fit slightly loose, prior to taping the bars. The cheesy shiny plastic sorts included with new tape are almost invariably the wrong size, to my experience. I favor the more malleable mountain handlebar plugs. The finishing tape included with new cork and vinyl tape is pretty cosmetic. It is not nearly as flexible as the grip tape itself, so nobody really uses it to finish the wrap. Electrical tape fills the role much better.

The control cables are supposed to be our faithful lieutenants, explaining our instructions to the components gathered below, but circumstance can lend the cables agendas all their own. Not much of anything may transmit through rusty cables, to take the classic example.

Excepting a few tandem brake levers and the oldest three-speed shift levers, cable-driven components will be meant to work with either road brake cables, mountain brake cables, or **DERAILLEUR CABLES**. These last, being the thinnest, arrive with the smallest heads. Little pinhead derailleur cables. But that's cool; their task is considerably less stressful than braking. The svelte dimensions also allow for greater imagination in the design of our shift levers. Which, like their cables, do not need to be overbuilt.

Italian component manufacturer Campagnolo decided the heads could be smaller yet, in fact, by precisely a third of a millimeter. In practice this means that while their cables will suffice for use with shift levers more generally, only Campagnolo-compatible cables work for their own equipment. Campagnolo cables themselves are also microns wider, at the very same time, so it's best to use some of their shift cable housing as well. Note that regular cable heads will get stuck in Campy parts, like boots in cement. You would have to drill them out.

Minneapolis wholesaler Quality Bicycle Products provides us with a decent but inexpensive Campagnolo-sized cable, fortunately enough, so you don't actually need to pay top dollar. Unless you want to, I guess. Q's version features two heads; Campagnolo's is stamped with a telling "C." You

chop off the end you're not using, prior to installation.

So long as we're on the topic, it should be mentioned that SRAM shift cables are evidently microns thinner than all the others. You would notice that they're far more flexible, as well. Alas their heads are of their expected dimensions, so they would not be able to fill in with the Campagnolo goods. I am quite sure they work well with SRAM shift levers, but in truth I've never had any troubles using those pulled from the garden. I hadn't even been aware of the distinction until Travis mentioned it, up at the old Freewheel one morning.

The **ROAD BRAKE CABLES** bear heads roughly similar to those we find on the derailleur cables, but with a second, wider section extending above the first. They may even be accepted into some of the simpler shift levers, in a pinch, assuming the wider brake cable housing was used as well. Only the thumbshifters, down tube levers and bar-end levers make inadvertent accommodations for their fat

heads; the modern shifter cable housing is too narrow to fit them. But we should stay focused; their central business is with the road brake levers.

Here again, Campagnolo has insisted on making brake cables at odds with the rest of the world. The dispute is with the cable housing this time; it suddenly becomes a hair too narrow. If the action on your Campagnolo brakes seems oddly stiff after lubrication, in other words, make sure that Campagnolo cables and housing have been used throughout.

We look to find a stout bar, pivoting across the typical road brake lever's interior, upon which to rest the cable's weary head. The pivoting is crucial, in that it allows the cable head to maintain a constant orientation as the lever is squeezed.

Those pivoting pillows featuring within Shimano STI dual control levers contain several smaller pieces, which themselves are inclined to pop out of the levers when cables are removed, so it is important to exercise due caution when working on these things. Each end of the diminutive cable head rest is capped with pairs of even tinier plastic washers, to provide for a more fluid range of motion, and the cable head itself is trusted to hold all of this in place. Alas the pivot assembly is only slotted into its position on the brake lever, and it jumps out of place pretty easily, once the cable's guidance is withdrawn.

Tracking down the four tiny washers can be difficult enough, but convincing the regrouped pivot assembly to crawl back into its cave can be a royal pain in the ass. It is easiest to install it independently of the cable, in those circumstances, but it would be better to avoid the hassle in the first place.

The next time you find yourself replacing an STI lever's brake cable, nudge the original's tail slightly forward in the housing, such that its head slips just a bit out of the pivot. You may need to get in there with a small pick or screwdriver, to lift the head clear of the STI shifting hardware, but as often as not it'll do as much on its own. This done, put a finger atop the pivot assembly, and hold it right there as you pull the old cable free.

The floating bars found in various older road brake levers are more reasonable. They allow small slots for the cables, which greatly simplify their installation. Only one side of the bar is drilled wide enough to accept the cable head; you may need to rotate it with a small screwdriver to see this. It might be useful to put some light behind the lever as well—with the expected modern aero-style levers at least, the cable must shoot out through a tiny cable-sized hole in the lever's mounting bracket. The hole needs to be small enough to prevent the cable's housing from charging back through; back-lighting the situation is often the easiest way to find it.

We will arrive upon the cable housing shortly, but circumstance advises a timely disclaimer. Any cable housing entering an aero brake lever must be denied the opportunity to press ahead into the cable's smaller hole, as the pressure applied with braking will inevitably encourage it to do. Its plastic sheathing will get hung up on the edge, while the firmer metal coil therein seeks to surge ahead, and the brake will start feeling more like a sponge in consequence.

Most manufacturers have borne this in mind, keeping such holes small enough to fend off anything wider than the brake cable itself. The ubiquitous cable housing caps (described momentarily) tend to become lodged inside road brake levers, where they are soon bent out of shape, so we do not use them in this particular application. That said, a reasonably common exception must also be noted. Many older Dia Compe levers anticipate cable housing wearing a distinct rounded aluminum bonnet instead. These DC cable housing caps have the same interior diameter as regular old M5 housing caps, but they are notably wider and rounded at the top, which in theory would have allowed the cable to exit at slightly more precise angles. The corresponding DC aero brake levers, in turn, will feature wider openings for the cable.

The **MOUNTAIN BRAKE CABLES** lay their heads flat, in plane with the cable, so that we see tiny metal lollipops. Their levers bear corresponding openings. Most also feature small slots, in order to facilitate the cable's installation. Such channels tend to slice right through the barrel adjusters and their collars. We line everything up like a combination lock, prior to installing or removing cables. Some of the oldest levers lack anything so useful; you may have to go in and feed the cable through from behind.

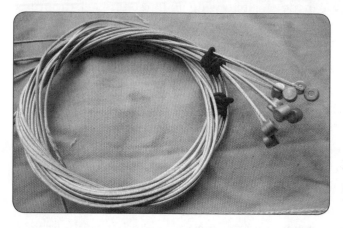

Any remotely modern control cable will feature at least one **BARREL ADJUSTER** along its length. The barrels thread into fittings on the frame or the components, or feature in-line along the cables themselves. Dialing them in or out decreases or increases a cable's tension, respectively. The great majority of cable adjustments require no tools, as we will see, because the barrels will suffice. We only need to make sure we keep them reasonably full. When doing more intensive work which involves cable adjustments—replacing the brake pads, for example—it is always a good idea to thread any barrel adjusters most of the way in, before tightening the cable's binder bolt. Cables do stretch with use, just as their housing seats itself more thoroughly over time, and of course the brake pads do wear down, so it becomes easy enough to find reasons to back the barrels out again.

Once the cables are installed through their respective components, we'll typically lop off their tails a couple inches past the components' binder bolts, up at the shop, but I leave those featuring on my own bikes a bit longer. The effort facilitates their reuse.

Most of our cable cutters also make provisions to crimp **CABLE FERRULES** to their jagged new ends. The tiny aluminum bullets, just hollow enough for a cable? Wider and narrower sorts can be found, for the brake and shift cables respectively. The cutters' jaws do their slashing just outside the tool's pivot; we crimp the ferrules in place where the arms cross just inside this point. Some cutters even have a pair of slight indents on the arms here, suggesting crimpage. The armpit of any old needle-nose pliers delivers an even better effect; the whole ferrule is pressed uniformly flat.

Some suggest you're also supposed to crimp the stainless steel caps meant for the wider-style 5 mm cable housing as well, but I don't bother. Crimping bends these all out of shape; they lose all interest in rolling with our barrel adjusters. Cable housing by definition is plugged into something or another, and the housing segments are not going to fray as the cables would; the caps can easily be reused if they're left unmolested. It would be remotely possible to damage the housing this way, if the cables are somehow made completely slack and then suddenly jammed back together, but this would be one of those situations where you would really have to try to fuck things up. So relax, you'll do fine.

The cables are secured to their brakes and derailleurs by means of the **BINDER BOLTS**, which clamp proprietary washers in particular orientations to a point along a given component's exterior. They're meant to work as a package with the part; the shapes fit with each other in particular.

You will notice, peering into their embrace, that at least one side features a telling cable-sized groove. This is where you want it to end up. The cable may want to spring out of position; pull it taut to hold it in place. The detail takes all of a few seconds' concentration, but it is a good use of your time. The little grooves prevent our cables from being crushed flat. We expect the cable's individual wire strands to gradually snap and begin to fray, in less exacting circumstances.

The **CABLE HOUSING** sections may begin to rust or crack, over time, so we often change them out with the cables. The bikes need distinct sorts of housing, for brake and shift cables. Make sure you grab the right stuff, especially with the brakes.

Close-up of rear derailleur cable pinch bolt.

Either variety proceeds from a similar plan. Some wire is encased in plastic, with a thinner plastic straw running through the inside. Yet where the shift housing is

Housing caps: 4 mm, DC aero brake lever, step-down, and regular 5 mm.

made of long strands of wire, the brake cable housing is wrapped as a sturdy coil. The one provides for a predictable, compressionless base for the increasingly strident indexed shifting systems, while the other is able to manage the occasional panic-yank on the brake levers.

One can often see the wrap of the wire, on brake housing. We expect a shift lever set up with brake housing to be marginally fuzzier, with 9- or 10-speed systems in particular. The shift housing is also much stiffer. You may suddenly be reminded of the distinction, if you pass over it here— the act of pulling the brake lever shoots a strident jolt of pressure down the line, which can make the shift housing

splinter. The outer plastic cracks, and the wires splay out in every direction. It is a spectacular little problem.

Personally? The coolest cable housing of all time is the old-fashioned stainless steel coil, which is not sealed at all. We can oil it by osmosis, in fact. Run an oil dropper along the length; soaks right in. A local wholesaler was once blowing out meter-long sections of this real cheap, made by Campagnolo no less, and I still have a couple lengths kicking around. But it compresses like an accordion box, and would likely encounter difficulties managing anything more complex than 7 speeds, were I so inclined.

The cables and their housing interact with the frame through the **CABLE-HOUSING STOPS**, which direct each along its particular course. They generally let the housing in one end, and block it from exiting the other; only the cable itself gets through. A frame may also sport cable

Oiling old school stainless cable housing by osmosis..

guides or cable housing guides, which are wide enough to pass either the one or the other. We usually spy some cable guides under the bottom bracket shell, for example. A few bikes, such as the lovely Surly Troll, make provisions for the cable housing to run the full length, from lever to component. This is actually a really good idea; the corrosion and grit is considerably slower in arriving.

Many new bikes arrive with their shifter cables in less than ideal routes. Of the two or three cable-housing stops featuring toward the front of the frame, each shift cable traces reflexively to the one closest: right side to right, left to left. This makes a basic kind of sense, in the same way that telephone books or airports might, but things work out better if we cross the right (rear) shifter's cable to the frame's left-side cable stop, and vice versa. This makes for an "X" where the two cables cross on their paths to the rear, under the down tube, or along the top tube. Looks nice and odd; makes not the slightest difference in performance.

Why? Because the stock cable routing puts an extra bend in the housing. The section needs to be of a certain length to allow a full rotation of the handlebars, and the slack always doubles up back by the frame. Ride in the elements long enough, and your cables will gather rust at the low point in this bend. You can just oil the housing and be done with it, but if you're going that far you may as well cross your cables.

"X" means this will not work on bikes with their cables zipped higher up the sides of the frame; you'd only scuff the paint all to hell. Sorry. Road bikes with down-tube cable guides make ideal candidates; the first-generation mountain bikes less so.

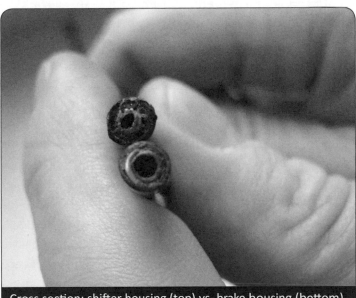
Cross section: shifter housing (top) vs. brake housing (bottom).

While we're on the topic of cable routing, we should talk about Klein, whose fat-tubed and square-tailed progeny feature prominently among those tucking the cables within the frames themselves. The streamlined effect to result is pretty unique—among the geared bikes, at least—but these sorts of **INTERNALLY ROUTED CABLES** arrive with maintenance issues of their own. If ever they're allowed to fully exit their quiet hallways, it can take some convincing before they deign to return.

Klein and other internally inclined manufacturers drill pairs of pinholes in the intended tubes, to put this in a nutshell, and the blind cable does not easily find the second in their series. There always needs to be a length of thin plastic straw, known as cable liner, stretching from start to finish.

Unless you can actually *see* a single segment of cable liner emerging from both ends at once, it is not a good idea to remove internally routed cables. If you're only replacing or installing the liner itself, slide any damaged liner segments down off the cable's tail, before sliding the new stretch into position. If you're replacing cables or housing, be sure the liner extends from both ends simultaneously, before pulling the cable out. The liner can be removed once the new cable is in, if need be, but there's no better way to get it in there.

It is possible to replace internally routed cables without the liner, sometimes, with patience. You bend and twirl, and bend, and twirl, and do it all over again. The only alternative would be the aforementioned "full line" housing throughout, attached with zip ties or similar, an option which Klein enthusiasts would likely find distasteful.

It is crucial that cable housing is just long enough to do the job. It should not have to bind or stretch at any point in the handlebars' rotation. Things can get messed up, quickly.

A bike's original housing may be a bit too long. Many manufacturers enlist a one-size-fits-all approach, leaving the housing for smaller frame sizes somewhat overcompensated. It would be best if this was corrected when first the bikes are assembled, at the shops—as we're lubricating the cables on new builds, for example—but this clearly doesn't happen as much as it should. Housing too long tends to snag on things, like railings, and this never does the bike any good at all.

To measure a correct length of cable housing, determine where the control lever in question is going to end up on the handlebar, stretch some housing from the mouth of its barrel adjuster to the first cable-housing stop it encounters on the frame, and make sure there is *just* enough slack to fully rotate the bars. (The smaller housing segments featuring farther back along the cable runs are much easier to measure, in that their end points are either fixed or not moving much at all.)

The **CABLE HOUSING LENGTH** also becomes an issue when we change out the handlebars or the stem. A switch to a high-rise stem, for example, renders all the cables just a bit short. You would need to replace the cables themselves—the longer ones, at least—but there may be things we can do for the housing situation. Do you see any loose brake noodles lying about? These trim metal straws are most often associated with the V brakes,

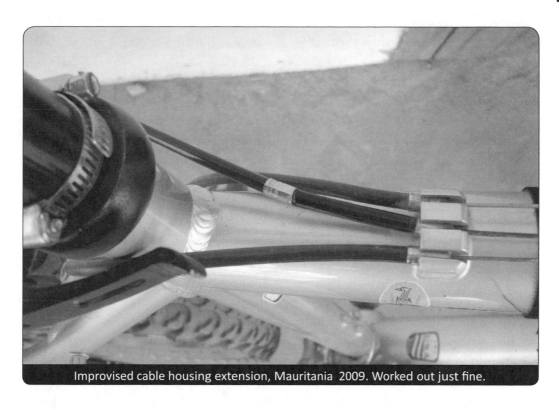

Improvised cable housing extension, Mauritania 2009. Worked out just fine.

as described on page 99, but they may fill in here as well. (These sorts of noodles cost more than cable housing; it would not make sense to buy new ones for this.) The housing slides right down into the brake noodle's base, absent the cable-housing cap, and its nose plugs right into the cable stop or barrel adjuster you're heading for. The fit becomes marginally more precise if you pull the noodle's press-fit nose off first, with your box pliers.

We may also noodle together distinct pieces of cable housing, to make for one long piece. The industry provides us with cute little housing bridges, which look like two housing caps locked in an embrace, but these gems are oddly expensive, looking around. At the same time, discarded brake noodles grow from the corners of just about any bike shop. These may be made somewhat straighter, with a

little effort, but their gracious curves will just as often coincide with our cabling imperatives.

Our extension merely removes the nose cone from the first noodle, to replace it with the tail section from a second. The cable simply jogs through this trim metal bridge, moving effortlessly from one housing situation to another. It is the Double Ended Noodle Cable Housing Extender. Let's call them **CABLE DONKEYS**. They carry from one place to another.

Brake noodles were themselves in short supply, among the ailing Peace Corps–issued Raleigh M50s I came across in Mauritania. Nor could replacements be found locally, and so it was that I chanced upon further shorthand. One doesn't necessarily *need* a bridge to join disparate lengths of cable housing, as it turns out, because the cables themselves might take up the role.

The rearward segment of brake housing was a bit short, on the bike I rode, and the only remedy at hand was to add a second piece in sequence to the first. The springs in the brake and brake lever conspired to hold things in place. The brake in question might have gained a degree of flex, going this way—cheap parts; hard to tell really—but it still stopped the bike just fine.

SRAM has in the past capped their brake noodles with chintzy plastic caps, molded around small aluminum rings. I'm not sure why; the plastic end piece still breaks. The plastic bit molds around a small alloy ring, which would need to be pulled off with the box pliers before constructing a cable donkey. The thing that

can be said for SRAM's infernal plastic nose cones is that they make releasing the cable somewhat easier.

The longer the cable housing, the more prone it will be to snagging on railings, branches or anything else that may become handy, and in such cases it is common that bends and kinks will be impressed to the cable and its housing both. You will need to straighten things out.

Remove the cable from its housing and grab it with your pliers, right next to any obtuse new angles, and bend it straight again. Not a big deal. Sharp kinks are often added to the cables just past the component binder bolts, as you'll notice, to route their tails away from moving parts.

The linear wires wrapped through derailleur housing settle a bit with use, such

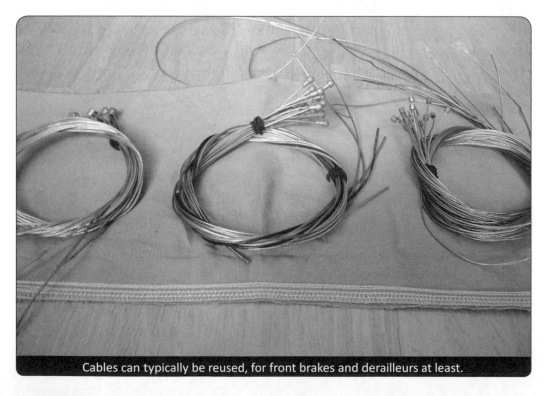

Cables can typically be reused, for front brakes and derailleurs at least.

that their length seems to grow over time. The wire ends stick out, suggesting haircuts. So we just snip the ends off. Reopen the plastic inner lining with your pick and put it all back together.

Ride On cables long inserted an extra plastic liner, between the cable and housing; not sure if that's still the case under their new management. Many more have been the various Teflon cables. Note that we're not supposed to need liquid lubricants, in either case—oil would only draw in the grit, which these others are trying to avoid.

I am a big fan of **REUSING CABLES**. I habitually spool up the useful remains of any stainless cables I am replacing, provided the time and opportunity. What can I tell you? It saves us some money. The shortened rear cables are probably still long enough for your front derailleurs or brakes. Not only that, but they're all done stretching out.

Stainless cables can last for a really long time. The housing, which is usually mere galvanized steel, rusts sooner. When you do reuse a cable, first make sure it doesn't have any sharp bends, especially across those stretches where it passes through the housing. But this is an obvious point; it would be like trying to force a triangle through a tube.

The only complication comes with putting the clipped cables back in. You need to make sure they don't fray. So you twist the hell out of the cables, continuously, in the direction they are wound. The hope,

of course, is that drama may be avoided by referencing the larger context. The fragile wires will not have time to become distracted, once they're spun fast enough.

I was less impressed with the servicing options available for some of the newer SRAM shift levers, at first, because for once this trick did not seem to work. I later discovered that one really just needs to twist the *hell* out of any used cables, which are suddenly asked to bend through some pretty unlikely angles. The cable spins easily across the fingertips, but it also happens you're gradually nudging it forward as well. (Some partial disassembly can quicken the cables into older SRAM shift levers, but this same task becomes far more arduous with some of the new jobs. The question is further explored on page 128.) More generally, any sharper bends in components or housing can make cable reuse more difficult.

The short segment flattened by the cable's binder bolt should not end up inside any cable housing. There would be too much friction.

Cables troubled by grit or corrosion can often be rescued with a bit of lightweight oil. Drip some on the rag; squeeze the cable through a few times. Check out the rag once you're done; the oil pulls that shit right off. Stainless steel cables are always likely candidates, but zinc cables sometimes become burdened with too much corrosion to deal with.

Everybody should have the options afforded by quality gear. Good bikes should not be associated with privilege; it is antithetical to their very nature. Poorly made bikes and parts are too often the easiest to sell, as with the department store bikes, but in the end they're only a reactionary tendency. A function of cheap gasoline, which only makes them all the more fragile.

The used bicycle market provides us a useful alternative in this respect. Generally speaking, you're better off getting a decent used bike instead of a bottom-barrel new one. The same point rings through all the more emphatically whenever suspension technology becomes involved. I must tell you, as your friendly mechanic, to ignore the scratches on the paint. Focus on the feel, the fit, the quality of the ride.

When appraising a bike, our first appreciation of its components often begins with the **BRAKES.** A worthy example can be reasonably expected to stop quickly, effectively, silently, and with minimum effort. We may even ask that they be simple, durable, and relatively lightweight, as well. None of this makes for unreasonable requests, considering the available technology.

We like the brakes to jump back from the rims just as soon as they're done, lest their pads become a drag. The brakes rely upon springs for such purposes, whose tension soon emerges as a major theme.

It is further expected—by most performance riders, at least—that the brakes do not feel spongy. Brake flex is largely a function of the materials used in construction, together with design imperatives, but cable lubrication can be just as important. Cables that stick along their housing encourage the brakes to flex. Brake cables often end up a bit looser than might be safe, for reasons we'll soon explore, but in no circumstances should a working brake lever be able to bottom out on the handlebar. (The appearance of hydraulics, incidentally, has put the bike industry in the habit of saying "mechanical" in place of "cable-driven." That's all "mechanical" means, with bicycle brakes: steel cables.)

As a mechanic, my principle concern is with the brake's stopping power. It is the crucial, on-the-ground, real-time

IX. Brakes

evidence of stunning success or abysmal failure. Yet it is another consideration, only casually related to this, that usually grabs the headlines. Let us all gather together and heap every curse and hex upon the real bitter-enders, the **SQUEAKY BRAKES.**

The rim-mounted brakes began their wailing long before the disc brakes were even gleams in their manufacturers' eyes, so we should start with them. A lot of the time, brake squeaks are revealed to be nothing more than hygiene issues. The pads sweep the rims clean, in the course of their duties, and this eventually covers their faces with a layer of hard and shiny debris—it is pressed flat, and ground into place. The sum of this detritus works away between pad and rim, slowly and methodically wearing away at the both of them, and eventually the brakes wail out as the process continues. When we hear the dreaded squeak, it often simply means that it is time to clean up.

This may be done with the wheels still on the bike, but I like to drop them out and do it in a truing stand. The wheel's trueness inevitably confronts any rim-mounted brakes; you may as well check the true while you're at it.

Brush away any dried-up crap on the rims, in advance of spraying them; just clear it out with a dry rag. The rims are best cleaned with rubbing alcohol, because it tends to be very thorough. You might use a citrus solvent or soap water, alternately. Anything short of oils! It's best to avoid hitting the brake pads with liquid cleaner, as this will complicate their own treatment.

Every once in a great while we come across some serious hard case, where the brakes still squeak after *all* other considerations have been thoroughly dealt with, and it is only then that I might consider **SANDING THE RIMS**. The task is kind of a pain in the ass; it's not something we just go and do for shits and giggles.

You need to take off the tire to sand down a rim. Sanding the tire down does not make a whole lot of sense. Steel rims are chromed or painted; it does no good to sand them either. It's just the aluminum hoops we're talking about.

There once was a time when I would habitually sand down a bike's rims if the horrible squeaking survived the most rudimentary pad-filing process, but I've since learnt better. The fine aluminum dust released by sanding rims can itself make the brakes cry out in alarm. I file the pads more completely, these days, because it is much easier. You take them off, clamp the post in a vise, and shave the faces smooth. If you are lacking in vises, lay a file on your bench and run the pads across that.

You can just leave the pads mounted, of course, but it is better to drop them out for a minute. The lighting is much better; you can do a more thorough job. A coarser metal-working file will also suffice from such an angle, rather than the harsh woodworking file we might otherwise use, and this will spare your pads some wear. You only scrape until the shiny buildup is gone; there is no filing competition.

The brake pads' angle against the rim, known as the toe-in, is often implicated in noisy brakes as well—the toe-in adjustments for each braking system are detailed in the pages following.

The brakes may have bigger problems, if a good cleaning and the right angle don't shut them up. Older and cheaper brakes are frequently characterized by wispy and even frail profiles, often rendered in weaker sorts of metal, and the sum of these shortcomings can cause the rapid vibrations we hear as squealing brakes. This comes up quite a bit, actually. The front brakes, less well-buttressed than their backward compatriots, have traditionally been somewhat noisier as well.

The cleaner and more rigid a given brake is, and the better it is supported on the frame, the less you would likely to hear anything about it. I really wish I could spell out a simple rule to explain away the squeaks, but I am not sure that would be possible. The horrible truth is that riding the bike makes the brakes squeak. Coaster brakes, drum brakes, and the fixes provide for alternatives, but a fair range of the elements make our disc or rim-mounted brakes scream their heads off— rain, snow, mud, dirt, anything. Angel dust. Even the famous

trophy bike, precociously reserved for use on those absolutely perfect days, will in time surrender its nubile pads to the ravages of time. I've not made it through so many decades myself, but I notice those brake pads that have tend to be pretty well toasted, like little rubber rocks.

Some pads and brake systems will whine less than others, but their blessed silence may only arrive at the expense of braking power. Road brake calipers squeak very rarely, for example, but they are not as powerful as V brakes, whose more ambitious designs leave them more vulnerable to the aforementioned vibrations, also known as "brake chatter." The

cantilevers, as well, are somewhat more exposed in this respect. With their power comes responsibility.

Growing up in Minnesota, the winters were something like a bike's final exams. Those that pull through earn our warmest thanks. Year after year, the huge volumes of salt and sand used on the roads present major challenges for the **BRAKE PADS.**

The pads work best when both their surfaces and the rims they face are clean and dry, but these circumstances cannot be maintained through the salt and snow, or the rain. We thus expect the brakes to squeak more in the winter. Their power may fade as well.

The pads also wear a lot faster. You can expect to replace them every spring, at the least, riding freewheeled bikes. I was inclined to stretch them as long as I could, back in the day, but you really don't want to push it. All the brake pads are built around metal spines, and it would do you no good to let these too near the rims.

Generally speaking, the harder pad compounds used by manufacturers like Shimano and Tektro tend to make less noise, while the soft compounds associated with brands like Kool Stop and Matthauser can be more effective, especially in wet conditions. This is true with linear pull brakes, and to a lesser extent with the cantilevers. The old Matthauser pads were favorites for many, but they are getting hard to find. The Kool Stop pads provide for similar performance, in terms of stopping effectiveness.

Cartridge brake pads are available from a number of manufacturers, for each of the major rim-mounted braking systems. They are the more sustainable option in any application, and over the long haul they're good and cheap.

The cartridges' rubber inserts are released and secured by means of small pins, in the case of the V brakes, or short squat bolts, with the cantilevers or sidepulls. Anything such would need to make it all the way back home, to be considered safe to ride: through both holes, or threaded in completely.

The expired pads can be pulled out with pliers, or pried away with a small screwdriver. The new ones should slide most of the way in on their own. Press any remainder in place against the edge of a sturdy fixed object, such as a vise, jamming the pad straight down into its base.

Note that cartridge pads are directional. Make sure they're correctly oriented to the rim. There are right and left pads, in other words. They should be marked as such. Exit always faces the rear.

Modern rim-mounted brakes feature vertical windows for pad adjustments. The pad's rigid metal spine cautiously pokes its way through, whereby it is thrilled to discover it can slide up and down to better meet the rim. The effort allows for a broader range of possible deployments.

Each distinct braking system makes provisions for its own particular pads. Cantilever brakes employ pads with smooth posts; V brakes anticipate for pads with threaded posts and stacks of washers; road calipers use pads with either bolts or short threaded posts.

We are usually able to convince the road brakes to accept V brake pads, if the washers get moved around. My old Trek 970 commuter is running some of the classic boxed-aluminum road brake replacement pads on the front V brake, at the moment. Less than ideal, perhaps, but they were cheap as hell, and (given their sturdy-as-hell alloy bases) they're nice and quiet as well.

Whichever sort of pad you're installing, you'll find its adjustments that much easier if you take a second to grease the hardware. Just dab a tiny drop into the nuts used to tighten the brake pads into position. Go easy, and don't get any grease on the braking surfaces.

Each system's arrangements allow us to set the pads precisely in line with the rims, which is good, because we don't want them carving up the tires or diving into the spokes. Most systems also let us consider the pads' angles, and this becomes useful as well. The correct angle can eliminate squeaks; by enlisting the wheel's rotational force to drag the brake pad faces better in line with the rims. We call this the pad's **TOE-IN**. Imagine a dime wedged between the rim and the pad's tail; that's what you're shooting for. Hold the pad at an ever-so-slight angle against the rim, as you tighten its hardware all the way down.

Linear and cantilever braking systems enjoy the most elaborate toe-in hardware, as we'll see, because the issue is more critical with these systems. Some better road brake pads are now coming with similar kit, but the traditional method for road brake toe-in was to bend the arm a bit with a big wrench. I shit you not. Rough, in the old days.

A slight reverse toe may quiet things down, where a regular one failed to do so. Unfortunately, such a reversal will effectively work against the braking performance as well. Squeaks that survive the original cleaning and toe-in regimen may be better served by a more thorough pad-filing process, a more extreme toe angle, or even new brake pads, before we even get to talking about sanding down the damned rims.

A. Sidepulls

Our screaming momentum first ended with the **SIDEPULLS**, also known as the caliper brakes. Other, more ambitious systems have since arrived on the scene, but none have yet become as svelte in their dimensions.

The name comes from the cable. Both arms reach over to meet it. The cable shoots down one side, dealing with each in turn, pulling them together in a tight smile. The arms pivot on a bolt above the tire; a spring of some sort holds them tensioned against each other.

Sidepulls have been with us for a very long time, and every opportunity has been taken to refine and profane each feature of their design. The arms have been both lengthened and shortened; brake-centering methods have been refined; the fixing bolt has ducked back into the frame. Yet their essential program remains blessedly straight-forward; the biggest complication may only be in finding the right one to fit your bike.

Sidepull brake.

The pinnacle in sidepull design has come with the dual pivots, as first popularized by Shimano. The pivot splits in two parts; the brake suddenly features three distinct pieces. The design offers much more bang for the buck. Anchoring a brake in one location directly above the tire is not the most impressive plan,

considering what we've learned since, but the dual pivot sidepulls suck it in and make the most of things. Kind of heroic, really. They do tend to be burlier and more compact than earlier renditions; there comes less opportunity for flex and play. They just do the job and that's it.

At the far, opposite end of this spectrum lurks the sidepull's worst-case scenario, the oversized generic steel monstrosity. Years ago, before corrupting first the cantilevers and then the V brakes, department stores afflicted some mountain and BMX bikes with the worst sidepulls ever. They were heavy and far too flexible, only grudgingly adjustable and barely functional in the first place. Paired with junk steel rims, as was usually the case, they can only further suggest an especially shady cynicism on the part of the manufacturers. Yet cantilever brakes soon entered the picture, sweeping away all the better mountain bikes, and the sidepulls were left with the luxury of focusing only on the road bikes. Their arms grew shorter to better grasp their newly refined responsibilities.

A sidepull's **BRAKE REACH** describes the distance from the mounting bolt to the spread of available pad positions down on the arms. The oldest frames tend to require longer sidepulls; more modern road bikes are clustered around the shorter versions. Most of Shimano's sidepulls claim a reach of 39 to 49 mm, last I checked, but they have a couple longer ones as well. Tektro comes in with 47 to 57 mm reach brakes, as well as a 53 to 71 mm pair and even a 61 to 78 mm.

Sidepulls are built around stout M6 mounting bolts, which originally poked right through the fork to meet a 10 mm nut. Newer sidepulls are born with **RECESSED BRAKE NUTS** instead, meant to work with a shortened mounting bolt of the same M6 threading. The brake bolt's exit hole is drilled out just a bit wider, to allow this to happen.

Road frames and forks have been thus drilled for a decade or two already, so this is one of those things we kind of have to get used to. The older non-recessed brakes can still be made to work on the new frames, assuming the arms are of a correct length; their tail sections only stick out a bit. We might also bring an older frame or fork up to date, with a drill bit just a hair wider than the recessed nut. Leave the hole closest to the caliper alone! Drilling straight through will do no good at all.

Whatever it is you find yourself doing, the brake needs to end up really tight against the frame. A loose brake will inevitably drag one of its pads on the rim, as would one that's been tightened at an odd angle.

Do me a favor, though? *Double-check the wheel's position in the frame, before moving to center the brake.* I would swear that maybe a quarter of all brake-centering scenarios are quickly resolved this way,

by correctly aligning the wheels within the frame and fork. The tire's center line should always line up with the frame or fork's midpoint; problems here would indicate either incorrect wheel dish or a poorly aligned frame.

Lacking as they are in refinements, older and cheaper sidepulls can only be centered manually. First confirm that the brake is mounted tightly, then grip both the nut atop the brake's spine and that fixing it to the frame or fork and turn the pair simultaneously. Slowly—it doesn't take much.

Better sidepulls incorporate thin wrench flats, mounted to the spine just before the bolt enters to the frame or fork. They measure 10, 11, 12, or 13 mm, depending upon the manufacturer. Or maybe 14 mm, if they're old Modolo. And I seem to recall that someone used 15 mm here as well, now that I think about it. The headset cups typically preclude the use of cone wrenches for these kinds of brake adjustments, up front at least. You would need to remove the wheel and attack from beneath.

The original sidepulls were built in easily recognizable patterns. The bolt was fixed with a slotted round block, with which to support a stout wire wishbone, bearing sturdy curly-cues to either shoulder. The two arms laid themselves atop this, with thin washers set between each piece to reduce their friction. Topping the deck, we found a pair of nuts, which are counter-tightened against each other, just before the arms began to bind. Popping one end of the spring out and stretching it has the effect of putting more zing in your brakes. A little cleaning and light oil may do just as well, depending.

The **DUAL PIVOT SIDEPULLS** use distinct centering methods. A small bolt is set to the top of one shoulder, to bottom out directly atop the brake spring. These things tend to be stubborn, like most other brake-centering bolts, and therefore quick to strip out: press down hard, and work slowly. The brake will grudgingly begin to rotate on its mounting bolt.

Campagnolo dual pivot calipers may feature small bolts set into either shoulder, each of which answers to a 2 mm Allen key. That appearing on the cable side governs the spring tension; its opposite concerns itself with the brake's centering. Or there may be slots for a 15 mm wrench, depending. SRAM Force and Rival dual pivot calipers provide wrench flats of the traditional sort, for centering purposes. Note that you would need to release the small fixing screw featuring upon the caliper's underside, before tightening its action.

It never hurts to drop a bit of oil in the mix, whichever sort of sidepull you're using. It is also a fine idea to overhaul a sidepull that has been piloted through the winter. The old- sters, at least; dual pivots can be more troublesome to put back together. With the tradi- tional variety, this only means undoing the bolts up top and cleaning everything up with a lightly oiled rag. Upon reassembly, keep in mind that there should never be lateral play along the pivots. The best adjustment would leave them with just enough freedom to smile and frown at their leisure.

B. Centerpulls

The **CENTERPULL** brakes epitomize dusty old ten-speeds. They mount in the same holes we use for the sidepull calipers, but none of the centerpulls were ever spec'd with recessed mounting nuts. Hell, I've known some to lack even the nylock in- serts. Centerpulls have longer and more flexible arms as well; everything about them dates to an earlier period.

Some of the very first mountain bikes used something similar, which was

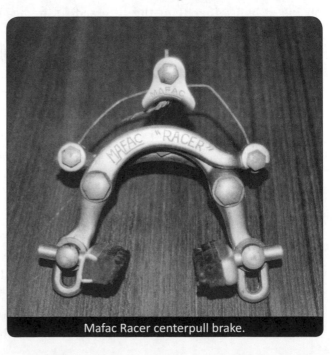

Mafac Racer centerpull brake.

called a **U BRAKE**. These were mounted in back, under the chainstays. The U's arms crossed each other, to meet a cable hanger and its straddle cable in the middle. The action ended up becoming similar to what we'd seen with their older cousins, the road centerpulls, which is to say that other braking systems would be lighter and more efficient.

GT was long alone among the major manufacturers, prior to their final debasement by Pacific Cycle, in that they refused to give it up. The only advantage the U brakes ever had was in their svelte profile—for a boss-mounted system, at least—but the linear pull brakes have long since strolled away with even this minor glory. Mountain bike geometry no longer affords the longish chainstays the U's had originally clung to, but some of the BMX bikes do. It's about the only place we find them, now.

The U brake's maintenance is fairly straightforward. Those mounted down on the chainstays get showered with a lot more mud; plan to clean them more regularly. The pads borrow mounting ideas from other systems; the cabling method mimics a cantilever straddle.

The original centerpull brakes were not possessed of any unique effect. A cable-housing stop of some kind suspends a straddle cable in a carrier; the brake arms cross each other to meet it. The design absorbs and misplaces a conspicuous portion of our energy, allowing for an unfortunate degree of flex. But they

can work, in a pinch. The coolest centerpulls were those made by Mafac. The design is a little better; they also look cool. A flat, curved arm with "Mafac" etched into it arches across the front, like a fine old bridge.

Centerpulls have no means for independent cable adjustment, so there needs to be a barrel adjuster at or before the cable housing stop.

Note as well that the straddle hanger needs to be made really, really tight. The straddle cable itself is of a fixed length, with buttons at either end; they pop in and out of the brake arms. These and their springs are bolted to a plate, which is fixed to the frame. The centerpulls are kind of a bitch to get back together, so I do not recommend disassembly. Just pull the pads and drop the thing in your citrus degreaser for a day, if you need to.

The centerpulls are not equipped with any dedicated brake-centering hardware. They are just that old. But that's cool; it means you finally get to use the hammer. You would want some kind of a punch as well, assuming you care for the bike's paint. A #2 flathead screwdriver is perfect. Center the brake as best you can by hand, first, and fully tighten its fixing bolt. Track down an M6 nylock nut for this, if there's not one up there already. Line up the screwdriver on the side that needs to move in, and knock on its tail with the hammer. Aim for the shoulders, right on top of the springs there. Tap, tap, tap . . . perfect.

C. Cantilevers

The **CANTILEVER BRAKES** were well-established and enjoying their zenith, when first I started working in bike shops. I would guess that the originals were made by Dia Compe, with an infant Shimano following soon thereafter. I've worked on the progenitors from each company; the Dia Compe design looks to be a bit older. Both examples were very stripped-down—more curious hot rod than established utility. Their designs are somewhat more graceful, but we find no specific brake-centering feature on either of them. And yet this was enough, because the frame-mounting protocol they began has prospered to this day.

The central advantage the cantis brought is in their leverage. The arms are able to lever against the frame, rather than simply pushing against themselves. If the sidepulls and centerpulls strain through their calisthenics in the airless void of outer space, the cantilevers are at least able to push off against the moon. This they accomplish by settling down atop the **BRAKE BOSSES**, which are installed to either side of the wheel. These are threaded metal stubs, 15 mm long by 8 mm wide, which act as pivots for the brake arms. They squat silent and motionless on the frame; the cantilevers pirouette above and around them. It works out pretty well.

Both linear pull and rim-mounted hydraulic brakes operate from the same bosses, in the same positions. It could be universal! But it's not, because BMX U brakes and their old GT admirers *and* the ancient roller-cam mountain brakes mount these very same posts in distinct positions.

The cantilever brakes each conform to a basic profile. The two arms are sprung out from the frame at angles; a straddle cable reaches down to each side from one central brake cable. The cantilever straddle thus ends up resembling an inverted "V," but it should not be confused with "V brakes," the popular slang for linear pull brakes. They're up next.

A stout M6 bolt pierces each brake arm, securing it to the brake boss. These bolts need to be tight. Manufacturers generally treat them with thread-locking compound. The outsides of the bosses, by contrast, should be lubricated with grease. Any rust you find here can get scuffed away with a light emery cloth or sandpaper, with an oily rag flying in to clean the dust away.

Crouched down in the back rows, just before the brake arms meet the frame or fork, we will *usually* find the end of a sturdy spring, tensioned between the brake arm itself and a hole in the back of brake boss. These are the engines which generates the brakes' action, by levering between the frame or fork and each brake arm.

The Dia Compe 987 cantilevers, Suntour self-energizers, Paul's Neo Retro cantilevers and others employ a slightly different approach here, anchoring the usually unworkable, actually. We sometimes use the top set, for older cantilevers, if the springs are all tired and worn out. Rarely, though. And so we see a second sort of brake boss, in which the three holes are clarified into the one.

The springs' collective energy must be equitably distributed, as means to create a more just society. The preferred method for this grand leveling relies upon a small screw, which threads into the base of one brake arm. The screw's tip bottoms out against one end of the brake spring; adjusting it will modify the spring's effective tension. Which, balanced against the opposite spring's fixed position, will make for a reasonably quick and accurate means to adjust brake centering. You turn the

Suntour self-energizing cantilever brakes.

springs to a nut set around the brake boss, rather than to the brake boss itself. You loosen the brake arm's fixing bolt and turn this nut, in order to adjust the spring tension or brake centering. These sorts of free-floating systems can be made to work well enough, but the others are simpler.

Most brake bosses will offer the springs their choice of three holes, lined up vertically on the base. Almost all the cantilevers will go for the middle one. The upper and lower extremes are

screw in to increase the spring tension, or out to release it. Increasing the tension on the one side eases that brake arm back away from the rim, and the reverse is also true. It can take a second before the impact of a given adjustment becomes visible—you can help things sink in by wriggling the arms back and forth across the bosses.

We should also discuss the **STRADDLE CABLES**, the wire wishbones which connect the two cantilever arms. We will see one of two versions, broadly speaking. A cable hanger may be bolted to the brake cable, with a separate straddle cable passing through it, or the brake cable itself will end up shooting down one side of a straddle assembly. (Shimano long ago experimented with an ungainly hybrid between these two—one which required the cursed "pro-set tools," as I described in *How to Rock and Roll*—but this crap is ever rarer. It can also be replaced.)

against the straddle cable. It should also be mentioned that old school and its imitators are also meant to work with distinct straddle cable hangers, rather than the streamlined straddle assemblies described below. In every circumstance, as with the centerpulls, it is crucial that the cable hangers become super tight. Squeeze the brake lever as hard as you can; see what happens.

Scott self-energizing cantilever brakes.

The general rule is that we like the straddle hanger's intersection to end up sitting just above the fender hole, leaving any fenders or reflectors just enough space to remain undisturbed by braking. Use this measure as your reference point, irrespective of how the cable happens to be set up. Not everyone necessarily knows how to set these things up, to put that another way, and a straddle hanger set too high will seriously diminish your braking performance.

The cable hanger is simple. It is fixed securely to an appropriate place along the brake cable; the straddle slips under the wire and reaches out to the brake arms. Where to hang? The angle formed by the two sides of this straddle cable should end up being around 90 degrees. Each side's angle against its brake arm should also be something similar.

Note that the original cantilevers and their more recent admirers were designed to lean out farther from the bike, comparing with more modern examples—their top edges become nearly horizontal, making for more acute angles

The end of the straddle cable itself gets fixed beneath a pinch bolt, on the top of one brake arm. The cantilever's **QUICK RELEASE** features on the opposite brake arm. We'll see a slotted round hole up top, meant to hold the straddle cable's round head in a tentative embrace. You will need to create some slack in the cable by squeezing the brake arms together, in order to open the cantilever's quick release.

A cantilever's cable may need to be tightened periodically, as the pads wear. Tightening our straddle cable or the brake cable itself challenges the mighty brake springs, as you would discover, but fortunately for our sake the prescient fourth hand tool arrives to save us the day. This operation in particular totally justifies its hook on the wall. The spring tension continuously encourages the straddle to escape, from under the iron thumb of the brake's binder bolt; the fourth hand is the only hand tool that might convince it otherwise.

The **STRADDLE ASSEMBLIES** are yet simpler. There are no extra pieces; the brake cable itself is routed down to the brake arm. It passes through a burly straw on one side, while a matching length of cable fills in as the quick release on the other. A flat interface, looking much like a squat fat coin, connects the two. Its backside features two grooves, separated by a tiny aluminum nub. One lines up at the end of the cable housing, and the other is centered under the handlebar stem.

We route the brake cable down from above, so that it falls in this first groove and shoots out through the straddle assembly's straw. This done, push the cable over the nub so that it is made to arrive through the central groove instead. Use your fourth hand to soak up the brake cable's overflow outside the brake arm, getting it up to that optimal 90-degree angle before tightening the cable in place beneath the brake's binder bolt.

Here again, finish any adjustments by squeezing the brake lever as hard as you can, to test the cable's purchase. It should stay put. The straddle assemblies do need to stretch out to their full extensions, so some especially tight set-ups are precluded as well—the rear brakes on some smaller women's hybrid frames, for example. You would want to substitute a regular hanger and straddle cable, in such a scenario.

We also see a short diagonal line, running across the front of the interface—this is meant to line up with the assembly's quick-release cable, once everything is set up. Which, set against the housing on the opposite side, makes for our pleasant 90 degrees. You threaded the barrel adjuster all the way down, right? Back it out again, just a bit, like a quarter of its length. This pulls the straddle cable up just slightly, to angles just less than our ideal. The pads are tightened into position right up next to the rim; this lets us back them off to more useful positions.

The brake pad's post will slide right into the top of a curious banjo-like bolt, which itself shoots through the cantilever's tall vertical window. A nut at the far end tightens their package into place, together with a pair of concave and convex washers. These coincide with the faces of the cantilevers' arms, allowing us to set the whole thing up at the most useful angles, to better meet the rim and to establish the pad's toe-in. The design was all the best of the 1980s—bodacious; gnarly; totally awesome.

The bolt is usually handled with a 5 mm Allen wrench. The nut is most often for your 10 mm box wrench. Their particulars vary occasionally, within narrow and reasonable parameters. Things will go a bit quicker if you kind of roll the nut to a starting position with your fingers first.

Veteran cantilever sets accumulate grit around the pads' hardware. It creeps up inside and just sits there, forever. As might be expected, this will complicate our pad adjustments. Take the hardware apart and clean it up with a dry rag, before setting up the pads.

Some brake pads have longer tails. The long end almost always points to the rear. The only exceptions I know of are some of Shimano's mountain cartridge pads, which flip the tails forward up front. But these are spotted easily enough, by virtue of their markings. The pads' ends may also be bent downward, to better coincide with the round of the rim. The pads' hardware should always become about as

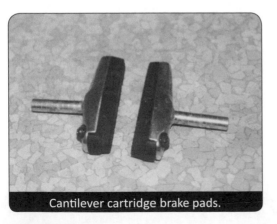
Cantilever cartridge brake pads.

tight as you can make it. Or just less than that, for really burly people. But you get the idea.

Shimano automatic toe-in washers: don't waste your time.

Our discussion might have stopped there, but it is also possible that your cantilevers are afflicted with **AUTOMATIC TOE-IN**. This was another bad idea dating from the 1990s. The guess was that adding springs in-line to the pad hardware could "automatically" set the toe-in. Unfortunately, in practice the effort shunts the pads out well beyond any useful angle. The solution, fortunately, is simple! You unscrew the pad hardware for a second, just long enough to ditch anything therein that looks like it may be a spring.

Shimano may have been the original culprit. They relied upon these truly goofy spring-loaded plastic washers, at first. These goof-gaskets were later replaced with more subtle spring-loaded washers: these bear slits, the sides of which bend in opposing directions, meaning thus to yield similar effects. This last arrangement crossed over to the earliest STX linear pull brakes, with cantilever-style pads, for some reason. Note as well that various generic cantilever

Tightening a cantilever brake pad into position.

own discretion. With each pad, dial the fixing nut finger tight before aligning the pad parallel to the rim, balanced between the tire above and the spokes below, with the back end sticking out just a bit further. This is another technique that sounds far more complicated on paper than it is in real life; basically you're holding the pad in just the right position while you tighten its nut down with the other. It gets to be reflex, with a little practice.

The Suntour self-energizing cantilevers were the coolest of them all. This was the name applied to WTB's rollercam brakes, when Suntour licensed them in the mid-1980s. I think that's what happened; I would have been just entering high school at the time. I have also seen the names Scott and Pedersen associated with this most worthwhile cantilever design, but I will leave it to the historians.

manufacturers buried their springs up inside the brake arms themselves—if your cantilever brake pads seem impossible to adjust, you may want to take them apart and see if you can fish out any extra springs.

Working to set up the cantilever brakes, the last thing we do is to align the pads on the rim and set up their **TOE-IN**. The front of the pad hits slightly before the back. That's all it means. Kool Stop pads are born with little lips that brace against the rim, which makes for a nice toe-in, but we're more usually left to our

D. Linear Pull

I was just cutting my teeth at Wheel and Sprocket, in Milwaukee, when the linear pull brakes started showing up. The originals were exclusively high-end, and also more complex. These curious old grandfather clocks installed tiny parallelograms between the brake arm and brake pad. These originals did offer a basic advantage over the cantilevers, in their improved leverage, alas the parallelograms loosened up with use, which meant that the brakes soon began to squeak.

Most recent versions have dispatched with the parallelogram. Thus improved, the linear pulls, more commonly known as **V BRAKES**, really do represent a meaningful improvement. The design allows a fuller portion of our efforts to be applied to braking. Persons who have trouble with less effective braking systems will do better on the V brakes.

A famous handful of the original test rides are said to have finished with riders going over the handlebars, actually. I have never seen it done; this may be urban legend. But ours has become a wantonly litigious society—denied real justice and security, we are asked to individualize such pursuits—so it should not surprise us that concerns around the V brakes' increased power have encouraged some manufacturers to engineer a degree of supplementary flex into their V brakes.

A small spring is added along those cables heading for the V brakes mounted on the forks of many lower-end bikes, precisely to modulate their power. (The rear brake's longer stretch and the diminished rigidity associated with entry-level parts accomplish much the same effect out back.) At the same time, as a characteristic this level of modulation is rarely associated with performance bikes, which effect crisper, more responsive components. There is no conspiracy; I merely mean to explain why some V brakes work so much more decisively than others.

Our adjustments are made in a different sequence, with the V brakes. It is best to set up the pads before arranging the cable. Their relatively long threaded posts are each adorned with two pairs of washers. One washer is concave, and the other convex; together the pairs allow for a range of adjustment.

The washers' sequence should be installed the same way, every last time: the concave washers form bowls for the convex washers' cantaloupe, which the brake arm slices in half. Only thus do we get the range of motion required to set things up right.

With each brake pad, you will notice that one of the concave washers is much thicker than the other. Which pair goes where totally depends on the bike. The V brakes' bosses are always set to the same distance from the hub, but diverse manufacturers' intentions around tire clearance and aerodynamics will find some brake bosses set farther *apart* than others. Thus do we see the thicker and thinner sets of washers.

Ultimately you want to make the most of the available spring tension, so the brake arms should be drawn together as much as possible, but not so much that the brake noodle rams the opposite brake arm. The best arrangement finds the arms parallel to each other, in line with the wheel. Depending how the brake bosses were mounted, this will find the fatter set of concave/convex washers on the inside or the outside of the brake arms.

It is easiest to set up the pads with the brake arms' springs disengaged. The spring's tail typically runs right up the side; you're able to pinch it out of the way with the fingers or a screwdriver. (A small handful of the Vs will pull the old cantilever thing, hiding the springs inside the brake arms. You would need to hold these to the rims, as the pads are tightened into position.)

The V brake's cable housing dives into the curved metal straw we call the **BRAKE NOODLE**. The left brake arm is topped with a hinged carriage, the end of which features a hole just big enough to accept the very tip of this noodle. The cable shoots out from the tip of the noodle, darts across the tire and ducks under a binder bolt capping the other brake arm. The noodle's graceful curve allows for the brake's quick-release feature, as well: you press the brake arms together with one hand, to slacken the cable, and pull the noodle back and free with the other.

Cables are sometimes flattened beneath the brakes' binder bolts, and this can complicate their interactions with the noodles. This is especially true of the plastic-tipped SRAM noodles, whose tiny nostrils are especially sensitive to such trouble. It's as if they tug at your sleeve, urging you to just snip the old cable and buy a brand new one. But you don't need to. A fourth hand tool will pull that cable right on out and back through again. (Next time, avoid this problem by making sure the cable is clamped down squarely within its groove under the pinch bolt, to keep it round and healthy.)

Recall our chat on the brake modulation? If the top of the noodle is noticeably taller and wider than its peers, it is probably concealing a small spring. It is easy enough to dig these things out with a pick, if you're so inclined. These wider noodles, unlike their peers, will also swallow a cable-housing cap—the spring needs to push against something solid—but this simply bottoms out in the base, once you clean the spring out of the way.

Brand new bikes invariably plug their brake noodles' nose cones into rubber boots, to cover the cable on its short trip across the tire to meet the pinch bolt. These things are meant to keep the tire's spray of grit from backing up into the brake noodles, but the boots can also complicate our

V brake noodles with and without modulation spring.

cable adjustments, by getting in the way of the pinch bolt. The cleaner your bike tends to be, the less you'd really need them.

At the very least, the cable needs to be tightened enough to prevent the brake lever from bottoming out on the handlebar. This minimum would still allow for plenty of slack, with the V brakes, which can be useful if the wheels aren't quite straight. The cables on a new or freshly tuned bike should be quite a bit tighter than this, which in turn will require a higher degree of truth from the wheels.

The brake centering comes last, after the pads and cable are set up. There are small screws installed to the lower sides of each arm, in the case of the Vs, which control both brake centering and spring tension. Dialing these in will jack up the tension, as with the cantilevers, and here as well the reverse is also true.

The screws do become progressively harder to turn, as the spring tension increases. You will definitely want to be pushing down nice and hard on the screwdriver or Allen wrench, to avoid stripping the screw. But the spring tension is our friend, and so as a default we'd rather turn the screws in than out.

You should end up finalizing the centering adjustment in small measures; half-turns on the screws. As you finish up, follow each tweak by jiggling the brakes back and forth across their bosses. The adjustment screw's stark commands can take a few seconds to echo down the length of the spring. This helps the brake arms absorb the news.

V brakes and cantilevers are of the same family, but they are not compatible. The V brake levers pull twice as much cable as the other mechanical braking systems. The linear pull levers can command other sorts of brakes—the cables can be set to ridiculously tight tolerances, in fact—but the V brakes themselves refuse to listen to anybody else's levers. And they get away with it, because shit is just like that. The brake cable's head comes to rest in slightly different positions on the lever, basically, and this changes the arc of its travel. There are some ambidextrous levers available, providing distinct openings for cantilever or linear pull cables, but most will need to go one way or another.

Cantilevers are not quite extinct. Avid and Paul Components still make a few nicer models; cheapos from Tektro and Shimano are also available. I would expect to find replacements so long as the lights stay on. There remain only a couple road brake levers which might govern the V brakes; the cantis are still pretty mainstream on cyclocross and tour bikes.

Dia Compe's 287V levers are designed to help smuggle linear pull brakes aboard the road bikes. By themselves, some of the new cross levers may be asked to do as well. If nothing else, the curious Travel Agent pulleys are able to trick the STI levers toward compliance.

E. Disc

There's nothing wrong with using a couple different brake systems on the same bike, so long as you honor the aforementioned details with regards to the cable travel. To the contrary, some bikes are interesting enough to require such arrangements. Ancient mountain bikes have cantilevers up front and roller-cams in back, and the tandems will commonly run a rear drum brake on top of their regular systems. Or, as with Coll and Sara's Co-Motion tandem, the V brake up front will balance a disc brake out back.

Disc rotor.

Discs don't represent an ultimate solution so much as a different approach. Their central advantage—to stop a bike quickly, without relying upon the rims' dirty faces—was first discovered with the simpler

and cheaper drum brakes. The discs are only more exotic, effective, and expensive.

Rim-mounted brakes create friction heat, which is rumored to have very occasionally become enough to flatten tires on heavily loaded tour bikes. Their positioning also leaves them exposed to the elements carried up by the rims, and thus do their pads wear more quickly. The aluminum rims wear down as well, albeit at a far slower rate.

DISC BRAKES, by contrast, sit right out in the wind. This allows the friction heat to more easily dissipate, which in turn allows for the use of more effective materials in the brake pads.

The arrangements allow both the brake pads and rotor to be replaced fairly easily. Changing out a rotor is quicker, easier, and cheaper than rebuilding a wheel. The rotors were originally mounted to their designated hubs with circles of six M5 torx screws, and many manufacturers still use this standard. Shimano's original disc brake hubs made use of the same six-bolt pattern, but their more recent offerings have adopted the **CENTERLOCK** interface, which carves yet more matching splines to the disc-compatible hub and rotor before enlisting a regular old Hyperglide-style cassette lockring to hold the two together. This is a pretty cool idea—it greatly simplifies rotor installation, and it lends a whole new purpose to a raft of lockring tools. (The aptly named Problem Solvers company produces a Centerlock adapter, which allows for the use of six-bolt discs on Centerlock hubs.)

The discs are inclined to squeak, just as the Vs are, but for slightly different reasons. They really, *really* hate oil. The traces on your fingertips are enough to make them squeal. This is revealed as the culprit often enough, actually—they're interesting; people want to grab at them. So they do, and the innocuous fingerprint oil gets all over the place, and we hear all about it.

This dilemma seems to be intrinsic to those compounds used to make the brake pads. And the fingers are not all that greasy to begin with most of the time; you can imagine the cataclysmic impact a few drops of straight chain lube may have.

The good news is that the discs can also escape the noise pretty quickly. It is easy come, easy go. Simply remove the wheel and clean the disc with rubbing alcohol, thoroughly. You can also slide a strip of emery cloth in between the calipers to sand down the pads themselves, if you really need to, but the juice usually does the trick. I am not aware of anything else that may work here.

Our friend Travis T. offers a further tip: do not dry-fire the disc brakes. In other words, do not squeeze the caliper without having the rotor in place between the pads. I haven't yet seen this in my own travels, but he has evidently needed to rebuild calipers and even bleed hydraulic disc systems to resolve such situations.

Discs don't bend easily, but it does happen. Your favorite local shop should have the means to true them. In the meanwhile, since the calipers invariably hang the pads incredibly close to the discs, the smallest deviation will either stop you cold or just rub, rub, rub until you really just wanna say fuck it.

The calipers must be installed to an especially precise position. "Almost there" is woefully inadequate. The mounting tabs themselves occupy standardized positions on the fork and frame; we only need the wriggle-room to account for the mindlessly tight adjustment parameters. The calipers can too easily be tightened at slight angles to the disc, and this in turn can prevent the wheel from moving at all. We must draw our inspiration from the microscopes and calipers; this really requires our close attention.

Cable routing is also more important, with the disc brakes, for the same kinds of reasons. Something so simple as pulling across another cable's housing can cause a brake pad to drag on its rotor. All these things can loosen—especially, as discussed, the front wheel skewers.

First make sure any bolts holding the caliper together are tightly installed, then confirm that the wheel in question is both centered and mounted securely.

The brake cable connects to the caliper by means of a pivoting arm, which moves in an arc: see to it that the cable is fixed such that the arm rests at a midpoint in its range of movement. We can fine-tune this later, to determine the lever pull, by reattaching the cable or fiddling with its barrel adjuster.

The main trick to setting up disc brakes is in ensuring that the pads become precisely parallel with the rotors. If the brake rubs, either the rotor itself is bent—less likely, and only if the rubbing is intermittent—or the disc caliper itself is not correctly positioned.

Loosen both the bolts fixing the caliper to the frame or fork, such that it can be scooted around on its base, and then tighten the caliper's fixed (inboard) pad all the way down. The inboard side of the caliper will typically feature a broad flat dial of some kind; turning this in tightens the fixed pad. Shimano Deore calipers enlist a 5 mm hex wrench for such purposes. Avid provides us a big red disc we dial with the fingers.

The rotor ends up firmly sandwiched between the two pads, and it is here that the caliper will be most aligned with its target. Firm the fixing bolts all the way down, once the caliper's death grip on the rotor has been realized, then loosen the cable pinch; the outboard pad should ease back from the rotor. Next back off the fixed pad, incrementally, *just* to the point where nothing is rubbing. This leaves it suspended as close to the disc as it may ever hope to be. All that remains is to set the other pad, by tuning the cable adjustment.

F. Leverage

Enough about the various calipers—let's talk about the brake levers for a minute. I am a big fan of the modern cross levers, myself. Those mounted upstairs on the drop bars, as if to mimic adolescent mountain brake levers. Their original intention was to update the old and decrepit "suicide levers," by providing for a secondary and more upright position on the road bikes' drop bars, which in practice makes for four distinct brake levers. The cross levers' action is also unique: the cable housing is made to move, rather than simply the cable itself.

The cross levers work out fine on their own as well, as with the solitary levers on fixed gears. They are just small enough to be gripped with a fuller portion of the hand, which might even improve our leverage—conventional brake levers have their advantage in length, but the palm can squeeze a lot harder than the fingertips. I had hoped to split a pair of these between a couple of my own bikes a few summers ago, but things were such that I couldn't even put together the wholesale price. Kind of a rough season. But at least one bike still needed a brake lever, so I started messing around, and eventually arrived upon something else entirely.

Recall that road brake cables can be made to fit with some shift levers? It happened that I had various dusty old shift levers scattered about the basement, broke as I was, and these provided materials for experiments. The earliest attempts were more dubious—pushing down with the thumb is *not* a natural way to slow a bike down, as it turns out—but the simplest aluminum thumb shifters can make for slick little brake levers, as it turns out. More, their steel clamps can usually be expanded to fit the drop bars.

The shift levers themselves are generally built around short M5 spines, but these may be drilled out and replaced, with something long enough to pass right through and engage a washer and nylock nut. The shift lever was not made with braking in mind; skewering it with a longer bolt renders this a more plausible ambition. The recipe does require a M5 screw long enough to pierce both lever and nut, and with a head flat enough to stand in for the original—one of those left over from your Kryptonite lock's mounting bracket, for example—its forgettable Phillips face can be made flush with the handlebar. You will also need to drill out the threads in the shifter's base to do this. But the big hole is already up in there; we can finish it off free-handed.

The new screw needs to be made just tight enough, beneath its washer and nut— you look for that fine balance, where the shifter's action is just loose enough to balance against the brake's spring tension. And that reminds me, one other thing? Do not use plastic levers for this.

With respect to the cable routing, the pursuit of this shortcut kind of implies that you'll work with what you get. It might make sense to mount such a lever on one side of the handlebar or the other, or perhaps beneath the bar, contingent on the cable's exit strategy.

The purpose of this odd little exercise? To illustrate how a shift lever may be used to stop a bike, if it really needs to— to reaffirm that we are making this up as we go along.

This was all a while ago. I have since managed to pick up a set of cross levers; they're on my wife's Terry at the moment. Back then, the important question was what to *name* this strange new fruit.

Soup spoon brake lever.

I consulted with my friend Xara, a local thinker of no small renown, but after endless brainstorming we were no closer to the light. It was only the next day that the answer landed before me—this high new device would be known as the **SOUP SPOON**. It gets us a bigger bite.

Soup spoons can be made from the old Falcon thumbshifters, which your friendly local bike shop can still score from Q, last I checked. These may also be the least expensive new shift levers you will ever come across—in metal, at least—and they suit our purposes brilliantly. You even get a spare, to pass along to your friend.

The Falcons do provide for a minor ratcheting mechanism, which is great for the shifting, but not for braking. You would need to get rid of this, to effect the soup spoon. But it's only a tiny piece of plastic, balanced atop a diminutive spring, pressing on the shifter's splined ceiling. It all pops right out.

G. Hydraulic

In terms of their stopping power, **HYDRAULIC BRAKES** cast those we'd begun with as more ornamental in nature. There really isn't any relation between lever force and braking force, with the hydros. This cuts both ways! If you're one to go really fast but not squeeze hard, hydros will stop you quickly, with only the slightest indication—you don't need to pull the lever so much as move it. If

you are accustomed to controlling speed more gradually, on the other hand, the sensation will be pretty abrupt. The awesome force delivered to the brakes corresponds best with sheer cliffs and sea changes; it is more closing down than slowing down.

Mechanically, hydros perch on their own distinct technical platform. Older, more common bicycle components watch bemusedly from the ground below. The hydraulics don't have to worry about rusted cables or anything boring like that, but this departure really launches them out into the void. They're picky, for one thing—each company's systems operate on their own distinct hydraulic fluid. Some, such as Shimano's mineral oil, are fairly common and somewhat benign. Others are imported straight in from more toxic automobile protocols.

Using the wrong juice can destroy the hoses. (The calipers would also need to be soaked in rubbing alcohol.) Where regular brake cables survive the occasional roughhousing, hydraulic lines begin to fail with the smallest pin prick. Stainless hydraulic hoses, available for many systems, fare somewhat better, provided they're long enough and routed correctly.

If your hydros do take a hit on the fly, there's nothing you can do about it. You have no more brake at all, wherever you happen to be. The tools and materials that might be needed to repair a damaged hydraulic brake would be a sizeable addition to any roadside repair kit.

Different hydraulic systems provide for various means to adjust lever reach and brake pad positions. It's usually just the two features; the controls' particulars will vary. Rim-mounted hydraulics, such as Magura, incorporate a quick-release lever behind one caliper. You pull the one side off its brake boss to remove a wheel. The rim-mounted hydraulic brakes really don't squeak at all, but the disc varieties will quite happily make just as much noise as their mechanical kin. As with their peers, caliper positioning will again become positively crucial. Squeakage is resolved in the same way, by cleaning the discs with rubbing alcohol, or flossing the pads with an emery cloth.

Broken or punctured lines are dealt with by replacing the fluid and the line itself. You drain everything, measure out and install an accurate replacement length of new hydraulic line, and then pump in the correct hydraulic fluid, until any air bubbles are gone.

Most of my own experience has been with the Magura hydraulic brakes. We need to begin with the full servicing kit, in order to either bleed them or replace any lines. Said kit should include a hose with a threaded fitting to drain the old fluid, a big plastic syringe for installing the new hydraulic fluid, and also a number of small metal rings. These rings, which Magura calls "olives," need to be replaced each time you take things apart. Tightening them into place changes their profile.

The hoses detach from their levers and calipers by unscrewing the compression nut, which turns out by way of an 8 mm wrench. This nut usually hides under a rubber sleeve, entering the lever. The short stretch of line connecting rim-mounted brakes together over the wheel is neither removed nor replaced, unless it is damaged.

Removing a damaged hydraulic line will empty any remaining fluid trapped therein, so don't be doing this over the Persian rug. Your friendly local bike shop should be able to set you up with a correct length of the appropriate hydraulic line. It will be proprietary, just like the fluid.

The particular length may be based on the original, provided it wasn't binding anywhere in the bars' rotation. Cut the new line to length with a razor. Or, if you have an advanced degree, maybe you can try Jagwire's hydro cable cutters. Not regular cable cutters, in any case. Lay the line flat on a sturdy surface and slice, aiming for a perfect 90-degree cut.

Slide the old compression nut onto the new line, and then the new olive. Plug the line all the way down into the caliper. It needs to be tight in place for the seal to hold. Slide the olive and compression nut down, holding the line firmly into its hole as you tighten the nut all the way back down. The other end plugs into the lever in much the same way.

Maguras run on what they call Magura Blood. No kidding. You unscrew a fill hole on the caliper, as well as a similar drain hole up on top of the lever. Fill the syringe, squeeze out any air, and thread its end piece into the fill hole.

Next, grab a can of something cold to drink. Got it? Pop the tab and slam it. This is important, because the empty can becomes the reservoir for the hydraulic fluids' overflow. Tie the can's pop tab to a cable somewhere, up there on the handlebars. The drain hose, which should thread into a second opening on the brake lever, will empty into the can.

You fill from down low, to drain up high. Gravity sorts out any air that gets in the way. Slowly pump the new fluid in, until such a time when no dreaded air bubbles are seen in the drain hose. Cap this top end first, securely. Unscrew the syringe fitting down below, once this is done, and put the screw back in there as well.

Other hydraulic systems will be purged and renewed along a similar pattern.

The luckiest bikes are born with righteous drivetrains. They will snap smoothly from gear to gear, weigh next to nothing and last for a good long time. Most bikes are not so fortunate.

I'd thought the drivetrains featuring upon department store bikes were the worst available, until I saw what was on offer in Mauritania. China does send the U.S. some truly lousy bikes, but it is to countries in Africa that they send their refuse. The dearth of options is striking.

The simple riveted pivot points found on cheap derailleurs' parallelograms allow their cages to sashay about of their own volition more freely—as you're trying to shift, or charge up the busy hill, and this oversight can drop you out of gear, usually all of a sudden.

This may be an issue with your own bike, depending. Grab the bottom of the rear derailleur's cage and see how much it can be swayed side to side. It's much easier to shove the cheaper ones around; older and cheaper ones, all the more so.

Bad drivetrain parts weigh too much, bend too easily, and break far too quickly. The cheapest specialty shop parts will often do little better, unfortunately. We find some relief among older components of quality, which are often considered devalued well before they actually wear out, but this is nothing close to universal. Old doesn't mean *better*, it means *maybe*.

It is difficult to describe the root of "most" shifting problems, simply because the discussion can branch in multiple directions. A given symptom may stem from a couple distinct issues, perhaps even simultaneously. The quality of your parts, the state of their health, your skill in using them, and even the weather itself can inform the situation. The more specifically you can describe a given problem, the sooner you'll be able to isolate its particular solution. Do things go haywire when you're upshifting, or downshifting? In some gears, or all of them? Do the gears only shift only hesitantly, or do they come and go more randomly? Are things always failing, or is it only when you pedal hard?

X. Drivetrains

All these things happen for a reason. A basic understanding of how drivetrains work will allow you to diagnose and correct the great majority of the problems that may arise.

A. Friction

The **FRICTION DERAILLEURS** have not been current for decades, but plenty of them were made well enough, and many are still on the road. They were designed to work with the eponymous shift levers, which at their best will hold a given position with nothing more than simple friction. You may remember this from when you were a kid: changing the gears just by their feel?

Front and rear friction derailleurs.

If nicer old parts interest you at all, it's worth recalling the friction shifting. The different component manufacturers' indexed rear derailleur systems, as we'll see, are not often cross-compatible, so the friction levers are the only things saving some of the nicest old parts from ornamental obscurity.

There must have been an enormous freedom, back then—the derailleurs did not really have to care about any rigid instructions shouted down from on high—there was just this flow. It was rad. The more modern indexed shifting systems are pretty well obsessed with the shift cable's tension, but the friction units are still only passively aware of this detail. They just don't care that much. They try to work with what they have. It is mellow and good.

Friction levers require a small degree of finesse, on the part of the operator; something on par with cooking breakfast, perhaps. As with any other derailleur gear reduction system, is best to ease up on the pedals before shifting—to avoid shifting under load, to get in the right gear before you start climbing the hill—yet the friction levers will require an additional level of discretion. You are charged with selecting the gears all by yourself, without the benefit of any helpful confirmation offered up from the shift levers.

The only adjustments to concern us with friction derailleurs are a few basic ground rules, which are also held in common with their indexed peers. All the pivot points should be oiled just enough, but not excessively, with lightweight penetrating oil. Those few bolts involved should all be tight, and the shift lever and cable should also be in good working condition. You may also attend to the drivetrain cleaning, as described on page 136. The limit screws, to be discussed shortly, need to be correctly adjusted as well.

The rear derailleur gets knocked around more than other components might, given its position. The force from such blows is not infrequently transferred right up to the frame's derailleur hanger. Bent derailleur hangers cause pronounced problems with the shifting—the chain will suddenly start dumping into the spokes, for example. This is actually a reasonably common problem. Moreover, none of the drivetrain remedies described herein will be effective until it is corrected.

Bent hangers are easy to spot. Looking from the rear of the bike, the derailleur cage should be parallel with the back wheel, the dropouts and the chainrings as well. An inward-leaning rear derailleur would suggest that the frame's hanger is bent. See the treatment on frame damage, beginning on page 19.

The derailleurs' cages may also be bent, though this is less common. The two pulleys are meant to be in line: anything less would indicate a bent cage. These can generally be straightened, if you take your time with it. You would need a vise. The pulleys are removed; each side is leveled individually. Modern front derailleurs often share odd lateral contours,

between their two cage plates, but all those I've seen on rear derailleurs are meant to be parallel with each other.

The rear derailleur's energy begins from a sturdy spring, which plays a constant tug-of-war with the stern yet whimsical shift lever. These springs wear out eventually; shifts into the highest gear would grow more sluggish, irrespective of all the appropriate maintenance. We sometimes see replacement springs, meant for some mid-90s Shimano derailleurs, but these are only mediators, meant to resolve an old dispute between rival component manufacturers. But this last we'll consider in due course, on page 129.

Rear derailleur limit screws: default location.

The derailleur itself is all of an articulated parallelogram, suspended between two pivot points. We need some method for preventing the bike's chain from diving into the spokes, or jumping off the edge of the cogs, and this comes with the **LIMIT SCREWS**. You should spy a pair of these threaded in somewhere, pointed into the parallelogram. Each bottoms out on a different edge inside, allowing the limit screws to govern the derailleur's range of motion.

Rear derailleur limit screws in a more traditional setting.

The screws are usually labeled L and H, for low and high. Older friction rear derailleurs often set the limit screws in line across the parallelogram's face, but at some point it became more fashionable to drill them instead into the derailleur's

Limit screws—front derailleur.

top section. Their function would be the same in either location.

There is one potential complication, with regards to the limit screws' positioning. For reasons beyond my awareness, the low and high screws have been traditionally set in a reversed sequence, such that the L screw features toward the high end of the derailleur's range. I can't imagine any clear purpose for this; it didn't need to happen. SRAM has since come along to sort out this detail, reversing positions for the two screws. The basic map is always the same, but its orientation will sometimes change.

We can check on the limit screws' adjustments by suspending the rear wheel and turning the pedals. Push the derailleur all the way in toward the spokes, to confirm that it can stop in time. Looking from behind the bike, the L screw's adjustment should prevent the chain from moving beyond the largest cog. Turn it in, if this is not the case. Conversely, if the chain is not able to reach that same largest gear, you would need to loosen the L screw. Work incrementally in either case, checking your work as you go.

The same principles are used when adjusting the H screw, which governs the chain's access to the smallest gear. We turn the limit screws in, to limit the range of motion. They are turned out only if the derailleur will not reach the cogs in question.

Travis introduced me to a novel way to test the limit screws, up at the old Hayes St. Freewheel. You turn the cranks, and you yank on the cables. It sounds rough, but it really works. Unless you're working on a carbon fiber bike, in which case you would want to be more delicate.

We grab the cable(s) as they pass along the down or top tube, in the more usual circumstances, and pull. This will tell us everything we need to know about the Low limit screws' adjustments. Does the derailleur secretly want to get up there and throw the chain at the spokes? Now's the time to find out! This cable-yanking business also has the effect of seating the cables and housing more thoroughly in their stops, which is useful for retaining our derailleur adjustments.

Note as well that you want to loosen the rear derailleur cable, before adjusting the H screw. (Or the L screw, with either the front derailleurs or the Low Normal rear units, to be described momentarily.) Their relationship is something like a see-saw; adjustments to the one become contingent upon the other. The limit screw sets the starting point for the derailleur cable to work from, so turning it will necessarily modify the cable's tension. The cable just goes tense and stays that way, past a certain point, nullifying anything else that the limit screw may have to say.

If the markings are not clear, or if you get the L and H screws confused, it is easy enough to determine which is which. Release the shift cable from its derailleur. Loosening one of the screws will allow the spring inside the parallelogram to further contract, moving the derailleur cage down the gear range. This marks its "high" screw out back, or the "low" up front. This marks its "high" screw. (Here, too, there are exceptions: we sometimes come across derailleurs too rusted or grimy to really give a shit either way, and more recently we also have Shimano's Rapid Rise/Low Normal derailleurs, which rearrange things such that the derailleur expands as its spring contracts.)

The derailleur would fold down to show you its resting position, once the two were removed, if it wasn't there already. You would be able to push the parallelogram all the way up to the other end of the range, alternately, to better understand the role of the opposing limit screw. (The Rapid Rise/Low Normal rear derailleurs reverse this traditional equation: the spring would be relaxed in the Low position, or tensioned in the High position.) You would be able to push the parallelogram all the way up to the low end of the range, alternately, to better understand the role of the Low limit screw. (The Rapid Rise/Low Normal rear derailleurs reverse each of these equations—the spring would be relaxed in the Low position, or tensioned in the High position.)

The limit screws are meant to be adjusted just once, when the derailleur is first set up. You put them where they're supposed to be, and you go ride the bike. Their threads are tiny, and often treated with thread-locking compound; they're not inclined to rattle loose.

I find myself adjusting the limit screws very occasionally, doing tune-ups. I always confirm the derailleur hanger's alignment, before doing anything else with the drivetrain. Bent derailleur hangers seem to be more common than maladjusted limit screws; either can just as easily toss your chain into the spokes.

Old-fashioned limit screw.

Each of the limit screws is dialed in to the point where the derailleur's pulleys can just *barely*, very slightly move past the final cogs. The textbook methodology has us stopping the pulleys directly above the high and low cogs, but I like to let them out just a hair past that. This seems to help. Stand directly behind the bike and imagine lines radiating out in plane with the cogs' teeth—we are comparing against those extending from the derailleur pulleys.

We need to get the rear derailleur dialed in first, in order to set up the front derailleur. This done, the first thing to do is make sure the front derailleur itself is properly installed.

The lowest point on its cage always needs to clear the top chainring by 2 mm. Pull it forward with the fingers, to check. At the same time, the longest section on the derailleur cage's outer plate needs to rest parallel with the chainrings. This may be toward the front or the back of the cage, dependent on the derailleur's manufacturer and vintage; the outer plates on really old examples are often perfectly flat. (Campagnolo again does the math a bit differently here, as we'll see, declaring that their front derailleurs' *inner* cage plates should be made parallel with the chainrings.)

Once the front derailleur is positioned correctly, shift the rear derailleur all the way up into its largest cog. While in this position, the inside plate of the front derailleur cage needs to barely clear the chain as well. I wish I could spell this out better for you, but this tiny distance has actually been shrinking with time. The more advanced front shifting systems do best with all of a millimeter's breathing room; older examples may require twice that. The only way to know for sure is to test it. The chain should drop down to the smallest ring without hesitation to, as instructed, but it should not be able to fall down onto the bottom bracket shell.

We dial the front derailleur's low screw to set the inner plate's resting position, and finish with the "H" screw, to set the outer limit up on the high end.

Shift all the way down to the smallest chainring up front, to start. Park the rear derailleur in its highest gear, then spin the cranks and pull on the cable, just as we did out back. If the chain hops off the big ring, you need to tighten down the high limit screw.

Any front derailleur further anticipates a good chainline, as well as a well-oiled cable set to a useful tension.

B. Indexing

The **INDEXED DERAILLEURS** are more recent. They are designed to work with matching shift levers, which provide for ratchet-like clicks in correspondence with the gears below.

Their approach has been ubiquitous for some time. The first popular example to really succeed was the old chromed Shimano Indexing System (SIS) derailleur. Indexing rear shift levers have been made in ranges of 5, 6, 7, 8, 9, 10, and 11 speeds, by a slowly growing diversity of manufacturers. Campagnolo has always enjoyed a small slice, but Shimano has long dominated the domestic market. SRAM is the new kid on the block, as far as the drivetrains go, yet their arrangements are increasingly popular. And suddenly there's microSHIFT, an exciting prospect we should keep our eye on. The salient point to remember is that the different manufacturers' parts are only occasionally compatible with each other.

The differences come in the spacing between the cogs, which in turn correspond to the amount of cable pulled or released with each shift on the levers. Shimano set the original standard, with their SIS. Suntour was the first to depart from their orthodoxy, by incorporating two slightly different cog spacing measurements. The cogs appearing across the lower half of the range were spaced slightly farther apart than their smaller siblings, to coincide with a distinct Suntour shift lever and rear derailleur, which themselves were no longer compatible with the Shimano products.

This may have been an odd thing to do, in retrospect, but such is the wisdom of our age. Suntour eventually acquiesced, back when they were still in the shifting game, producing a series of cog sets meant to work within Shimano, which were marked as "Powerflo." The question of their original parts' compatibility has become somewhat less relevant, with the passage of time, but some of their better components were certainly built to last.

The cool thing about Suntour's old 7-speed parts is that they're not all that far removed from the contemporary Shimano protocols. I've been running Suntour shift levers with Shimano-compatible derailleurs and cassettes for many years, actually. What can I say? Suntour made some damned fine shift levers. Which, I do realize, is something like saying that heavy metal was better before all the damned power ballads.

The challenge with any such adaptation, of course, is that the adjustment parameters (for the cable tension, most specifically) grow markedly narrower. Shimano's own 7- and 8-speed parts are not even cross-compatible, strictly speaking—the cogs end up spaced just slightly differently, across each range— let us say for now that the rules of indexing comparability are not necessarily carved in stone, and with a bit of imagination they're not quite as tight as our favorite component manufacturers will sometimes suggest.

Jtek Engineering of Minnesota produces seven distinct ShiftMate adapter pulleys, which modulate the control cables to translate among Shimano, SRAM, and Campagnolo indexing drivetrain parts.

Derailleurs are essentially parallelograms, which—excepting Shimano's aforementioned Rapid Rise/Low Normal platform—are pulled to more extreme angles by their springs. It becomes possible to see an even rectangle, shifting the rear derailleur through the midrange, and the dimensions of these boxes delineate the schisms which define indexing compatibility. Where Campagnolo's box is tall and thin, SRAM's is short and squat. The Suntour, Shimano, and Sachs boxes fall between these.

Campagnolo indexing systems were not designed to work with those from other manufacturers, and—as with their rivals— some of the newer products don't work with their older peers. Yet there do come other, special opportunities with Campagnolo, as when updating the Ergopower levers to 9- and 10-speed for example.

SRAM is the fruit of a union between Sachs and Grip Shift, both of which had previously produced Shimano-compatible parts. Once together, they soon brought out a wholly new indexing standard, for their nascent mountain bike range. The SRAM cog sets are still spaced to the expected Shimano distances, but modifications to the derailleur design have succeeded in doubling the cable travel associated with each shift. The precision of a healthy indexed drivetrain is largely governed by the tension on its shift cable; doubling the interval involved allows for a much more generous range of useful adjustment.

1. Rear Derailleurs

Working with the indexed rear derailleurs, we may also come upon a **B-TENSION SCREW**. It is often overlooked, for it claims no major role. It doesn't even show up on older friction derailleurs, actually. We'll typically spot it right up next to the hanger, behind and below the mounting bolt.

The B-tension screws started coming in when manufacturers began putting springs in the top pivots on derailleurs. The two elements face off against each other, such that the B-tension screw determines the derailleur's resting angle in relation to the cogs. The derailleur's mounting bolt becomes the pivot point; adjusting the B tension rotates it back and forth across this axis. The intention is to better accommodate different ranges of cogs with the same rear derailleur. Top cogs are generally pretty small across the board; we're speaking more of those spreading out behind them. We turn the B tension out to better reach smaller cog sets, or all the way in to fit larger ones. Just about everyone has settled upon the bigger mountain-range cog sets, so in practice this means we generally want the B-tension screw dialed in.

The only time you actually need to adjust the B tension is when the derailleur pulley rides up against the largest cog, in which case you'd want to dial it in. You'd need a derailleur with a longer cage, if this did not solve the problem. No B-tension screw can provide the wee road derailleur the courage to conquer a huge mountain gear range.

The oldest Campagnolo derailleurs omitted the B-tension screws, just as their contemporaries did. They eventually began showing up around the derailleur's mounting bolt, as we may expect them to, but around 1999 they snuck down under the derailleur's knuckle. Their function remains the same.

Excluding SRAM's MRX and Shimano's Alivio, both of which top off around 30 teeth, new mountain rear derailleurs are expected to accommodate cogs up to 34 teeth. The longer the cage, the more teeth it can deal with. It is with the road derailleurs that things really shrink. Campagnolo's derailleurs finish off on cogs between 26 and 29 teeth, last I checked, while Shimano's road range accommodates cogs up to 27 teeth.

My shelf once featured an ancient Huret Allvit derailleur, which bore some of the world's very first **DERAILLEUR PULLEYS**, which were simply round biscuits. Someone eventually must have noticed that these poker chips weren't necessarily required to roll with the chain at all—they could just sit the whole game out, if they wanted to—and so teeth were duly carved to their edges.

The interior was made to feature a bushing, held in place by a screw, shot through a pair of protective washers. And so began their mission, to guide the chain through the forest of gears. The pulleys have grown successively narrower, scaling up to meet the 8th, 9th, 10th, and 11th cogs used in the modern age. The wide old relics could not be asked to fill in for their svelte progeny. Shimano has also brought us the curious floating pulley, which leaves the bushing just slightly wider than the pulley itself, allowing it to slide back and forth on its axis. This affords the indexing derailleurs a useful discretion, rendering their jumps from gear to gear more free-flowing and natural.

These pulleys are stamped "Centeron." Other manufacturers have picked up on the idea as well. They couldn't steal the name, of course, so we just look for the essential feature instead—the pulley is able to slide just a bit, along its axis. Any of these floaters would need to be mounted in the positions nearest the cogs, in order to do any good at all.

More exotic yet is the sealed bearing pulley. Many are machined from aluminum, nakedly displaying the cute little sealed bearings at the cores. The pulley bodies are sometimes thinner than bike chains; we set a washer or two to each side to make things work. Shimano renders its sealed bearing pulleys in ceramic, rather than aluminum, but the uppers in such pairs still retain the useful floating feature. Shimano sealed pulleys are also more modest, covering the bearings with dust caps, so that they look a lot like regular pulleys. Keep that in mind, when next you get around to soaking the high-end derailleurs in any kind of solvent, which will lick the grease right out of the bearing cartridges.

Shimano has more recently taken to putting larger-than-usual lower pulleys on many of their rear derailleurs. I'm not sure just why—I suspect marketing, frankly—but I don't think it's a bad idea. We can expect these big 13-tooth derailleur pulleys to last a little longer than the usual 10-tooth ones; their extra teeth spread the chain's ravages across a slightly wider range of teeth.

The SRAM pulleys are off in a different place entirely, in that they're much more integral to their cages. The SRAM X.O and 9.0 use sealed bearing pulleys; 7.0 and 5.0 use replaceable bushing-style pulleys. The 3.0 won't give the pulleys up at all, for the cage is all one piece. Cheesy.

The single most important thing to remember about any

of these other derailleur pulleys? Always, always, always make sure their mounting bolts are tightened securely. They do not tend to loosen on their own, but they just *might* if they're not made fully tight on reassembly. Dab a mild thread-locking compound on the threads, if ever you do take things apart.

2. Front Derailleurs

As a rule, the **INDEXING FRONT DERAILLEURS** require more precise adjustments, with regards to the cable tension. The front derailleur cages have become increasingly specialized, bending and expanding to focus upon various different gearing ranges—mountain and road examples are each distinct, in cage shape and profile and perhaps the frame mounting particulars as well. The fresher schisms dividing 7/8-, 9-, 10-, and 11-speed component groups also factor in.

Their rules of their compatibility are still kind of Wild West, to some extent at least. Manufacturers present their inevitable dictums on what is right and proper, but we'll sometimes find a little

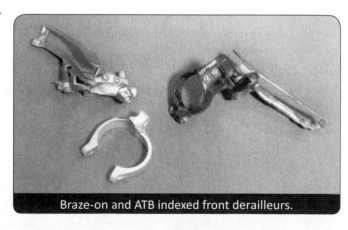
Braze-on and ATB indexed front derailleurs.

wiggle room. I was charged with upgrading an 8-speed Shimano Sora-equipped Peugeot to 9-speed, not so long ago—while the chintzy steel chainrings stamped as "8-speed" made the jump just fine, the clumsy Sora derailleurs did not. What were those books called? Choose Your Own Adventure?

The compact road cranks may or may not require special derailleurs of their own, to take a more common example. Campagnolo provides such kit to accompany their new compact cranks; Shimano's R600 compact is said to work with a regular Ultegra 10-speed derailleur.

Beyond the compatibility issue, a given front derailleur would need to coincide with the features of its intended frame. The cables travel to meet the derailleurs from either on high or down below, for one thing; each route requires distinct accommodations, in terms of the cable routing. More, those indexed front derailleurs with frame tube clamps will be in one of two different styles. "High mount" (or "traditional") front derailleurs wrap their clamps higher up on the frame than the "low mount" (or "top swing") examples. Note that the placement of the frame's water bottle fittings will often preclude us from swapping the one for the other.

Additionally, the front derailleur's mounting parameters have been broadened to include five distinct methods.

Most will be built around clamps designed for one of the three seat tube diameters currently in use—28.6, 31.8, or 35.0 mm. (Note that this measure is distinct from the seatpost up top; it is the outside diameter of the seat tube.)

Some of the nicer road bikes have succeeded in eschewing the clumsy old clamps entirely, favoring instead the **BRAZE-ON FRONT DERAILLEUR**, which is bolted onto a tab brazed to the frame's seat tube. These work well enough, provided they are mounted correctly. The bike drops a few more grams; its lines grow a touch cleaner; everyone wins.

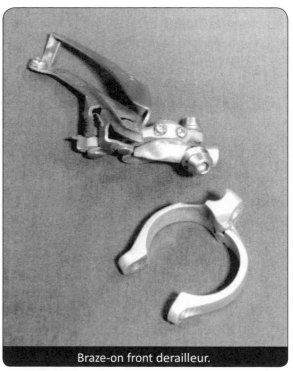
Braze-on front derailleur.

Shimano has more recently presented the front derailleur's fifth mounting option, known as the E-type. It snubs the expected clamp as well, favoring instead a burly steel plate, which mounts around and just beneath the bottom bracket's fixed cup. The plate does eliminate the problem of dumped chains, up front and on the inside at least, but by fixating so thoroughly on the bottom bracket, it also precludes the use of different-sized chainrings. We would not be able to move the derailleur up and down the seat tube to accommodate different rings, as we normally would. Far and away the Happy Meal, among the front derailleurs.

To put all this in a nutshell, any replacement front derailleur would need to match the original in certain crucial respects: you might have all of a couple options, from among dozens of quite similar pretenders. The wrong example either works poorly, or it doesn't work at all. Hope you saved your receipt! An outsized clamp might be accommodated by enlisting a metal shim of complementary dimensions—I've had to do it that way a couple times, actually.

Shimano is the only company able to provide a full range of front derailleurs, for the moment at least. This includes a midrange compact mountain front derailleur equipped with a set of shims, which allow it to transcend our three tube sizes. Some of these work extended cable grooves into their pivots as well, permitting the cable to run from either on high or down below.

Shimano's indexing front derailleurs rely upon more dynamic cage profiles.

Their long boxes appear more wedge-like, when viewed from above, and it is the longest edge featuring therein should line up parallel with the chainrings. This is usually, but not always, the front corner of the cage's outer plate.

Braze-on front derailleur mounted on frame.

As with the front derailleur's other adjustments, this is only determined by testing out the shifting. The end result usually leaves one or both sides of the cage's tail splayed out to either direction, to better accommodate the chain.

Campagnolo figures things somewhat differently, suggesting that the inner plates on their products are meant to become parallel with the chainrings. But their serene road drivetrains allow for more natural cage profiles, comparing against all the jumpy mountain cranks; they're easier managed with simple rules.

The cages are very occasionally bent farther still, in truly spectacular crashes, and there is not much we can do in such circumstances. You'd need to compare against the cage profile of an untroubled example of the same specifications, in order to know for sure. It's difficult to replicate a front derailleur cage's original profile; the damaged front derailleurs are usually done. But the fearsome cranks and the frame itself will likely step in and take the hit before forsaking the neurotic front derailleurs. It is quite rare that we actually get to this point.

A given road front derailleur will be inclined toward double- or triple-chainring cranksets. The doubles' cages are thinner and more fin-like; those found on the triples demonstrate more of a stepped effect. The inner plates on triple-ring front derailleurs extend considerably lower than their outer halves, which in turn are taller and more pronounced than those found on their double-ring peers. The effort allows for more productive exchanges with the smallest chainrings. This is something you would notice, trying to run a triple crank with a double-ring derailleur; it really makes a difference. A triple derailleur on a double crank, by the same token, will reliably dump the chain onto the bottom bracket shell.

We also want the front derailleur cages to faithfully match the contours of the chainrings they're focusing upon. A good fit will find the cage's outer plate maintaining its 2 mm gap against the chainring; or against the tallest point on the top ring, in the case of elliptical chainrings. The frame's seat tube rests at a fixed angle, which provides us with a reference point. (Some of the recumbents do their own things in this respect, with their diminutive front derailleur stalks. These are often kicked back to

deeper angles, to better support the larger chainrings commonly associated with the smaller 'bent drive wheels.)

The double-ring cranks were long set aside for the road bikes, until just lately. SRAM paved the way with its 2x10 mountain drivetrain; Shimano duly followed suit with something similar. The rise of 2X10 testifies as much to the unique challenges of keeping front triple indexing systems in proper adjustment, as to the gearing redundancies they inevitably contain.

Braze-on front derailleurs can be knocked out of alignment, so it is a good idea to secure their bolts with a mild thread-locker. Some clamp-style front derailleurs tend to rotate slightly out of place on the seat tubes, as they're tightened into position; hold things down with your free hand to prevent this. The final position is best realized with the clamping bolt just slightly loose, so that the derailleur can be usefully nudged toward improved positions. Just make sure the bolt gets nice and tight once you do settle the derailleur on a good position.

Road derailleurs always anticipate a bottom-pull control cable, last I checked, and for the most part they eschew the ungainly top-swing ('high mount') design as well. It is with the hybrids and mountain bikes that things can grow confusing. There once was a very simple solution, back when first the top-pull derailleur cables appeared—a small brass pulley, mounted to the seat tube behind and below the front derailleur—but this, too, seems to have vanished unto the ether. We can assume it went buried with mud, flung down from the back tire.

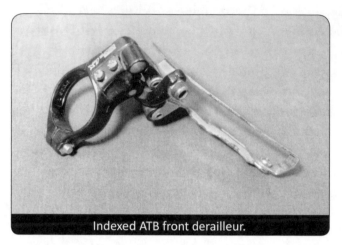
Indexed ATB front derailleur.

SRAM and Shimano have both tackled the very same question, in recent years—for the compact mountain gear ranges, at least—and of the two, SRAM's solution is more righteous. Where Shimano's approach runs the poor cable through an unlikely roller coaster of obtuse bends to accommodate both top- and bottom-pull cable routings, SRAM simply fixes two cable binder positions to opposing sides of the same pivot point. The SRAM design also plucks the derailleur spring from its dusty old dungeon behind the cage, relocating it to within the pivot assembly, where it is likely do somewhat better.

3. Indexing Derailleur Cable Adjustments

An indexed derailleur's precision is governed by the tension of its control cable. Adjustments to the cable's barrel adjuster—found on the derailleur itself, at the frame's cable stop, at the shift lever or in-line on the cable housing—should provide us all the flexibility we need for to accomplish this adjustment.

A healthy indexing drivetrain further requires all the correct adjustments with regards to the derailleurs' limit screws and positioning, as described on pages 111 and 114, for rear and front derailleurs respectively. With regards to indexing rear derailleurs, the correct adjustment is best seen when the chain in the second position, one shift removed from the derailleur's resting position. We make the adjustment while the chain is on second smallest cog, in other words. (Unless you're working on one of Shimano's Rapid Rise/Low Normal rear derailleurs, in which case you'd want to conduct the following steps with the chain on the second *largest* cog.)

Our test is simple: when the shift lever is moved from the resting position to its second, the chain should jump precisely one gear, and it should stay right there once pressure is released from the lever, without riding up against the adjacent cog. If the chain does anything more or less than this, you would need to adjust the rear derailleur's cable tension. Turn the barrel adjuster out to increase the cable tension, moving the derailleur further away from its resting position, or dial it in to do the reverse, moving in half-turns either way, checking the results of your work as you go.

The more cogs you run out back, the more precise this adjustment needs to be. You may even slim down to quarter-turns, on the cable's barrel adjuster. The first shift is meant to set the pattern for the rest—once the correct cable tension adjustment is accomplished, its fine reason should echo across all the chain's interactions with the rest of the gear range.

Expanding the number of available rear cogs has complicated the front shifting as well, in that the wider range necessitates a couple distinct positions for each chainring, in order to prevent the chain from riding on the front derailleur's cage. Shimano STI and SRAM dual control road levers provide two positions apiece for each ring in their care, but Campagnolo trusts us with a whole range of minor clicks with which to manage the front shifting, as do some of the SRAM/ Grip Shift ATB levers. This adjustment, known as **TRIM**, represents a sage compromise between indexing and the friction, yet as with the friction drivetrains more generally it does presume that the rider will know, more or less, how to cook their own breakfast.

All indexing front derailleurs anticipate the interventions of a barrel adjuster, at some point along their cable's length. Dialing this out moves the derailleur cage toward the big ring, and the reverse is also true. More recent Shimano STI levers are somewhat easier to negotiate with—those awarding each chainring a pair of indexed positions—but the originals can really test the patience.

The triple is best evaluated with the chain in the middle ring, from which it should be able to hit all or at least *most* of the rear gearing range without grinding on the derailleur cage.

The correct cable tension only yields an indexed double clear access to the gears we're actually *meant* to use, in other words. Older seven-speed systems generally provide their chains full and clear access from this middling position; modern 8- and 9-speed setups run the chain against its patient minder at either or both extremes. Cross-geared combinations—from the big ring to the two biggest cogs, or from the small ring to the smallest two cogs—are not good for the health of the drivetrain parts, and the double-ring indexed front derailleurs strive to warn us of the fact, by grinding on the chain in such positions.

C. Shift Levers

The original shift levers first clustered around the down tube, but it wasn't long before a few of the more adventurous sorts ventured up toward the handlebar stem. Others developed ratcheting mechanisms. A further minority, led by the inspired pioneers over at Suntour, had already begun the determined trek out to the ends of the handlebars, to become bar-end shift levers.

A protracted conflict has since opened up on the handlebars, and the old guard has suffered horribly. Excluding a few

Suntour Command Levers.

but their children have become increasingly confused. In so blithely discounting any faith in the breadth of our capacities, the ever-more-ubiquitous shifter pods represent the very crucibles of imperial presumption. Pods are only the obvious example—the relentless novelty drapes our village like a leaden blanket, blocking out the sun.

especially gifted creatures, the new bikes were long made to shun and fear the original shift levers. Anonymous hordes of vain and neurotic plastic "shift levers" laid siege to the dwindling encampment of trustworthy alloy levers we long relied upon, threatening to smite them unto memory. More recently, however, new outfits like microSHIFT and Retroshift have hastened to join the old stalwarts at Paul Component Engineering and Kelly, and on finer days fortunes nearly appear to be turning.

Things looked bleak indeed, for a spell. It wasn't so long ago that bar-end shifters, the only righteous levers brave enough to remain visible, had been relegated to an ever-smaller portion of road bikes. The noble thumbshifters witnessed their own tragedies as well—those few remaining were largely been reduced to plastic.

Their presumed replacements, generally speaking, sought to remove anything remotely emotive from the shifting process, much like the Daleks on *Doctor Who*. The first Grip Shift levers were pleasantly simple, if less than durable,

Yet the future, mercifully, at least appears to be brightening: witness the range of microSHIFT's thumb and bar-end shifters. And then there are the gems which come to us by way of the inspired wizards out at Retroshift, who face road brake levers with down tube-style shift lever mounts. Genius! And V-brake compatible, unlike most other road levers on the planet. They even have a crash replacement policy. Anyway, if ever I do succumb to the many charms of the more-modern world, scoring a set of these would probably be my first stop.

The Daleks' future may not be so bleak either, dependent on the point of view. Our friend Travis T. once showed me a useful method for regenerating some of Shimano's rapid-fire pods, for example. The pod's action is based upon a pair of delicate palls, ratcheting away beneath the cover, and the lubricant these things are born with seems to dry out after a while. So you remove the lid, dose a bit of

T9 or similar around the palls, and very carefully work this in with your small screwdriver. Sway the palls lightly back and forth, until their tired little springs are convinced to return the things on their own.

Shimano's original Rapidfire pods featured useful escape hatches for cable replacement, but these were eventually sealed with clumsy plastic plugs, which have more recently been paved over with awkward contoured plates. These last, while distinct to each of the shift levers they afflict, are invariably held in place by pairs of especially tiny screws.

A Shimano Rapidfire pod spills its guts: not a pretty sight.

You need a smaller Phillips screwdriver to attack these itsy-bitsy screws, which are very small and light. Each might be convinced to balance briefly atop the screwdriver, with a careful hand. Exercise caution when pulling away, lest the tiny spike tumble forever into the abyss—you may never find it again; you could only wail and remember and write poetry. Cup your hand under the screws, until you're able to stash the both of them and their damned plate in a jar lid while you work.

It was not so long ago that even the fancy shifters didn't plug up their cable holes.

It was in my livelihood to service these for quite a while, and I cannot imagine a valid reason for the change. Beyond any marketing value, this new hermetic-sealing tendency could only possibly be useful if you were out trolling the handlebars through mud puddles or something, and it's still not clear how this imposing darkness represents any meaningful improvement. We would want to strip the shifters down and clean them up after a night like that. The sealing impulse works quite well in other applications—some bearing cartridges, for example—but it comes off a little ridiculous, perched up on the handlebars there. Come on. The mud is all the way downstairs, on the ground.

All the Rapidfire shift cables are ultimately removed by the same method. Shift all the way down to the derailleur's resting position, so that the cable is as slack as it ever may be, and release its tail from beneath the derailleur's pinch bolt. You would need to snip off any ferrule or frays, to pull it back through the housing. There may even be a kink or two to bend out with the box pliers, as well. The binder bolt may have flattened a small stretch of the cable—this might be made roundish again with the box pliers, if we're lucky, but in more extreme cases you may need to pull the cable free with your fourth hand tool.

However it comes to pass, the cable's head should ultimately be able to retreat back out of its foxhole in the shift lever. The derailleur generally needs to be parked in the slackest gear, in order for this to happen. Unless you can actually see the thing, as with the older and simpler sorts of shift levers, we can assume that the cable head comes around a bend as you downshift, remaining inaccessible until the very end.

Shimano's **STI DUAL CONTROL LEVERS** (known more colloquially as **BRIFTERS**) have grown to be more reliable over the years, by some accounts, but in essence they are still disposable components: we can't do much for them at all in terms of maintenance, beyond lubrication. Campagnolo's Ergopower levers offer more specific hopes for redemption, through replacement parts and expertise available at Campagnolo dealers. I've yet to find the opportunity to work with SRAM or microSHIFT dual control levers.

BAR-END SHIFTERS tend to be made well—I've never encountered any burdened with redundant springs, or built using structural plastic—the design doesn't really support anything that doesn't need to be there. Many are still able to run well on the otherwise-extinct friction mode, and this makes them quite universal. The originals, made by Suntour, were set to a basic ratcheting friction on both sides. The mounting hardware slips into the handlebar; the shifter bolts to its face. Said base is built around a further bolt; turning this counterclockwise expands its tail inside the handlebar.

Campagnolo still makes these, but I've come across all of a few pairs in my life. The last time was on an M5 I saw in 2002, if memory serves: nice and crisp action, smooth design; artisan, but also obscure. Shimano's top-end Ultegra and Dura Ace have been far more common to see. They're relatively expensive, but they will last. You would need some kind of active conspiracy to destroy such equipment.

The shift lever itself is essentially a down-tube shifter. The profile is only a bit different, to better suit its new station. The world had previously agreed upon a set of standardized bosses upon which to mount the down-tube levers; the bar-end hardware simply brings the pair upstairs to the balcony. Your old Shimano down-tube shifters can serve for spare parts, in other words. Grape Juice, my battered old Trek 970 commuter, runs a 7-speed 105SC "bar-end" shifter at the moment. The Shimano bar-end mounts are installed first; the shifter bosses are pushed through their sides.

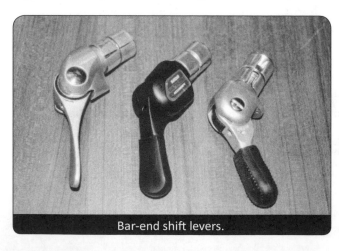
Bar-end shift levers.

Note that bar-end shifters do not fit in the ends of flat ATB-style handlebars. You would also have a tough time sneaking them past any serious curves in road handlebars: plugging flipped-and-clipped drop bars, for example. All they need is a bit of straight pipe, in the road dimensions.

The dusty old 3-speeds began borrowing the **TWIST SHIFTERS** from motorcycles some time ago, but the idea did not really take hold until Grip Shift arrived on the scene. Their original shift levers accomplished their business with a linear spring set between the body and its shell, which allowed the pair to ratchet away contentedly, all but oblivious to the clamor all around. The original plastic springs did not hold up so well, but we're able to replace these with more useful metal ones.

Newer SRAM shift levers are more complicated. An unlikely and entirely redundant spring is jammed into some of the newer high-end levers, such as the 9.0, in order to change the way the lever feels when in use. The effort recalls Suntour's short-lived F7 and F8 lever settings, an earlier attempt to blur the borders between friction and indexing.

A Grip Shift lever's adjustment would follow the same map outlined on page

122. Cable replacements with SRAM and Grip Shift levers can seem complicated at first, in that various different methods were used over the years, but it all becomes pretty intuitive with practice.

Grip Shift (and the SRAM Corporation, which ate them) have parked the derailleur cable's head in different places, over the years. Old-fashioned examples will sometimes bury it up inside the stationary portion of the lever—a cable head may be just visible, up a shallow hole on its innermost side. These can likely be replaced with a new, uncut cable, but you need to take the lever apart to reuse cables. Lots of bends inside; cut ends fray all to hell.

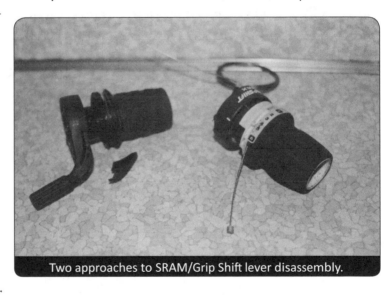
Two approaches to SRAM/Grip Shift lever disassembly.

You may just have to take the thing apart anyway, if you don't see a cable head somewhere on the stem side of the lever's base, because some older levers hide the cable heads beyond view.

The body and its shell may be held together by a molded triangular U-shaped clamp in such cases, mounted just in from the lever's barrel adjuster or cable housing stop. This would be released by way of a conspicuous slot at its base— you stab this shallow opening with a big flathead screwdriver and turn, to slide the clamp aside. Other models rely upon more prominent Phillips-head release screws to keep the lever together, which feature as the noses on slightly curved triangular faces, mounted in the same positions. Yet others are simply pulled apart. Be sure to look for a release screw or the screwdriver-sized slot of a clamping plate, before yanking on things.

The humble SRAM MRX levers showed up with a better plan. Its grip section features exactly one rubber corner, which is pushed aside to reveal the cable head's escape hole. (This becomes a conspicuous rubber flap, with various other SRAM levers.) Here as well, you do need to shift the lever to its slackest position, to spy such an opening.

And yet it may not be so simple, because SRAM also wants to make sure the cable head is not able to back out of position, and thereby employed various methods to hold it down. A trim plastic lip clips just over the top of the cable heads, in the case of SRAM 7.0 levers; this is pried aside with a small screwdriver. The 9.0 levers thread a tiny cable-set screw down atop the cable head itself—the very one we see used with some of their planetary hub cables, actually. It turns out atop your 2.5 mm Allen key.

To summarize, be advised that the SRAM/Grip Shift amalgamation has tried all kinds of things over the years, with the cable routing in their shift levers. The one true path should become obvious enough, once the lever is taken apart—look for an unbroken, extended cable-sized groove, and follow it. Note that this will *sometimes* find you forming a loop with the cable, before reassembling the lever.

We typically anticipate a sharp 90-degree bend in the cable's path, just before it exits to cable housing. Taking the levers apart allows us to thread used cables through this channel. Some of the newest SRAM shift levers secret this channel away in darkness, which discourages us from reusing cables. We can still manage, but only by really twisting the *hell* out of them as they are installed. This is always useful in preventing frays, of course, but with these cans in particular we need to take it to logical extremes. You're vigorously rolling the cable in your fingers, while only gradually, almost incidentally nudging it forward into the shift lever.

The only other alternative here would be to pull the lever apart. It snaps together, lengthwise. But this becomes five times as stupid, because the new design makes this erstwhile basic task more arduous as well. Remember that extra spring, forced in by the marketing team? It sits directly opposite the shifter's working spring, and the two will struggle against each other, as you try to press their cage back together. You may be camped out for a while, actually. Does this really need to happen?

Secure the handlebar in a vise, or see to it that the bike remains quite still, and get in there with your smallest screwdriver. Try to jam the new spring back in place, while carefully easing the lever closed. As this happens, you also want to make sure the gear indicator's wispy neon straw is correctly aligned in the appropriate position. Have fun!

Shimano's derailleur springs are meant to work with smaller, counterbalancing springs set up in the shift levers, and the early Grip Shifters lacked any such thing. Their timid linear springs were no match for the bold and furious Shimano derailleur springs, and the result was an unfortunate propensity to drop out of gear, especially over time. Retro-fit derailleur springs were thus made available, to balance things out, but these were always kind of a half-measure.

SRAM currently produces shift levers meant to work with either Shimano derailleurs, or their own. The SRAM flagships—those bearing the revolutionary 2-to-1 cable actuation ratio—are identified by odd numbers. The 3.0, 5.0, 7.0, and 9.0 each have twice what it takes. Other SRAM levers feature names like MRX or Rocket or Attack, or perhaps an even number, and these are meant for the Shimano derailleurs.

SRAM's original MRX shifters have another distinct concern. The plastic lips holding them together can wear down over time, with the result that the lever keeps coming apart, over and over again. The wrap of the cable has a tendency to push the shifter apart, and this they do. The levers end up being held in place by the stationary portions of the grip.

Concurrently, by unfortunate coincidence, many handlebar grips supplied with inexpensive new bikes began to demonstrate a conspicuous tendency to loosen up with use. The hands end up rolling them away from the stem. And, since the aforementioned issue with the cable wrap too often leaves these things in charge of holding the chintzy MRX shift levers together, this essentially cosmetic problem manages to become more damning. The shift levers come apart, as the grips loosen, and after a point we can no longer shift the gears.

You might have better luck with some of the more durable aftermarket grips, but last I checked SRAM still pumps out plenty of their fragile MRX flowers, to suit triple-chainring systems employing five through eight cogs. The longer half-pipe MRX models available for 7- and 8-speed drivetrains have at least as many problems in this regard; their shorter grips loosen even sooner. (In fairness, it should be noted that the MRX name is also applied to a smaller number of sharper-looking and more worthy levers, which do not share this liability.)

These sorts of soft and mushy "comfort" grips must be convinced to stay in place, in order to partner with the original MRX levers. I've never had much luck with the grip glue products, and it's not like grips don't wear out. The summer of 2002, when first I focused on this stupid little dilemma, my fix-it-for-free rental bike approach was zip ties—the grips on our dozens of MRX-afflicted rental units were duly strapped in place, with a little help from the mighty fourth hand tool. Alas our clients found the new arrangements untenable—however much we trimmed them down, the zip ties on the grips inevitably proved a distraction. A month or two after we'd shuttered the rental shop for the season I finally realized the best solution to the dreaded MRX dynamic: bar-end extensions, a useful upgrade in the first place. You get some extra hand positions; your crappy little shifters get some solid guidance on keeping it together.

Later still, putzing in the basement on a crisp winter afternoon, I began to wonder how setting up every last MRX-afflicted rental unit with its very own bar ends would square with the famously slim margins associated with bike rental. And I realized the cheapest (and best) MRX solution yet: BMX handlebar plugs. Their protective role can be flipped around, to prevent the grips from escaping, which in turn keeps the shoddy MRX devices

from unraveling. Their tendency to come apart is my principal complaint. They worked well enough for the rental bikes, thus improved.

Performance-minded riders may find solace in SRAM's higher-end rotor shifters, but Shimano's Revo-Shift inspire no such passion. It is nearly a caricature of a disposable component, especially when joined to the overbearing gear indicator known as the Central Information Deck, which draws in a pair of odd new cables from the shift levers as means to run its super-cheesy plastic display window.

The CI Deck itself is entirely superfluous to the shifting process, and this is just as well; they're all fragile as eggs. We're able to remove the decks easily enough, but their wires are dug in a bit deeper. You have to pop of a couple more of Shimano's odd plates, which are attached with the same ridiculously tiny screws.

Worse yet is the horrible SEC Shift lever. But this may be obvious enough; the shifting action just sucks. The shift up is like climbing a dangerous hill, while the return action feels perpetually on-the-way-out.

"SEC Shift, U.S. Patent" is all we can read on their smug little faces: no model name, no manufacturer, no nothing. There is only the patent number, scratched in far too small to the underside, where

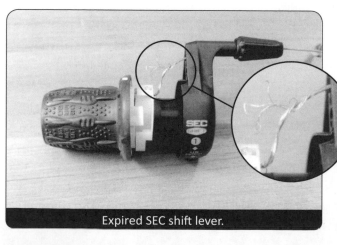

Expired SEC shift lever.

it was never meant to be read. This level of communication suggests that these things were probably hashed together on the whims of bitter cynics, which would indicate all you'd need to know about warranty service and replacement parts.

These things arrived on our 4 KHS Tandemania rental tandems early in May, a few summers back: of the eight SEC levers involved, five broke down and stopped working before July was through. So I went ahead and replaced the remainder, lest their failure rate strive on toward completion. The bikes in question sold for $700 or $1,100, new. What the royal fuck? Those enlisted as rental bikes are abused more often, perhaps, but so was everything else in our fleet: in my four years as the rental mechanic, I cannot recall any bicycle component with so atrocious a record. SRAM's poor little MRX lever, once improved, quite handily flattens the miserable SEC to the ground.

D. Planetary Gearing

The derailleurs become straightforward machines, once you begin to understand their role. They lack subterfuge—their moving parts are out where you can see them. This does leave them more exposed to the elements, which may or may not become an issue for you.

The alternative is to move the shifting indoors, to the hubs. Or, in the case of Schlumpf's heel-activated Speed and Mountain Drives, to the bottom bracket. This aesthetic and inward tendency is known as **PLANETARY GEARING**.

You can probably imagine the original planets—they are the curiously thick chromed canisters that move the old 3-speeds. A closer inspection often reveals the manufacturer as Sturmey Archer. We know they were made well, by virtue of the fact that so many are still on the road. The production year is often stamped on the hub body, actually. It is not uncommon that we find examples three or four decades old, still tooling about.

These originals provide for an oil port, right there on the hub body. It sticks out, topped with a little plastic cap. We want to drop some Phil's Tenacious oil or motor oil into this now and then, like a couple times each year. Planetary hubs needing more oil often make more noise. Most hubs do fine with regular bearing grease, but in this case it would only slow the planets' motion.

A rod running through the axle is charged with dragging a drive gear past different orbiting gears in the hub shell. Our original examples put diminutive indicator chains in charge of the planets, but modern versions have managed to usefully update this interface. This classic steel model has been edged toward the museums, really—its shiny steel body is a bit heavy and no longer quite fashionable; the 120 mm axle spacing is fully quaint in its antiquity; a paltry 3 speeds is no longer enough to get excited about.

The old and quite proprietary Sturmey cables are unique, in that they're already sized to length. They have two heads, in fact, distinct to each end. A prescribed length of cable housing spans a portion of their middle distance; moving its stop up and down the frame tube sets the ground floor for the cable tensioning. We also find a barrel adjuster down by the hub, for purposes of fine-tuning the same. You attach the cable at both points, then slide the housing clamp up the down tube until the slack disappears. Pretty special. If you do have troubles with a Sturmey, you want to check the cable first. Make sure the housing is anchored securely where it needs to be, and that the cable itself is not hung up on anything.

Adam Cornell went into some detail on these in *How to Rock and Roll.* As he suggested there, you really don't want to take a planetary hub apart just for the hell of it. It would be a good idea to hunt down a schematic drawing particular to your specific project, prior to beginning.

The small rod at the end of the indicator chain threads into the larger one in the hub, shooting straight out through an elongated axle nut. Its top is beveled inward, like a mouth opened in surprise; our indicator chain snakes off the lip and quickly hooks up with the cable. It is an absolute dwarf compared to the regular bike chain—strong enough to transfer a shift into the hub, but not nearly rugged enough to handle much for impact. Three-speed indicator chains die all the time. Some more interesting bike shops may yet have a few kicking around in

back somewhere. A small hole drilled to the side of the oldster's elongated locknut provided a glimpse of the indicator chain; marks on its end piece and the hole itself mean to line up when the hub was shifted to second gear.

The hub interfaces aboard newer Shimano planetary hubs provide for more judicious outcomes. Everything transpires beneath a sturdy metal shelter. Its lower section comes off with a small screw, and the shelter is revealed to hold only a binder bolt mounted on a pivot point. This is pressed against a one-piece push rod, which disappears into the hub. The rear of the metal shelter features a small window, to help with calibrating the adjustments.

Hub gears, like the external drivetrains, are governed by the shift cable's tension. Planetary hubs tend to rely upon barrel adjusters, set somewhere along the cable run—at the shifter; on the indicator rod; outside the hub—but at least one more basic system, the SRAM Monsoon TS200, seems to manage without. Those examples I've worked on, at least. Planetary hubs are more generous with the cable tension parameters than some derailleur systems; the Monsoon gets away with it.

SRAM's Monsoon, together with the old 3 x 7 hub and various others, links the indicator chain to shift cable by means of an **ADJUSTMENT SLEEVE**. This is a small plastic box, wedged in front, bearing the tip of a linear brass spring on one side. The opposing end of this spring is pressed against the indicator chain's threaded end piece, such that we can press the exposed tip to release the chain. The chain's end piece is simply pressed forward in the sleeve, alternately, to increase the cable tension. The shift cable's tail passes through one nostril set in the sleeve's narrower end, where it is clamped by a cable-set screw and sent out another exit to the rear.

This airy sleeved approach is fully lilting and melodic, comparing with the original planetary hubs, yet newer systems such as SRAM's Dual Drive or the Shimano Inter 3 owe much to old school, in terms of how they are adjusted.

The cable interface features a small window; our cable tension adjustments only need to align a couple brightly colored lines. Additionally one can actually see if the tension is off, with the adjustment sleeve-equipped hubs—the sleeve itself balks and jumps around, as you try to park it in second. Or, if the cable's too tight, the hub simply does not go into its last gear.

Each of these hub gears is best matched to its own specific lever.

DUAL DRIVE pairs SRAM's 3-speed planetary hub with an 8/9-speed freehub body, allowing 27 speeds with a single front chainring. It updates the 3 x 7 hub, which featured a 7-speed freehub body. Everything is run by a solitary lever over on the right side, which becomes reasonably intuitive when you see the thing.

The Dual Drive incorporates the **CLICKBOX** downstairs, which basically shoots the cable right down to the end of the axle. The top side of the Clickbox features a simple button that functions as a quick release, as well as a small plastic adjustment window. The cable pinches down to a pivot with a sharp yellow line drawn across its top, which is what you look for to check on the adjustment. The barrel adjuster is right there on the Clickbox. (The one featuring up on the Dual Drive shift lever itself is for the rear derailleur.)

It is not complicated to remove the Clickbox, when you need to drop the wheel out, but putting things back together may take a little work. The Dual Drive's particularly tiny push rod just barely peeks out of the hub, before ending with a little cap, which is meant to slip under a catch on the Clickbox. It comes off easily enough, but you may have to kind of wiggle things around to get it back.

When installed as original equipment on new bikes, the Dual Drive's cable is typically clipped just past the binder bolt. Pinching a cable so close to a fresh cut invariably results in a spiky bouquet of frayed wire, which is less than ideal. You forget it's there; you rush in and jab a finger, blood everywhere, it's crazy. Lucky for us, SRAM was nice enough to provide for an out. The rear of the Dual Drive's interface features a small plastic plate that snaps into place, the bottom of which features a nice big hole a proper cable tail may pass through. The bike's original handlers may not have been hip to this, but there's no stopping you. Just let the cable flow out a short distance, next time you change it, so you can clip and cap its end properly. You will have to put a couple small bends in the cable to get this going, but it will work.

Rohloff has also enjoyed some success, with its legendary 14-speed internal hub. No cassette is able to fit on top of this one, but the 14's range works out to be wide enough already. We also have the Speed and Mountain Drive planetary bottom brackets from Schlumpf. The Speed adds an extra accelerator range on top of an existing drivetrain; the Mountain provides for more generous climbing gears at the bottom. Your number of gears is essentially doubled, in either case. I have played with these, and they also seem quite worthwhile. The spindle bolts are hollow; the heel kicks a rod back and forth to change gears. Said rod wears decent-sized caps on its ends, which may be further shielded by crisp wings coming down along the crank arms.

E. Chains

The ⅛″ **BICYCLE CHAIN** is the widest in common use. It caters to bikes with single cogs on the rear wheel—BMX, cruisers, track bikes and various older 3-speeds. The next size, the narrower and more common ³⁄₃₂″, carries over from the original derailleur bikes. Modern ³⁄₃₂″ chains are meant to work with 5-, 6-, 7-, or 8-speed gear clusters. Ancient 5- or

6-speed equipment may sometimes balk, but more often the cogs will be of workable widths.

The world has narrowed, with the arrival of 9-, 10-, and 11-speed gear clusters. The chain, the cogs, and their spacers are fractions thinner than all else before, with each successive step.

The 8-speed cog sets had previously reached what may be described as a useful limit to our shifting parameters: 8 had already tacked a spare cog to the back side of 7, and for a long time at least the resultant width was thought to be about all we could reasonably ask the wheels to deal with. This is a function of the wheel dish, as described on page 207—too much baggage on the hub can shove the spokes into awkward angles, basically. Yet some of the new mountain bikes have been showing up with rear hubs spaced to 150 and even 165 mm, just lately, and it's not hard to imagine how such expansive real estate might be asked to support even *more* cogs. I guess we'll see. Regardless, it is hard to imagine how the chains might be made any narrower than the 11-speed example Campagnolo has already provided. To wit, Shimano opted to widen the cassette body by about 2 mm, when they introduced their own 11-speed group.

Note that the chains need to be uniform throughout. We cannot safely assume distinct manufacturers' links are compatible with each other. This is especially true across the different chain widths, from 7/8 to 9-speed for example.

New chains arrive to our world coated with an especially thick and luscious lubricant, but it is only the packing grease. It had previously been suggest-

7, 8, and 1-speed chains.

ed to me that this stuff was some kind of awesome factory super-lubricant, a theory which the service crew up at the Freewheel found amusing. It was normal there to oil brand new chains with a bicycle-specific chain lubricant, such as Rock "N" Roll.

It is very much worth your time to do the math, when **INSTALLING AND REMOVING CHAINS**. It's not at all common for chains to break under load, but when it does happen we'll typically trace it back to improper chain installation.

Shimano chains are assembled with their proprietary **HYPERGLIDE CHAIN PINS**, which are twice the length of their fellows. They have pointed front sections, which are meant to smooth the way for the wider tails. These nose cones snap right off with pliers, once the rear is in place. Distinct Hyperglide pins are used with 7/8-, 9-, and 10-speed chains. Each is a bit shorter, and their steel enjoys three different hues as well.

The pins are one-shot deals; you use them once and they're done. Nor do we want to break a chain upon a previously installed Hyperglide pin; their tail sections widen out the chain plate holes just enough to preclude this. A new Hyperglide pin can only replace a regular chain pin, in other words. You'll be able to spot the difference, looking closely. Plan to follow the pin's installation with adjustments in the chain tool's upper saddle as well, as described shortly on page 139.

Campagnolo 10-speed chains feature interior and exterior sides—only the latter is stamped with a production batch number. Also note that their chain pins are designed to be installed from the inside. Campagnolo pins are capped with big plastic noses, which slide into place between the plates, but only to stake a claim for their cargo. They pull right out, once this is in place. The 10-speed master pin means to protrude an even 0.1 mm from the inside chain plate, when you finish.

Campagnolo's chain pins can only be fired the once, just like their Shimano peers, and they actually cost a few bucks apiece. Wippermann's ConneX **MASTER LINKS** work just as well, in the same role, over and over again. Their use with Campagnolo or Shimano chains has not been officially sanctioned by either party, but it has become common practice. It is a bit dicier with Campagnolo; their chain pins and plates are narrower. The 8-, 9-, and 10-speed ConneX links are sold individually or with the full ConneX chains.

We enjoy no such shortcuts with the Campagnolo 11-speed chains, which must be assembled using the company's $200 chain tool. The new PowerLock master links supplied with SRAM 10-speed chains have more in common with the chain pins, in that they are not meant to be disturbed after installation, let alone reused. You'd need to attack from another location, breaking the chain again. Good thing we have the ConneX 10-speed chains and master links, right?

Lacking such conveniences, or to shorten a chain, we need a chain tool, which

SRAM master chain links.

Chains are best broken and reassembled with the chain slack. With the derailleur-equipped bikes, this condition is realized when the chain is shifted down to the smallest gear combinations. E-type front derailleurs excluded, you might even set the chain aside on the bottom bracket shell while you work.

When breaking a chain, it is important that the pin is not pushed all the way through. Its tail end must retain a toehold on the *inside* of the chain, in order to facilitate reinstallation. You'll want maybe 4/5 of the pin's length to end up on the outside of the chain. The chain is bent sideways a bit, to break. It will snap back together in much the same way.

We do not expect the chains to break of their own volition. I first suspect some confusion in the chain's installation, when they do fail. The chains are replaced periodically—we'll look into that in a minute—but we more commonly break them for purposes of **CLEANING THE DRIVETRAIN.**

presses a fairly sturdy pin down atop one of the chain's more transient pins, as means to shove it the hell out of the way. Be sure to center the tool's pin right atop one of the chain pins, prior to beginning, as it may snap if you thread it down off-center. We use the tool's lower saddle to break and reconnect the chain; the upper position is only used to fine-tune a link's tightness.

This is a glorious spring ritual, equally messy and joyful, meant to celebrate the arrival of better seasons. Bikes in regular use earnestly look forward to this, especially if they've been piloted through the elements, but the sad truth is that drivetrains are not cleaned nearly enough. The lucky summer bike's chain may go a couple years without being cleaned, provided it is fed just enough wax or gel-based chain oil, but everyone probably knows what we're trying to avoid here—the greasy black liquid snake, eager to stain anything it might touch? Things don't have to be that way.

The old-fashioned wet chain lubricants make some sense in the winter, just before we take the drivetrain down for its cleaning, but they draw in all kinds of gunk. The remedy is a bicycle-specific citrus degreaser, such as Finish Line or Zep Orange. (I have experimented with some of the more common household degreasers; they don't seem to work as well.) Pour some in a big old Tupperware container; something with a tight lid that can be safely shaken. Stopping by periodically to agitate the parts tends to hurry the process along a bit. You will notice that your undiluted citrus degreaser bath accumulates a layer of fine silt, with repeated use: pour the liquid off into a surrogate container, once this has settled, and clear the muck away before using the solution again.

Any of these degreasers can be diluted with water, but they become that much weaker. It makes more sense to do this right the first time. The good news is that you can keep using the same batch, over and over again. Many of the parts-washing machines at the shops are already doing this, actually.

Your soft broth will turn to coffee after a while, but it still works just fine. I did a good bit of work out of my old basement on Oakland Avenue in South Minneapolis, the years I lived there; I think I may have changed out the Finish Line all of once during that time. I can't even tell you how many parts that batch cleaned. Do make sure you keep the lid in place, to prevent evaporation.

So the chain comes off, as described, and you toss it in the soup. You want to let it sit for a night or two, ideally. Make sure you stop by and shake it up a few times, to help loosen the gunk. The chain's grimy companions also need to take the plunge. The hub gears and the cranks are both more properly introduced later on, on pages 167 and 148 respectively; suffice it here to say you can remove them for cleaning. The derailleurs also need to take a bath, provided any sealed bearing pulleys are first removed.

Your spider crank is probably not going to fit in the Tupperware dish. You may remove and clean the individual chainrings, if they look really bad. The cheap cranks won't let you do this, because they suck.

Gear cassettes can get dunked, but this is not a good idea for freewheels. Soaking them in solvent wicks away any lubricant they manage to squirrel away. Leave it on the wheel, hit the cogs with lightweight oil and floss them clean with a rag. (The freewheels contain moving parts, but they're rarely disassembled anymore. It's like cold fusion or something; theoretically possible but entirely uncommon.)

You want to let the parts dry thoroughly, whatever it is you're working on. At work, we enlist an air gun for such purposes. You might set yours by the window for a day, instead.

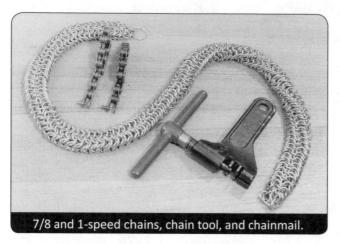

7/8 and 1-speed chains, chain tool, and chainmail.

Avoid spraying the freshly cleaned parts with oil, once things are dry, as this invites the gunk right back on board. The spray cans only waste our time. Grab your trusty oil dropper; drip a bit in the derailleurs' pivots. Work it in a little; wipe away the excess. The chain should get oiled with a wax or gel-based lubricant once everything is set back up, and then wiped dry.

Everything goes right back where you found it. Procedures for reinstalling the derailleurs, cranks, and hub gears are each described elsewhere in this volume.

It is with the chain's reassembly that we really understand the brilliance of the new SRAM-style master links. You set them in place, and you pull the chain taut; they lock right into place.

Absent a master link, our work becomes somewhat easier with the creation of another basic tool. Run out back and find a spare spoke somewhere, and crimp a

90-degree bend to its midsection. Bend the ends again, by similar measures. You now have a **CHAIN HOOK**, with which to hold the disparate chain sections in union. You slip each end into chain links a few links outside the break, and there it sits while you work. The rear derailleurs' spring tension might try to pull the chain apart, lacking such intervention; this device makes it easier for you to concentrate on the task at hand.

We are looking for two things, with the chain's final adjustment. Each end of the chain pin must pass *precisely* the same distance through the outer chain plates, and the link itself must also be just loose enough to pivot freely. The chain tool presses the links together, across the pin it is focused upon, and this intersection generally needs to be spread out again.

Chains anticipating master links will end on two inner links, because the master link would plug 'em both. Those awaiting our manual reassembly need to finish on one inner and one outer link; trim the length as required.

Line up the inner link inside its mate, once the chain has been correctly routed through any derailleurs, and set their hard sandwich in the chain tool's lower saddle. The tool's pin will thread down to press upon that protruding from the broken chain. You first push the chain pin back in place, until its length is almost but not *quite* centered between the outer plates. See to it that one end of the pin extends just a hair farther out than the other end—the "fine" in our fine adjustment—and then level things out, by pressing it another quarter-turn in the chain tool's *upper* saddle, such that the pin ends up centered between the chain plates, with each end protruding by the very same measure. This should loosen the chain link just enough to avoid binding. The chain's farther plate is not braced against the tool's body, in the upper saddle, and this lets the chain plates expand.

Neglecting this last step will usually leave us with a **TIGHT LINK**. These are easy enough to spot, on derailleur-equipped bikes; we only need to spin the pedals backward. Does the chain bump around, passing between the pulleys? Your suspicions about a particular link may be confirmed by bending it between your fingers. Get in there with the chain tool, and let its upper saddle work its special magic.

As mentioned, Campagnolo 11-speed chains can only be safely assembled using the company's UT-CN300 tool. No kidding. I haven't yet encountered such exotic fruit myself, but my research suggests we really are denied any shortcuts here.

We start to think about **REPLACING A CHAIN** when it starts to skip.

All bicycle chains stretch over time, just as their cogs (more gradually) begin to wear down. Neither condition is necessarily obvious to the eye, but their tedious conspiracy will cause the chains on derailleur-equipped bikes to skip out of gear, under pressure. You may know just what I'm talking about, from that last time you tried to charge up that big hill?

Make sure the shifting systems are healthy and well-adjusted, as described on page 122, before concluding any drivetrain parts are worn out. A maladjusted derailleur can affect a skipping chain, as can rusty cables; check everything out before replacing anything.

The chains can be replaced independently of their cogs. It is always a safer bet to replace the two simultaneously—they do wear together—but changing out the chain alone may stop the skipping, if you catch it in time. Nothing is immortal, but we are sometimes able to stretch a single cog set to cover the lifespans of three chains, using this method.

Checking chain wear.

Park Tool's Chain Checker describes a chain's wear on a scale between 0.0 and 1.0. We are encouraged to replace chains registering above 1.0, but in practice you can *generally* avoid replacing their cogs as well if you catch them at 0.75. Try it, at least; see if the bike still skips. ("Chain stretch" is the phrase we all use, but it's not strictly accurate. The rollers wear down, straining against the rows of sharp teeth; pulled taut the chain appears to have stretched.)

A worn-out cogset quickly reduces a new chain to its own level. That's just how it works; think of it as corruption. The smaller cogs are usually devoured sooner than their larger kin, because the chain's attrition is more concentrated. But the only way to really know for sure is to get on and go, using an uphill test ride as our proof.

The chainrings up front wear as well. A toasted chainring feels sandy or grainy, when pedaling. Its teeth would also be much sharper, comparing against those found on a new ring—less flat-top; more sharks' tooth. If a bike's chain and cogs are both pretty toasted, it'd be smart to change out its chainrings as well. Those in regular use, at least.

The fixed gear bikes have a greater tolerance for worn drivetrain parts, as do the singlespeeds. Anything that lacks derailleurs, actually: the chain would have nowhere to skip off to, absent their distractions. We merely pull the wheel back in the frame dropouts as required, to increase the chain tension. The chain tension is only enforced by small springs, on the derailleur-equipped bikes; a toasted drivetrain essentially pits these crickets against the strength of our legs.

I have heard different things about the particulars—fortunes vary, with riding styles and the quality of the drivetrain—but with luck we might milk 3,000 miles from a chain. Replace it as you need to; in advance of some grand tour for example.

The wear can be gauged by measuring the chain's actual length, if you forget your chain checker at the bus stop. The distance from the center of one chain pin to the next is precisely 1″, when the chain is new, but they stretch as they wear. So find a 12″ ruler; see how the pins line up against it. The difference from good to toast need not be much; a worn-out chain will have stretched fractions of an inch over the course of the foot.

When installing new chains, we also need to make sure the **CHAIN LENGTH** is correct. The stock length proves a bit too long for most bikes; recumbents tend to require chains twice as long.

A chain too long droops down when shifting to the smallest gear combinations. (That's usually what this is, at least: worn-out derailleur springs can manifest similar effects. But we are able to spot these easily enough: the pulley cages will be less than parallel to the ground, when shifted to the smallest gear combinations.) A chain too long also has more slop to it; the shifting may not be quite so precise.

Chains too short are not able to wrap around the largest gear combinations. Lacking better judgment, the rear derailleur inevitably tries to climb all the way up regardless, just like it used to, and riding the bike like this will destroy the rear derailleur. This very thing happened to a pair of our Specialized FSR rental bikes, actually. The bikes' stock Shimano chains had evidently failed at some point, and enterprising renters had re-assembled them minus the broken links. And rather than simply fail again—as we may have expected, in the absence of proper Hyperglide chain assembly pins—in both cases the shortened chains managed to reduce the bikes' firm Shimano Deore LX rear derailleurs to spaghetti, by the time they came through for service.

I have no idea what could have caused the original breakage—busy fleets of rental bikes get up to all kinds of crazy shit; that's really all I can tell you—but we must strive to learn from examples such as theirs, lest more innocent derailleurs perish in vain. Our pedaling force is transferred straight down to their pivot points, in such situations; they carve themselves to bits.

You can get away with running a short chain, if you do lose a link—or, as the case may be, if you're building a bike from scraps—you'd only need to make a commensurate adjustment with the derailleurs' limit screws. Turn in the rear derailleur's L limit screw to block off

access to the top cog or two, as required. In the most extreme cases, dialing in the front derailleur's H limit screw to block off the biggest chainring would magnify the same effect.

We can confirm the chain length by a couple different methods. Simplest is to shift down to the smallest two gears, in order to check out the rear derailleur

Confirming correct chain length in the big/big combination.

cage's position in this setting. If the two pulley bolts form a parallel line directly above the lower chain run, the chain is presumed to be just long enough. This quick guess is usually accurate, but it is not the ultimate science. The better way to check chain length is to measure things out in the largest gear combinations. When wrapped around the largest cog and chainring at once, the chain should still have a little slack to it. We would not want to ride a bike in such a gear combination, as the angles involved would precipitate undue wear on the drivetrain, but shit happens sometimes, so it should still be at least theoretically possible.

The manufacturers' official chain length formula for derailleur-equipped bikes generally adds two pins' worth of chain, after its length has been stretched straight across the biggest gears, without running through the pulleys. You measure the chain first, before using the chain tool to remove the remainder, and then finish by routing it through the derailleur cage and connecting the ends.

Chain links occasionally bend, if a rider is especially forceful with the shift levers. Bent links may be straightened, using two pairs of your sturdiest pliers, but the scientist in me would encourage you to replace them.

Someone busts out with a new shaft-driven bicycle transmission system, every few years or so. I'm not sure why. The famous and inevitable drivetrain wear, which reliably results from the transfer of our energies? Any shaft-drive system concentrates all of this upon a pair of nervous transition points, rather than displacing it along the full length of a chain. How long can we expect any shaft teeth to last?

BELT DRIVE represents a more interesting development. Reputable manufacturers such as Spot have offered belt drive bikes for a few years already, and the approach has more recently been mainstreamed by Trek, with their Soho and District bikes. Belt drive might best be considered as more of an option than a particular improvement—a different way of doing things, rather than a better one.

The belt, which needs neither oil nor grease, is lighter, quieter and cleaner. A well-maintained chain transmission is more efficient, and much more versatile in its range of options. The chains don't exactly thrive on mud, but they'll also manage it better than a belt would. The belts in use come with strong recommendations from the world of motorcycles, so there is no reason to fear they'd snap under pressure, but this cuts two ways. The belts are so solid, in fact, that the intended frames are made to accommodate them. At this writing, a belt-driven bike requires a door of some kind in the chainstay, through which to pass when installed. That would be an expensive and quite possibly dubious retrofit at the least, and more likely a whole new bike.

F. Pedals

Most bikes ship with plastic pedals—nylon pedals, whatever the hell they want to call them. The older black ones tend to be crap; some of the more colorful newer versions do a lot better. Either sort will also be nicer to the shins when things go south. Yet the originals fared poorly within the 70-bike rental fleet I maintained for years at a Minneapolis rental shop, and so became a particular nemesis of mine. What is supposed to happen, stomping on the diminutive plastic box over and over again? It will crack. And you will hear an annoying creak every time you ride the bike. But it might also persist, because the plastic may be somewhat resilient as well. And so maybe the pedal won't up and fall off the bike—someday, perhaps; you never really know—but its crack will conspire to fester and grow, until such a time when the pedal is able to drop away and be done.

Unfortunately, the plastic-bodied pedals smuggled within chintzy metal cages may actually be worse. Our basic Specialized Crossroads rental bikes came with these, my first three years at Calhoun Rentals. Left to their own devices, the steel pedal cages simply unscrew and fall off. But we couldn't let that happen, so I got in the habit of checking them out, every time I put a Crossroads up in the stand. I needed to make sure the pedals were not falling apart, of all the useless things! I've never had to do this anywhere else, before or since.

These things said, the discredited original format has been usefully revisited in recent years, with respectable manufacturers producing a new wave of plastic pedals incorporating better designs, color choices and even sealed bearings. Alas the dark old toxic forest continues to grow around these interesting new fruits, crowding out the light—mass-market bikes, far and away the most common sold in the U.S., still feature the sorts of cheap plastic pedals we'd do best to avoid. Some are inevitably pressed to hard duties regardless, over the miles and through the elements, and it falls to us in the service department to explain why the ensuing repair bills get to be so steep. Or, as is more often the case, to explain just why it is that most bike shops

refuse to service department store bikes at all.

This, too, is part of the job. But let's look at that: what if I don't want to sell someone the alloy pedals their bike needs, because I can already tell both the rear derailleur and the tires are not going to make it through the season? Should I "Go on, take the money and run"? Wal-Mart sure as hell did, right? But maybe I can't encourage the rider to save up and buy a real bike, as I would like to do, because this person works a crap job and makes even less than I do. The bike is a disaster, but it really needs to ride tomorrow, because there's no bus out to the job. How is all this suddenly my problem? It's not, but it is, because I live here too.

The good news is that it has become more and more possible in recent years to direct riders to shops selling used bikes and parts. Therein we'll find a wealth of salvation: I'd take old metal over new plastic any day of the week. Every day of the week.

The pedal axle threading is broadly universal, across a pair of sizes; any plastic pedals you may come across would be replaceable. (I've never seen plastic pedals cut in the old French threading.) Most adult bikes use pedals with $9/16''$ axle threading; most children's bikes use $1/2''$ pedals. The two sizes are easily distinct from each other. The confusion arrives with the threads' directions. Looking down from the bike's seat, *the one on the left is always reverse threaded*. Why? Because it has to be, basically. (A search on the topic at the venerable SheldonBrown.com yields a more detailed explanation.) It is only the drive-side pedal which enjoys the conventional threading we're familiar with; righty-tighty and lefty-loosey. Many pedals have "R" or "L" stamped to the ends of their axles for just such reasons. The threads themselves are fairly pronounced. They're under a good deal of stress; they need to be.

How to keep track? Imagine lines tracing out in plane with these threads, extending out to the front and the rear of the bike: they would angle in to form a triangle in front of the bike, when it is

Left pedal with "L" stamped on the axle.

right side up. But it is much easier to install and remove the pedals with the bike upside down, if you don't have a repair stand, and this finds the same lines intersecting to the rear. Get in the habit of visualizing such lines, and you will know which pedal goes where.

Many high-end pedals are installed and removed with 6 or 8 mm Allen keys, which slot right into the backsides of the axles. The wrench ends up kind of under the bike. More often we're using a pedal wrench. Its handle is long enough to provide for some torque, and the jaws are just narrow enough to fit the thinner wrench flats we find with many pedals. The regular old box wrench may be too wide to fit; the cone wrench is too narrow to deal with the torque.

Here rises the mighty Park pedal wrench, serenely surveying the vast forests of hardened steel pedal axles, to present jaws of precisely the best dimensions. We are lucky the tool is so dedicated, for it might have few other roles. It will make for a passable war-club, once civilization collapses. But I bet you'd want something bigger, unless you were fighting it out in tunnels or something.

But let's first **INSTALL THE PEDALS**, shall we? You want to avoid misthreading the pedal, and you want to make sure it ends up nice and tight.

The pedal axles should always be greased. We leave tubs of grease sitting around at work, for just such purposes. Wipe the threads clean with an oily rag before applying grease, if they appear especially rusty or gritty. Dip the axles up to their knees or something; the grease will spread everywhere it needs to. (If the crank threads appear unhealthy, it is best to get them both re-tapped at your favorite local bike shop.)

The pedal should go in perfectly straight, and their journey should not be difficult. Anything else would make me wonder if I was stripping out the crank's threads. Back the pedal out and begin anew if ever you are unsure about its trajectory.

You'll be able to thread the pedal most of the way into place with your fingers, if both the pedal and crank threads are nice and clean. Switch up to the wrench toward the end. Pedals should be installed about as solid as can be—tight, tight, tight. Some manufacturers provide washers to install between the cranks and pedals, to forestall damages that over-tightened pedals may impart to the crank arms. Nobody ever used to do this—must be a carbon fiber thing.

Were there some dispute with the steel or titanium pedal axles, the modern aluminum crank threads would always lose. The dead crank threads may be removed and replaced, by means of an old and fading technology known as the Helicoil, but you can expect to search for this. Helicoils take a bit of time and work; many shops find it more cost-effective to simply sell you a new crank arm.

A misdirected pedal axle will sometimes erase only the first few threads on a crank. In such cases—where a majority of the threads are still healthy—the axle itself might be convinced to work toward reversing the damage, once installed from the back side of the crank arm. Grease it up good, start it into the intact threads out back, and then use your pedal wrench to slowly press it forward through to the end. This doesn't repair the damaged threads so much as arrange their rubble in useful rows, but the pedal only needs to get a good grip on the healthy threads, once installed through the front again. I used this technique to rescue an injured crank on the bike I rode in Mauritania, and things worked out just fine.

Park offsets the jaws on its newest warclub to opposing angles, and this does seem to help, but the handle is also longer, and this proves very useful when **REMOVING THE PEDALS**. You will first want to ensure that the leverage is directed toward actually removing the pedal, rather than simply turning it, and this we can do by balancing our force against its mate. Flip the bike upside down, if you don't have a repair stand, and hold the one crank firmly as you bear down upon the pedal opposite. Better yet, tie the one you're not working on to the nearest chainstay with a toe strap.

Many pedals shine their wrench flats in a few distinct orientations, and this can work to your advantage here. You acquire the most leverage by squeezing the wrench and crank arm together, clasped tightly beneath your hands.

The pedals are supposed to be firmly installed, and some of their number inevitably becomes seized in place as well, so we can expect them to release rather suddenly. You will want to anticipate this—make sure your hand is not positioned to slam into the chainring, once it gives.

Is that going to do it? Maybe not. Our odds are improved easily enough, with the power of the **JESUS BAR**. It slides right over the end of the wrench, turning its period into an exclamation point. The opposing pedal keeps you from doing something similar for the crank, but you probably don't need to.

The Jesus bar will accomplish its singular mission, in most circumstances, but some hardened and especially unrepentant pedals may still refuse to believe. But that's fine, because our crusade begins with the supreme advantage. We have the means to fuck with their reality. Pull the crank arm from its spindle—this procedure is described with the cranks, page 154—and clamp it lengthwise and level in a good vise. Swaddle the crank arm in a rag first, if it's all fancy or pretty or whatever. Get in there with the wrench and the bar again; I expect you'll have better luck.

You can literally put your whole body into the effort this way. The sum of your being, focused on loosening a pedal axle? The fucker never had a chance. I have taken seized pedals to just such points many times myself, and this final option has yet to fail me. I cannot even remember the last time I required heat to remove a pedal, in fact. So you just put the torch away, OK? We have no need to burn the heretics.

The civic-minded road pedals may be the least popular, for they eschew the crenellations associated with gnarly mountain pedals, but this only makes them more specific. The mountain pedals, known in the Midwest as the **RAT-TRAPS**, face their cages with rows of pronounced teeth. This can make a big difference with the traction, on rainy days. Simpler examples couple steel cages to aluminum bodies; better sorts use alloy throughout. The best among these, upon which I rely extensively, are built around sealed-cartridge bearings. The detail jacks up the price a bit, in the short term, but I've burned through enough of the lesser pedals. Their dust caps fall off, the grease wicks out, and the bearing adjustments become loose.

The more basic pedals are finite in this sense, like the chains or the brake pads. We are not able to improve their condition, because we lack the means to mess with their bearings. We would need to move a socket within a socket, essentially. This is possible, theoretically—I bet this has happened often enough with the nicer old pedals, many of which were built to last—but the effort can seem to be more trouble than it's worth, especially if there is any cheap plastic involved.

The **TOE CLIPS** are attached to the front sides of the pedal cages, with pairs of screws. Their straps sneak through flat openings to the rear of the pedal bodies. Most road and mountain pedal cages have a front and back—or an upside and a downside, dependent upon the perspective—and we see this most clearly when we're mounting the toe clips. The two holes needed to attach the clip may only feature on the front of the cage. Its rear features a large tooth, midway along its bottom edge. We press this down with the toes to flip the toe clip up into position.

You may even find the clips in a distinct size or two, looking around. Wellgo produces their stubby Mini Clips as well,

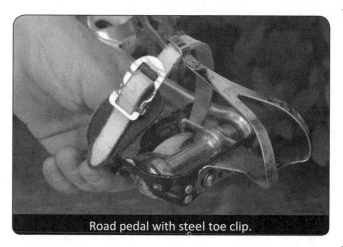
Road pedal with steel toe clip.

last I checked, which have no straps. The Power Grips do away with the clips themselves—they're only double-wide straps, cutting at diagonals across the pedals, attaching at angles to the front and rear. These have been outmoded by all the new double-wide strap systems, such as that from Brooklyn's Hold Fast.

Shimano released the first **CLIPLESS PEDALS** in the early 1990s, if memory serves. A cleat is fixed to the sole of a cycling shoe; a corresponding face on the pedal catches and holds it. The particular characteristics associated with the clipless pedals' endless catch-and-release have been further developed through manufacturers' various cleat and pedal sets. As they fit with the shoes, a majority of these have aligned with Shimano's

original two-bolt cleat mounting pattern, which cuts a pair of long slits to each sole, just beneath the balls of our feet. The cleats themselves also provide smaller degrees of side-to-side adjustment, allowing us to refine the position further still. The endless clipping and unclipping perpetually threatens to shake them loose, so make sure their bolts get to be nice and tight. These cleat bolts should also be greased, lest their charges rust in place.

Those cleats following Shimano's lead are fairly well recessed into the shoes; it's much easier to walk around in them. The road versions offered by Time, Campagnolo, Look, and others instead use much larger plastic cleats, built around a distinct three-bolt pattern. Performance is evidently improved; walking is more duck-like.

The various clipless pedal systems offer varying ranges of rotational movement, known as "float," while clipped in. As with the cleat's positioning itself, a pedal's float tends to become important to the continued health and happiness of the knees.

Different pedals and cleats are not meant to work together. You may come across lucky coincidences, among those systems that closely mimic Shimano's cleat pattern at least, but you want to test any of these thoroughly. A poor match will not catch or release as well as we'd like it to, and this can become supremely important, riding along next to the cliff.

We step forward and down with the foot, to engage the pedals. The tip of the cleat catches on the pedal; you push the heel down; it clicks into place. The springs executing these transactions can usually be coaxed toward more and less severe adjustments, by means of tensioning screws. Make sure both sides are adjusted to similar positions, with the double-sided pedals.

Releasing from the clipless pedals is simple enough as well. We rotate the heel out to the side, maybe 30 degrees or so. Clipless pedals release with less effort than that required by the toe clips, actually. You don't have to kick the foot back; you only rotate to the side just a bit. Be advised that the cleats do wear over time. Worn cleats can be more difficult to release.

G. Cranks

Glancing to the insides of the pedals, our gaze falls upon the crank arms. There should be exactly two of them. Their pair is known as the crankset.

The most basic example, the **ONE-PIECE CRANKSET**, is found aboard cheaper kids' bikes and various oldsters as well. It is one long metal stick, bent to nearly right angles passing through the frame, drilled and tapped for ½" pedals at each end. Their frames' bottom bracket shells need

to be quite a bit wider, in order to accommodate this passing business. These American-style bottom bracket shells are notably larger than the more contemporary European BB shells.

The one-piece bottom bracket cups are press-fit into their American shells. As with the headset cups upstairs, we like to do this with a special press. The neutral side pedal needs to be removed, in order to pass the crank out the drive side of the shell. Their bottom brackets are described in greater detail on page 158.

The wider American bottom bracket shells are also sometimes host to high-end BMX renditions, in which distinct spindles are suspended between sealed-cartridge bearing cups. The crank arms are fit to their spindles by means of a threadless headset-style preload bolt, which passes through the spindle itself. A few different manufacturers offer proprietary splined spindle and cup arrangements; those I've seen are attached with pinch bolts set perpendicular to the spindle.

This last detail brings to mind another older system, the **COTTERED CRANKS**. These are identified by their cotter pins, which are also laid across the spindle ends. Every set of cottered cranks I've ever seen has been made of solid steel, which is too bad, but people just didn't know any better back then. (Department store bikes and a few unfortunate others later enlisted steel for cotterless cranks, but these were layered with plastic to hide the truth.) Steel cranks become lead weights upon the wings of our destinies; they're as obsolete as coal. The bottom bracket's balls and cups you can maybe reuse. Any other cranks you find to fit will be smarter and lighter both.

The cotter pins have an obvious slant to one side, which corresponds to a matching angle cut into the spindle. The short, threaded end section of the pin slips out on the other side of the crank arm, where a nut tightens everything into place.

Whenever we come across such a system, the natural temptation is to wind that nut off and pound the hell out of the pin with a hammer. This has been known to work, but you should know that cotter pins are made of softer metal. They are meant to adapt the profiles they encounter descending into the old cottered cranks, and the upshot of this is that you may just smash the head flat, leaving the pin's wider body in place.

Park Tool once made the CR-2, the sole purpose of which is to loosen these cotter pins. It looks like an oversized chain tool, and works in much the same way. Turning a handle threads an extractor down, to push the cotter pin out. You can probably locate a shop that still has one, buried in some bottom drawer in the service department. Failing that, an approach outlined on the Bicycling.com forum seems like a reasonable alternative. Remove the cotter pin's nut, and then track down a much bigger nut, one with interior dimensions taller and just a bit wider than the pin's protruding tail section. Find a regular old C-clamp to hold

this nut in place over the rear of the cotter pin (under a coin, if need be), and use the vise grips to wind the clamp down. The pin should ease right out.

Cottered cranks were still very much in use in Mauritania, the year I lived there, but the developed world has long since moved toward the **THREE-PIECE CRANKS**, also known as cotterless cranks. Their same label describes the cottered cranks, technically speaking—or even the high-end, one-piece sets mentioned earlier, for that matter—but in common speech at least we're discussing the majority option here. The bottom bracket shell is smaller and threaded, as with the old cotters, but the crank arms attach themselves in a much better way. The spindle ends are either splined or tapered, and their ends will feature uniform threads.

Bottom brackets appear in force somewhat later in our story, but I must tell you a few other things about them, as a means to draw out and develop the major cranks. The spindles' aforementioned factions, the tapers and the splines, are distinct and non-compatible crank mounting platforms. Each also shelters a number of more subtle variations, which together serve to direct particular cranksets to the most appropriate bottom brackets. We need to use Campagnolo cranks with Campagnolo bottom brackets, for example, because the angles and lengths to their tapers are just slightly different than those used by Shimano.

These taper disputes are not easily distinguished with the naked eye—we look instead for stickers or engravings on the bottom bracket's midsection, to navigate ambiguous situations—but the split

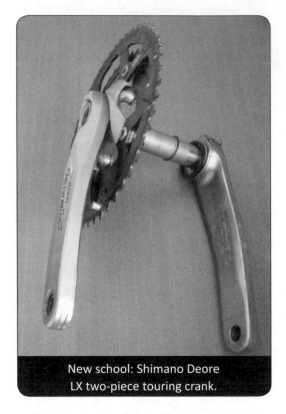

New school: Shimano Deore LX two-piece touring crank.

between the tapered spindles and the splined pipes is much more obvious. The new pipes are considerably wider, because they are hollow.

Splined bottom brackets have settled upon a pair of overall lengths, for the most part, for use with double- or triple-ring cranksets. The old tapered spindles, by contrast, may be found in a half-dozen lengths from 107 to 127 mm, to correspond with the numerous crank profiles favored over the years. Older cranks sit farther out, on longer spindles. Newer styles are considerably more svelte; some completely obscure their spindles.

The ground began shifting again in 2004, with the advent of Shimano's Dura Ace Hollowtech II crankset. Its selection of materials allowed it to become marginally lighter than previous examples, but the design also represented (the proper introduction of) a whole new design concept. The **TWO-PIECE CRANKSET** skewers our Euro BB shell with an even wider hollow pipe, itself anchored to the interior of the drive-side crank. The pipe slips through a lightweight sleeve to settle within external bottom bracket bearing cups, which thread into the frame in the usual method. The neutral crank is then drafted to help press this new sandwich together. Brilliant.

Other leading lights duly noticed and pounced upon the idea, rendering it anew under color of their own flags. SRAM's version enlists a GXP Team bottom bracket with outboard bearings; the neutral arm incorporates an integrated extraction bolt.

We also have the crank arms' length, their pedal threading, and what we call the bolt circle diameter to consider, if ever you're swapping parts around. Pedal threading, really, we can almost dispose of; just about every last crank we find is threaded to English standards. The larger ⁹⁄₁₆″ size is used with three-piece cranks; the smaller ½″ with the one-piece cranks. The two sizes are readily distinct; there should be no confusing the two. Recall that the neutral side pedals are reverse threaded, in either case. A small number of the cranks found on older French bikes are burdened with obsolete

French-threaded pedals, but these can only grow less common.

The crank arms are measured center-to-center, from pedal threads to spindle hole. The length is almost always stamped somewhere along the crank arm's inside surface, in diminutive script. We come across three-piece cranks in kids' sizes every once in a great while, but the shortest common crank length is 165 mm. The two most common crank lengths are 170 and 175 mm; 172.5 and 180 mm make more occasional appearances. Shorter cranks are more suitable for shorter people, and the reverse is also true.

The **CHAINRINGS** appear on what we call the **SPIDER CRANK**. They may or may not be integral. Cheaper examples rivet steel rings directly to their spiders; better ones let you change out the chainrings. The rings can indeed require replacement, following extended use. In most circumstances they might be exchanged for big-

Chainring with bolts.

ger or smaller sizes, which can result in a dramatically hastened or moderated gearing range, respectively.

The different rings link to their spiders through another curious measurement known as the **BOLT CIRCLE DIAMETER**, which is the loop formed by their bolts. Manufacturers tend to stick with the safest and most fashionable BCDs, while they're current. This measurement is usually etched somewhere, with the aluminum chainrings.

The grand old favorite is 110 mm, which has featured upon rings from 34 to 62 teeth, suiting everything from older mountain bikes to the small-wheeled recumbents. Most 110 cranks also have a second set of holes drilled on the inside, for a 74 mm BCD granny gear.

For road bike cranksets, the world standard is the 130 mm, which may arrive in sizes from 39 to 63 teeth. (Triple-ring road cranks pair the 130 with a 74 mm inner ring.) Campagnolo set their standard at 135 mm, which is a bit awkward, if not unreasonable. The chainrings have long been available in a wide range of quality levels, and in this case the Italians' fabled exclusivity affords a modicum of control over which in particular come to associate with their cranks. Campagnolo did see fit to go for a standard 74 mm inner ring, on their triple cranksets.

The **COMPACT ROAD CRANKS** have come on strong in recent years. They pick up on the classic old 110 BCD pattern, to sport chainrings in the range of 34 to 50 teeth. Our svelte double-ring road gearing range becomes less macho and more generous. Which, given that spinning faster is generally healthier and more efficient, makes a good deal of sense.

The 144 BCD is kind of an odd track bike thing, as memory serves. More recent, if not exactly new, is Shimano's Compact 58/94 BCD mountain bike standard. Such rings tend to be a few teeth smaller than the older 110 BCD rings, which typically went up to 46 or 48 teeth. Similar reductions occur out back, with the smallest cog shrinking from 13 to 11 teeth. Some enterprising soul had pointed out that parallel reductions front and back would make for a matching gear range with a slight weight savings. Suntour began doing this with their Microdrive system many years ago, but then their spaceship exploded. This is all history, in any case—58/94 is no longer spec'd for use with the new bikes, yet as with 110 parts can still be had. And so we spy dozens of fiercely territorial chainrings, organized as best as might be possible, collecting dust on the back shelves of bike shops all over the world.

Everything mentioned so far features a total of five bolt holes, in the circles. Improvements in materials have more recently allowed some of the more self-conscious ATB mountain spiders to ditch an entire digit. The road cranksets are still on the five-bolt patterns—the larger rings seem to require it, for now—but the smaller mountain cranks have regrouped around the new, pleasantly symmetrical four-bolt spiders, leaving

us with even more BCD patterns. Little 58 mm circles are ambidextrous, or androgynous or something—we find them with both four and five bolts—but these other new throwing stars are on their own. The 64, 68, 104, and 112 mm, at last count, each register as distinct four-bolt BCDs.

We can also find special intermediaries, known as gear adapters, meant to work with **SPIDERLESS CRANKS**. This is an option for newer Shimano Deore LX, XT, and XTR cranksets, among others. The drive crank is set up with odd splines and a short stack of threads; a proprietary spider and lockring settle atop these. We are afforded some discretion as to the BCD, using these—gear adapters are available in a couple patterns—but their grander purpose is to allow the spider be replaced independently of the crank arm. (I can't say I'm sure why this is suddenly so important. Spiders get bent sometimes, but almost all can be straightened in a vise. You just can't be a spaz about it. Remove all the rings and work slowly, lest the alloy snap.)

Everything so far coincides with standardized **CHAINRING BOLTS**. Shorter and taller versions are available to better pierce single, double, or triple chainring sandwiches. We will occasionally spy narrower examples on very old cranks, but broadly speaking the chainring bolts have long been of standard sizes.

Spacers for either chainring bolts or their (wider) nuts are occasionally inserted at points between the two, to compensate for slight differences in thicknesses among various chainrings and the spider crank bolt shelves. Steel

Chainring bolts and spacers.

rings are often a bit thinner than their aluminum superiors, for example. The judicious use of spacers allows their teeth to sit in the same place in relation to the other rings, which is important, because both the chain and any indexed front shifters rely on this measurement.

The chainrings may also have different profiles—a given example may extend straight out in plane with the crank arm bolt shelves, or it may lean forward just a bit. Differences here can probably be resolved with chainring spacers, to fit in front of or behind a particular ring. Remove the crank and compare it against a new one, or one you know to work well, if ever you're in doubt about the chainring spacing.

Aluminum chainring bolts are lighter, as we would expect. Do not use them on your fixed gear, because they aren't as strong as their steel kin. As with the SRAM-style master links, they were not designed for use with the fixed application.

With the derailleur-equipped bikes, it is also useful to install the chainrings in their correct orientation, in terms of their timing on the spider. The individual rings generally feature small engravings, at some point in their circles—the number of teeth, generally. A well-timed example finds each of these ducks lined up in a row.

The starting point for the chainrings' timing is determined by the outer chainring, which typically incorporates a small free-standing post at some point in its circle. This pin means to line up directly behind the crank arm itself, to keep the chain from jumping between the two, and it is often complemented by solitary inward-pointing teeth on the smaller rings. Note that the inner and outer surfaces of the chainrings are distinct as well, in that they may or may not provide indentations to better seat the chainring bolts.

As with Shimano's Hyperglide cassette cogs, the chainrings' timing serves to make the shifting easier. Many of the better multi-speed chainrings rely upon combinations of ramps and shallower pins to facilitate smoother shifting; any such detailing relies upon the rings' relative timing. Some Truvativ chainrings are even stamped with the year of manufacture, in fact—they're meant to be used with others of the same vintage, with their date stamps aligned.

The smallest rings on triple cranks wear out very rarely, because they are generally used less than their peers. The middle rings will sooner expire. You would start to feel a curious grinding sensation, while pedaling in a worn ring. Its teeth, seen from the sides, would have earned a meaner shark-tooth profile as well. The big rings displace the chain's business among greater numbers of teeth, and thereby wear at slower rates, but nobody lives forever. Bikes that have earned a new cog set and chain may well be up for a new ring or two.

Chainring bolts are small and unobtrusive, comparing with the burly **CRANK BOLTS**, which pin the crank arms to their bottom bracket spindles. We need to use steel crank bolts whenever we install a pair of cranks, but here as well the aluminum option is available. Note

that the latter are merely placeholders; the torque required to tighten a crank securely in position would tear their threads to shreds. You'd need to install the cranks with regular steel bolts, in other words, before replacing them with alloy ones.

The hardened steel business versions always need to become about as tight as you can make them. Manufacturers' instructions yield more precise readings for your torque wrench, but this is essentially what it comes down to.

It is a very good idea to periodically confirm the tightness of a bike's threaded fittings, the cranks and pedals in particular. It is a bad thing to ride loose cranks, because after a point their soft aluminum underbellies are left rocking around on the hardened steel spindles, and soon enough they become too loose to tighten at all. More shiny new paperweights.

It would be better to **REMOVE YOUR CRANKS**, if and when you need to, using the appropriate socket or Allen wrenches. And, in the case of most of our three-piecers, the appropriate crank extractor.

We spy the cranks' wispy extraction threads, once the bolts and their dust covers are removed, The extractor winds its body up into these, fully but

Crank bolts, nuts, and dustcaps.

also quite carefully, and only then does the tool's spine thread down the interior to push off against the bottom bracket spindle.

With the tapered spindle cranks, make sure that you dig out any washers parked beneath the crank bolts. These are common enough, and they tend to stay put as their bolts are removed; leaving them in place would cause the crank extractor to destroy the extraction threads. Peek inside; there should be nothing in the way. Also be sure to firm the body into the crank threads with a big wrench, *before* the spine comes down to face off against the bottom bracket spindle. Crank threads are easy to strip! You want to make sure the tool is threaded in as far as it can be, before doing anything else.

The success of this mission may be critical to the bike's future. Stripped extraction threads will effectively cement the cranks in place, trapping as well any demons lurking in the bottom bracket. One could only pull the bolts out and ride up the big hill, over and over again, until the cranks' dry husks finally clatter away to the pavement beneath. Automotive gear pullers are also rumored to be helpful in such situations, but I am not personally familiar with these.

This is why the **SELF-EXTRACTING CRANK BOLTS** are so cool. They take full advantage of their situation: their sharp aluminum dust caps squirrel down in the crank's extractor threads, to surround a distinct crank bolt and washer. But the dust caps are burly little fuckers; they hold their positions as the bolt is released. The crank bolt, in other words, is given the authority to actually attach and remove the whole crank.

SE crank bolts may be released with 5, 6, or 8 mm hex wrenches. They were becoming more popular, just before everyone went galloping after the two-piece cranksets which effectively rendered them obsolete, and for a brief moment there some of the nicer bikes were even born with them. It's easy enough to test for them, of course, but we also look to see two small spanner holes in the dust caps. These are installed or removed with Park Tool's diminutive CNW-2 or small needle-nose pliers.

The cranks' extraction threads are nearly universal. I know of only a pair of exceptions, in fact. I came across a pair of fairly modern Stronglight cranks on a Quintana Roo tri-bike the other day, the extraction threads of which were reversed. They also bore their own self-extracting bolts, fortunately. I understand Campagnolo once pulled this as well, producing a corresponding extraction tool to match.

You only have to screw this up once, to learn the hard way. I first blew my chances with a nice old Stronglight spider, several years back. And so it totally amazed me, a couple summers ago, when I managed to strip out an innocent STX spider crank. I had not realized that I'd grabbed the wrong **CRANK EXTRACTOR**. This was Park's black-handled CCP-44, newly introduced at that time, which I had never seen before.

This tool was meant to be used exclusively with the new-style splined "pipe"

Octalink crank, but only an old CCP-22 tool? Get that button in there.

bottom brackets, as it turns out. Its face is wider; to better greet the new pipes. It will bottom out inside the crank arm, instead, when faced against one of the thinner tapered spindles. Which, if pressed, strips out the fucking crank. "Wow," I recall thinking, "this sure is pretty tight." Then came the dreaded evil feeling, where the extractor pulls the crank's wispy aluminum threads out into the daylight.

I am not proud of that day's work. My purpose in relaying the ignoble tale is merely to caution the reader. Both sorts of crank extractors are also available as shop versions, without the conveniently color-coded handles described here. Make sure you have a match, before doing anything else. New pipe bottom brackets are typically sold with a solid metal button, which allows for the use of a tapered-style extractor, but this horse pill provides for the only exception.

A given crankset is meant to run with a specific bottom bracket. Shimano and Campagnolo both make their parts available as component groups, marching right up the income ladder, and it is safest to assume that each successive layer does its own math in this respect. There is no "standard" spindle, in other words, outside the model year of a particular component group. But the particulars have evolved over time, with the goal of drawing the chainrings as close to the frame as they may become. This aligns them more precisely with the hub gears to their rear, which is to say it provides for a better **CHAINLINE**. A good chainline is more efficient. It also shifts better.

Differences in the length of the tapered bottom bracket spindles relate more to a crankset's vintage than anything else. The **CRANK PROFILE**—the lateral positioning of the drive crank's spider—has moved in toward the frame's center line over the years. With the notable exception of some newer downhill mountain bike equipment, we expect only the oldest cranks to sit wider apart, straddling the long 122 or 127 mm spindles.

The spider crank is the great crouching tiger among its kindred components— it defends itself well enough, with but the slightest prompting. Its enemies are forced to attack from angles. While damaged pedal threads may be replaced with the brilliant Helicoil inserts, as described previously, the same cannot be said for the crank extraction threads. Some shops have the shallow and obscure tap used to clean up gritty extraction threads, but that's about all we may do. Stripped cranks make for bar bikes.

Crank arms also break very occasionally, across either the pedal threads or the spindle hole. This happened to me once, when I was a courier in Minneapolis, coming down off a curb. Freaked me the hell out, it did. **BENT CRANKS** are slightly more common. Using the front derailleur cage or the chainstay as your reference point, some spot in the spider crank's rotation would appear to be out of round. If only one chainring sways, that would be the problem. If two or more rings bow out simultaneously, this would suggest that the spider crank itself is bent.

If only one chainring in a set is bent, it is sometimes possible to slowly lever it straight with a pliers, or a big screwdriver. Make sure all its bolts are tight first, and be careful not to lever the other chainrings out of round. You tweak it a little and rotate it past the derailleur, to see how it lines up.

Given the opportunity, it would be preferable to remove the rings and straighten any bent ones in a vise. Compare chainring teeth to vise jaws; gradually bend or lever as needed, rotate and do it again. Easy. The big old crescent wrench is useful in this operation, particularly when single teeth are bent out of line. You really get a sense of its leverage, doing this.

We can do something similar for bent spiders, using the vise. Or, if you lack in vises, remove the rings and retighten the denuded spider upon its spindle. It will be one of the bolt tabs that bent; you'll be leveling it against the others with the big wrench. Aluminum is not nearly as resilient as steel; work slowly and carefully.

H. Bottom Brackets

Having dispatched with the cranks, it is time to discuss the **BOTTOM BRACKETS**. We begin with several distinct possibilities—one-piece bottom brackets, three-piece units, sealed-cartridge versions of each, as well as the two-piece cranks' external bearing sets. These different camps, in turn, are well sprinkled with additional variables tossed in by the different manufacturers over time.

All the bottom brackets accomplish the same functions, to varying degrees of grace. An axle, burly enough to support the considerable force created with pedaling, is suspended tightly between two parallel sets of bearings.

The unthreaded American bottom bracket shells, measuring 2.02″ across, are distinctly larger than their peers— they are very popular with older bikes and children's bikes. Tandems make use of them as well, for chain-tensioning purposes. An eccentric bottom bracket featuring offset European BB threads is installed therein; rotating it fore and aft accomplishes the chain tensioning.

The English/ISO standard, using 1.37 x 24tpi threads in a 68 mm shell, is far and away the most common in use today. This same threading was adapted for the wider 73 mm bottom bracket shells in the 1990s, and more recently for the 83 and 100 mm shells as well. Note that the drive-side cup is always reverse threaded, with English bottom brackets. High-end Italian bikes will often insist on distinct 70 mm Italian bottom brackets, threaded to 36 mm x 24 tpi. The old 36 x 1 mm French standard hasn't been used for decades, but replacement parts can still be found. Phil Wood makes a nice set. If ever you do manage to strip out your bottom bracket threads, all hope may not be necessarily lost: go and get yourself one of Velo Orange's Grand Cru Threadless Bottom Brackets.

1. One-Piece

The hoary old **ONE-PIECE BOTTOM BRACKETS** are usually the simplest. The crank makes its lazy 90-degree bends, passing through; the bearings' cones rest upon its shoulders. That featuring on the drive side will be in a fixed position; a threaded cone and locknut opposite allow for our adjustments.

We should also spy a thin, keyed washer set between the cone and locknut, to better accommodate their settlement. The nut may be loosened with either your

30 mm headset wrench or the big old crescent wrench, but the cone itself anticipates Park's HCW-11 wrench or similar.

One-piece bottom brackets are generally thirsty for our attention—they often show up on older bikes, and rarely do they have much for bearing seals. Remove the neutral side pedal, to start, and thread both the cone and its locknut out of the way. This lets you pull the crank right out through the drive side. The one-piecers run on huge $\frac{5}{16}''$ bearings in retainer cages—the massive red dwarf stars, compared to the other bearing systems—heavy, but durable. It is best to throw everything in the undiluted citrus degreaser and let it sit overnight, given the opportunity.

The bearing cones are rarely pitted, on these burly old contraptions; their races even less so. At the worst, they are replaced quite cheaply. The proper bearing adjustment echoes that which we find with the headsets, or the hubs—things end up just tight enough to prevent any lateral play, with cone and locknut supremely tight against each other. As with the other bearing systems, this may find you over-tightening the cone initially, as means to back it out in the final adjustment.

2. Sealed-Cartridge

The bearing adjustment is already set, with the **SEALED-CARTRIDGE** bottom brackets. We can find sealed bearings to fit with the overstuffed American-style bottom bracket shells—and Fly's newer, slightly smaller Spanish shells as well, for that matter—but the term is typically associated with threaded European bottom brackets. A complete bearing and spindle set is installed to the frame from one side; a corresponding hollow cup threads in from the opposite side to brace the far end. These are the big no-brainers—they'll either work, or they won't.

Sealed-cartridge bottom brackets are removed with various spanners and extraction tools. Shimano's BBT-2 is presently the most universal among these. Its splines will coincide with many cheap generic bottom brackets, as well as some newer ball-and-cup sets. Campagnolo's Record and Chorus bottom bracket cartridges are installed and extracted with their UT-BB080 tool, which is the same one we use with the company's cassette lockrings. Their AC-H, AC-S, and SC-S cartridges are extracted with the UT-BB100.

How do the threads look, in the frame? Any rust or other damage is better dealt with before installing a bottom bracket. Your favorite local bike shop should have the expensive tap set required to chase the threads clean. Get in there with a rag and some lightweight oil, failing such treatment, to clear out any grit.

We paint the frame's threads with plenty of grease, prior to installing any bottom bracket. An ungreased cartridge will probably creak like hell, after a few rides. You would also just be begging the thing to rust in place—which, with the cartridges in particular, is something to avoid. The torch we might eventually call upon in such situations may only burn away the cartridge's seals, in the course of its work. This in turn might leave the mechanism loose as well, which would suck all the more, if you weren't able to remove the thing.

You may or may not want to grease the bottom bracket spindle ends, before installing the cranks. Shimano recommends greasing the spindles, so that is what we do, for their products at least. Campagnolo, by contrast, encourages us to degrease the spindle before installing the cranks. Truvativ splits the difference—where we were pointed toward "clean, grease-free" conditions for the company's tapered-spindle bottom brackets, we're encouraged to grease their splined spindles. The strongest words on the topic may have been penned by Chris Bell, in his Highpath Engineering notes. "Anyone suggesting that grease shouldn't be used [on bottom bracket axle tapers] either hasn't got a very good mechanical understanding or has a vested interest in shortening the life of your cranks," he says.

The sealed-cartridge bottom brackets are installed in a particular sequence. The hollow cup is installed first. It will usually, but not always, feature on the frame's neutral side. Do not thread it all the way in: stop a couple threads back from leaving it flush with the frame.

The hollow cup's interior will now provide for a shelf, which becomes useful when installing the bearing cartridge.

This last is somewhat top-heavy going in, as you'd notice, and thereby somewhat inclined to challenge the threading, lacking such guidance.

Thread the bearing cartridge all the way home, using the appropriate extraction tool; this piece in particular should become about as tight as you can make it. This done, firm down the hollow side as well, as far as it will go.

The hollow is almost always threaded to fit the frame's neutral side, with the cartridges—the side without the gears—but there was a period in the 1990s when Shimano and certain imitators anchored the bearing mechanism to the neutral side instead. Shimano's more recent BB-7410 Dura Ace canister pulled the same switch as well, as have likely others; just keep an eye out.

As was mentioned, the English BBs used with most bikes are reverse-threaded on one side, not unlike the pedals. How to keep track? Imagine the frame is not there for a second, and look down at the cartridge in question: anything written or etched on its body should be legible, from your vantage in the seat. This is your orientation; it tells you which side is which.

Alternately, simply look at the threads. They will be cut at slight angles to the cups, to coincide with those they find in the frame. Excluding the tiny cliques formed by ancient French-threaded bikes or exclusive Italian-threaded racers, the bottom bracket cups' threads both point slightly inward, toward the bike's rear end, when it is right side up. (The reverse is true once again, when you flip it upside down.)

Whichever the case, our final test comes with the execution itself. *You should never feel like you're forcing anything through the threads.* A cup's outside edge remains perfectly parallel to the frame's bottom bracket shell, as it threads into place. This is how we know if it went in straight.

We should also discuss the new splined pipes. Truvativ's ISIS Drive, which set ten even splines to the ends of a hollow 21 mm pipe, was the first popular example. The applied wisdom evident with the frame tubes—that hollow can be lighter and stronger at once—had finally made it down to the nether regions below. Alas Truvativ enlisted tiny ball bearings in their original design, as means to fit the wider spindle. This defied decades of industry precedent, and lo did their strange new icon begin to crumble. Bottom brackets have traditionally relied upon ¼″ balls, and this original ISIS arrangement became known for its problems.

Shimano's Dura Ace neatly circumvented the problem, relying upon needle bearings instead of the tiny BBs. Yet neither do these first-generation Shimano pipes enjoy stellar reputations, among mechanics I have known—the originals were not well sealed, and thereby were left more vulnerable to road grit, which becomes a bigger problem with needle bearings.

The next logical step, again first demonstrated by the Dura Ace, was to mount the bearings outside the bottom bracket shell. The circle is made wider, allowing for both the pipe and properly sized bearings at once. This new Hollowtech II design has since worked its way down their parts hierarchy, and other manufacturers have duly followed suit.

Two-piece external bearing bottom bracket.

Shimano's needle bearing formula has been usefully updated as well. It has spawned a child of its own, in fact: where the original V1 spindle will fit some newer DA, Ultegra, and 105 cranks from that period, the longer and wider V2 spindles are meant for the contemporary Deore, LX, and XT mountain cranksets.

The Octalink and ISIS drive systems use fat 15 x 1 mm crank bolts. Some of the better Shimano units are held together with hollow bolts of the same dimensions, which answer to the big 10 mm hex wrenches. Finally, another use for that thing.

There is one important thing to keep in mind, when installing cranks atop any of these splined pipe-style bottom brackets. Many of the intended cranksets incorporate the clever self-extracting crank bolts, which save us the trouble of tracking down the correct extraction tool, but these need to be removed, to safely install the cranks on their spindle.

It is easy to install these types of cranks at slight angles to the bottom bracket splines, which would render them paperweights. The only way to make sure this is not happening is to turn the bolts out. The SE jobs feature a pair of symmetrical holes across their face; we attack these with a small pliers or spanner, such as Park's CNW-2.

Wider still is the unthreaded **BB30**, which replaces the 24 mm steel spindle used with most two-piece cranks with a 30 mm aluminum tube. Cannondale originally introduced the idea as the SI bottom bracket back in 2000, promoting its use as a more universal standard. Manufacturers including Specialized, SRAM, and Full Speed Ahead have taken up the design. Its case is compelling—the BB30 is lighter, stiffer, and not vulnerable to the range of complications that may visit with more conventional threaded bottom brackets. The design eschews bottom bracket cups altogether, much like the internal headsets, an approach better suited to the more uniform forces channeled through the bottom bracket axis.

BB30 bearings are only removed when they need to be replaced. Park's BBT-39 set includes a punch designed to knock the bearings out as well as bushings to guide reinstallation, meant for use with their headset press. Note that you'll want to avoid damaging the bearing-stop clips mounted inside the shell directly behind each bearing.

Yet other manufacturers have set off to establish their own standards, based on novel interpretations of the very same math: BB83, BB86, and so on. Most prominent among these is the system Trek used with the 2010 Madone, which enlists a 90 x 37 mm threadless bottom bracket shell. The design's profile annexes the land external bearings might otherwise have occupied, and the broadened platform to result allows for wider frame tubes above, which in turn garners those concerned a few more percentage points' worth of efficiency and performance. As with the BB30, cartridge bearings are press-fit into sockets.

3. Three-Piece

I first learned **THREE-PIECE BOTTOM BRACKET** overhauls back at Wheel and Sprocket in Milwaukee, in the early 1990s. Complete bike overhauls were already becoming a little easier, way back then, for the sealed-cartridge bottom brackets were just beginning their invasion. The ease and convenience represented by these new cans of joy was

truly remarkable, comparing against other contemporary arrangements, and it wasn't long before all the better bikes were relying upon them.

Adjustable bottom brackets were increasingly rendered conspicuously old-fashioned, relics from a dark time when the world knew no better. Yet the sealed cartridges bear at least a passing resemblance to religious zealots, in that there's no talking to them. Every last one is meant to be hermetically sealed; simple adjustments are rarely even possible. Their silence tempts us to leave them to their own devices—for years at a time, as the case may be—and this very license encourages them to rust in place, which itself may put an end to the frame's useful life. The saccharine comfort of maintenance avoidance tends to express itself dramatically.

That said, I do run sealed cartridges on a few of my bikes—the ideological supermarket, as they say, is only good for raiding. But I also save all the healthy old **BALL-AND-CUP SETS** I come across, because among these at least there really is some hope for redemption. The

Ball and cup bottom bracket cup set.

great majority of those I've seen can be returned to service again.

A fixed cup, outfitted with 10 loose or 8 caged ¼″ bearings, is threaded all the way down over on the drive side. A sturdy axle, known as the spindle, flies in to pin the balls against the cup's interior. A further piece, known as the adjustable cup, scoops up more bearings and threads down from the neutral side, trapping the spindle between their two sets. A lockring spins down atop the adjustable cup, finally, making official its new position. And you can turn the crank.

As with bearing systems more generally, the better examples will incorporate polished bearing races and distinct rubber dust seals. More basic ball-and-cup bottom brackets are all of brown metal rods, which happen to coincide with the bearings—their cups lack any refinement. The fancier ones have always a minority; most of those I've rescued have been of the simpler variety. The ends to the original bottom bracket spindles were threaded, to be capped by sturdy nuts, but it was eventually decided to simply thread bolts into the spindles instead.

All of the adjustable bottom bracket's component parts must be firmly installed. I have known too many of these to hold adjustments for years on end; there are no secret bottom bracket demons, craftily upsetting our work in the dead of night. The bearings need just enough freedom to spin evenly; any slop beyond this measure should always be dispatched.

The tools typically required to overhaul a ball-and-cup bottom bracket begin with a fixed cup wrench such as Park's HCW-4, or a 1 ⅛″ [36 mm] headset wrench, failing that. Over on the adjustable side, you will need a lockring wrench and a spanner; most likely either Park's HCW-11 or their SPA-1. Both cups will need to be removed. These and their spindle can get cleaned up with an oily rag; any caged bearings should sit in solvent or degreaser for a night. The frame's threads should at least be cleaned up with a rag and lightweight oil and then greased anew, before reassembly.

Lay a couple fat donuts of grease in both cups and plop the bearings down therein, once they're clean and dry. Even the loose ball bearings should just stay put like that, assuming for nice and fat donuts. Note that any bearing cages should face the *outsides* of the cups, away from the spindle.

The fixed cup goes in first, all the way down. The spindle dives in next, pinning the bearings to the inside of the cup. The drive side of the spindle is probably longer, but the best way to confirm its orientation is with the numbers and letters invariably stamped on the spindle's midsection. However this ancient code happens to translate, it should read right side up from the vantage of the seat, assuming the frame didn't interfere.

The deal is clinched with the adjustable cup, which dials in on the neutral side until its bearings bottom out on the spindle's bearing race. Spin a rag rapidly across the ends of the spindle, to help the bearings settle into their grease, before introducing the lockring. Keep your tool firmly atop the adjustable cup, as the lockring is tightened, lest the cup merely go with its flow. When the adjustable cups are held with tools in fixed positions, the BB lockrings have the effect of pulling them ever so slightly out from the frame, as they are tightened into place. You may want to compensate for this, by beginning with an adjustment just a bit too tight.

The final exam drops the chain onto the BB shell, before rotating a crank arm parallel with a chainstay. The bearings should spin quite smoothly, and there should be no lateral play at all across the crank arm and the stay. It can take a few tries to get this adjustment right, but this is one of those things that is worth practicing.

Of all the bicycle's bearing systems, the **HUBS** are the most traditional. More than a century after the advent of bearing retainer cages, and decades past the popular adaptation of sealed bearing cartridges, the great majority of hubs still incorporate loose ball bearings. A small number of hubs have experimented with bearing cages, and many more incorporate cartridge bearings, but the majority option is conspicuous, in that the better headsets and bottom brackets gave up the loose balls with disco.

All the loose and caged bearing hubs require occasional overhauls. Think every few years, at a minimum—rolling the axles with the fingers, any hub that feels less than smooth would be a good candidate. As we will see, there are things we can do to nurse decades-old hubs back to health.

Excluding the sealed bearing hubs, whose numbered cartridges span a fair range of sizes, *nearly* all the rear hubs use nine ¼″ balls to either side. Almost all the loose bearing front hubs sport ten ³⁄₁₆″ bearings in each race.

Most bikes on the road today were born with **THREADED AXLES** incorporating bearing cones, locknuts, dust caps, and axle spacers. All of a given hub's component pieces tend to be replaceable—bearing cones may get to be pitted; axles are sometimes bent—but we will generally need an exact match. A replacement bearing cone, for example, would need to match the original's height, width, threading, and profile.

Shimano's axle threading standards—9 x 1 mm front; 10 x 1 mm rear—have really become predominant, by virtue of their monopoly. There are exceptions, to begin with Campagnolo. Top quality steel bearings can be found quite cheaply these days; the finest grade 25 balls will cost about a dime apiece. Lower-quality grade 200 bearings are best set aside for the bar bike. The ceramic bearings presume for disposable income; apparently they're lighter, rounder and more durable than all the others.

The working surfaces of both the cones and the bearing races are meant to brace the bearings in one particular orientation. Balls too small—or too few—will screw things up. By the same token, the wrong cones will present the bearings

with angles they were not expecting, leaving them to skate around the edges, assuming they're able to roll at all. Every part of a hub really needs to fit the rest of it, right down to the bearing seals.

Better cones and races are polished to finer degrees. The races themselves are rarely damaged—the bearings' blazing comet tails streak across reasonably broad surfaces—but pitted bearing cones are not uncommon. Any maladjusted hub may earn a pair, if it's ridden too long. They would need to be replaced, before riding back up the mountain.

The longer and weaker an axle, the more likely it will eventually bend—a not uncommon problem among the old freewheel-equipped solid axle hubs, to take the most famous example. Newer hubs enlist better designs and stronger materials to circumvent this issue, but it wasn't always so easy.

The distance from the tip of one locknut to the tail of its opposite is known as the **HUB SPACING**. The hubs and frames are meant to coincide with one of a few common hub spacings, and their fit should be snug. Not loose, or binding, just snug. You should never need to use much force to install a wheel—not anywhere it is meant to be, at least. Any serious frame stretching can be expected to fuck up the bike's alignment. Pressing a frame together to meet a narrower axle, conversely, puts extra stress on those fixtures mounting the wheel to the bike.

Front hubs with threaded axles are wonderfully predictable. Nearly everything is

spaced to 100 mm. Many compact folding bikes have 75 mm front hubs, but the wheels are also tiny; you almost expect to see it. I have also heard of some old 90 mm BMX hub measurement, but I've never seen one in real life.

BMX rear hubs start the listing for the threaded axle hubs out back, with the slim spacing of 110 mm. One gear; they get away with it. Both track bikes and the old-fashioned 3-speeds share the 120 mm gap. Note that the 3's axle is maybe a bit narrower; its frame dropouts would need to be filed down to accept a track hub. That was my friend Amelia's experience, at least. Some really old road or city bikes have also have been 120, but 126 mm is the real old-fashioned road bike standard. Fades a bit every year, but we remember.

I have seen only one reference to 128 mm rear hub spacing; I'm guessing it was also an old road bike. Modern road bikes are more recently at 130 mm, for many years now. And we can tell the mountain bikes entered production during this time, because this 130 is also the original ATB rear hub spacing. The big common coin for threaded axle hubs is 135 mm, found with all the modern mountain bikes, hybrids, recumbents, recumbent trikes, and many others. Odds are good this is you.

Tandems may be found with any of the aforementioned rear hub spacings—except the 110, hopefully—but modern tandems are all using wider hubs. They support the weight better; they also allow a drag brake to slip in on the wheel's neutral side. We're talking 140, 145, or 160 mm, dependent upon age and manufacturer.

The various axle sizes are expected to correspond with matching frame dropouts. In recent years, a growing number of the mountain bikes are arriving with **THROUGH AXLES**, wide smooth pipes which are not threaded. Those frame and fork dropouts anticipating the through axles clamp all the way around their charges, eschewing any need for quick-release skewers. It is a heavier way of doing things, but also sturdier. Tullio's 20 mm front axle was the first of these, to the best of my awareness—its arrival coincided with certain pressing new questions around the use of disc brakes with conventional Q/R front hubs, as described on page 24, and the ensuing controversy helped advance the design.

Phil Wood tandem hub.

Through axle wheels may be mounted or removed with 5 or 6 mm Allen wrenches, or perhaps a 14 mm box wrench. The 20 x 110 mm through axle has become standard for front wheels on downhill bikes. Specialized introduced a wider 25 mm version as well. There are also 10 and 12 mm rear through axles to fit hubs of 135, 150, or 165 mm width.

A. Freewheel

The hub gears either thread on as a complete package, or they slide down the splines of an existing mechanism. The threaded **FREEWHEELS** came first. Their effect is easily taken for granted, from the wizened modern perspective, but the freewheels were revolutionary in their time. Our cadence was shifted from perpetual motion to full-on casual, by nothing more than a basic mechanical duplicity. A circle of bearings and spring-loaded palls was inserted between cog and base, and away we went.

The freewheel perches upon a stack of wide, flat threads rising from the drive-side hub flange. These threads should not be confused with those found on track hubs, which are stepped in two distinct sections, the smaller of which is reverse-threaded. The freewheels enjoy the traditional right-handed thread orientation, which in their case means that riding down the road serves to continuously tighten them in place.

We (very) occasionally come across French- or Italian-threaded hubs and freewheels, but both are endangered like the species. We also have the BMX Mini threading, used to accommodate the diminutive 14t singlespeed freewheels. Everything else you'd find would bear threads cut to the English 1.37" x 24 tpi standard. Whichever their nationality, the hub threads should always be greased before any freewheel is installed.

The freewheels are made of steel, by virtue of their strenuous responsibilities, and the hub threads are typically aluminum. This makes for yet another tedious power relationship. The angry freewheels are only too happy to erase the hubs' more fragile threads, given the slightest pretext. Installing a freewheel at odd angles will end the hub's useful life. The thing should just twirl on like butter, threading into place with the slightest push. Back it off if it fails to do so, using the appropriate freewheel removal tool, as will be described momentarily.

Freewheels are available in various sizes and gearing ranges, from the BMX singles up to clusters of 7 or 8. Neither 9- nor 10-speed freewheels exist. The technology that renders freewheels obsolete came to the world years ago already, back when everyone was still on 7-speeds. In this respect, 8-speed freewheels are kind of a fluke.

Having played with the freewheels awhile, we're given a sense of certain shortcomings particular to their program. The design

Chain whip and freewheel extraction tools.

leaves the drive-side bearings well back from their frame dropout, under the wide threaded section. The axle is thus not well supported across the remaining distance out to the frame; it becomes much more vulnerable to bending. Some high-end examples are able to persist regardless—the old Mavic threaded hubs spring to mind—but their lesser peers simply cannot be trusted with much for weight. No larger riders; no loaded tours.

One needs a good deal of force, in order to remove a freewheel from a hub, and perhaps a bit of cunning as well. The freewheels are only removed by means of their extraction splines, some of which are shallow indeed, and the wrong kind of shove could easily render these useless, marrying that particular freewheel to the wheel in question for all of eternity. The hub didn't need an overhaul or anything, did it? Not the kind of union we'd like to promote.

I'm not quite sure how many distinct freewheel removers were called into being, when they were current—I want to say a dozen, at least—but some are far and away more common. Any remotely modern freewheels will answer to Park's FR-1, and almost all singlespeed freewheels are removed with their FR-6. We also find occasional uses for their FR-2 and FR-3 extractors, for two- and four-prong Suntour freewheels respectively. With these last two in particular, it is important to use the right tool. Others may look quite similar, but they will wreck you.

You will also want to make sure the extractor stays plugged in tightly to the freewheel, once you begin applying force. *Finger-tighten either the Q/R lever or the axle locknut atop the extractor, to the point that it cannot move around at all, before applying any force.* The freewheel's actual removal is best accomplished in a vise—clamp across the extractor's flats, get a solid grip on the wheel and turn it counterclockwise. You might do as well leaning over it with a big wrench, alternately.

The freewheel will be on the hub pretty good. It will only begin to give all of a sudden. Once it does begin to loosen, pause to back off the skewer or locknut before proceeding. This done, the freewheel should just spin right off the hub.

B. Cassette

The freewheels fuse the clutch mechanism to the cogs, to varying degrees of permanence, and this makes individual cog replacement either difficult or impossible. But this only means the **CASSETTES**, which fix the clutch mechanism to the hub itself, are fucking brilliant.

The cassette hub replaces the freewheel threads with a splined cylinder, known as the **FREEHUB BODY**. A gear cassette bearing matched splines slides down around this, and a lockring secures it in place.

The hub's drive-side bearings make the most of the new situation, migrating down toward the outer end of the freehub body to rest just under the cassette lockring. Their job becomes much easier—they've no more awkward gap to worry about. For this reason the cassette hub axles are much less inclined to bend.

Freehub bodies have appeared in a few different styles, over the years. Most are either rare or obsolete. Suntour had distinct 7- and 8-speed cassette hubs, for example, back when they made hubs. Campagnolo has additionally offered various freehub arrangements, for gear cassettes ranging from 7 to 11 speeds.

Freehub bodies compatible with Shimano's 7- and 8/9/10-speed Hyperglide cassettes are the most common. The Hyperglide platform improves upon Shimano's original 7-speed Uniglide prototype, the top cog of which settled into threads around the original freehub body's exterior. It has since been demonstrated that lining up the cogs just *so* tends to make shifting the gears a lot easier; the Uniglide's odd old locking cog would have precluded this from happening. Thus do the Hyperglide cassettes anticipate distinct internally threaded lockrings instead.

The splines radiating around the lockring's underside ratchet away against matching splines found atop the cassette's final cog. A well-installed lockring will be tightened just to the point when the pair cannot ratchet any further. The cassette splines' profile has also changed, with Hyperglide—one especially wide stripe has appeared, forcing the cogs to line up in a predetermined orientation.

Shimano's 8/9/10-speed freehub body is a little longer than the 7, as may be imagined. It is possible to update or replace either sort, with the Shimano cassette hubs at least. Minute distinctions in cone and dust cap dimensions set many of the freehub bodies just slightly apart—the true scientists among us will note the model number on the hub body, before ordering any replacement parts.

Chain whip, freewheel, and cassette removers.

Shimano cassette hubs hold the freehub body in place with a hollow bolt. The axle passes right through it. The big 10 mm Allen key slots into position, once the axle is out of the way, to release this fixing bolt. We would of course want to be sure it was well greased and thoroughly tightened, upon returning to duty. These things loosen quite rarely, but to the untrained eye it can make for an especially bleak and existential problem. This happened to my friend Shelly's bike, on our

long ride out to Portland, and at the time I was left absolutely slack-jawed.

All freehubs have just a bit of play, to allow for their mechanisms to whirl, but this becomes less and less perceptible with the better examples. Shoddier hub manufacturers marry the freehub body to the hub, as one solid package. Cheesy. There are no flats for the 10 to grip, because there's no fixing bolt in the first place.

Campagnolo cassettes arrive aboard curious plastic decks, which are meant to slip right over their freehub bodies, allowing us to simply slide the goods down into place. This we should do, because the cogs and spacers are arranged in a particular sequence. The slices are not all of uniform thickness; losing their order would leave an indexed derailleur very confused.

The Campagnolo cassette's lockring looks quite similar to those we see with the standard SRAM and Shimano products, but they're attached and removed with the distinct Campagnolo UT-BB080 extraction tool. They made a couple of them, actually; the lockrings supplied with 1998 and older Campy cassettes are not compatible with the more modern freehubs. Different threadings.

Excluding the aforementioned original model, Shimano cassette hub systems are more standardized. The very same Hyperglide tool will fit modern road and mountain gear clusters from 7 to 10 speeds, as well as their imitators from SRAM and Sunrace.

All cassettes are removed by the same method. Two hands are required: one presses the cogs clockwise, and the other twists the lockring off in the opposite direction. We enlist a vise and various specialized implements to expedite the process up at the shop, but only to save a few seconds. A chainwhip will suffice to brace the cogs, and a big crescent wrench will hold the lockring tool; the two are levered against each other.

You will notice that the cassette lockring splines are pretty shallow. As with the freewheels, we need a means to make sure the extractor doesn't simply jump out of the way under pressure. For this we have a couple of options. Park's FR-5G cassette extraction tool features a long spine, which dives into the Q/R axle once its skewer is removed. Alternately, the FR-5 can be held in position with either the skewer or an axle nut, in the case of bolt-on cassette hubs. As with the freewheels, finger-tighten the extractor atop its target before applying force, then back it off once the cassette's lockring begins to loosen.

A loose lockring allows the cassette itself to sway back and forth on its freehub body, presenting something of a moving target above the derailleur's precise and hopeful clicks. The situation becomes obvious enough; the cogs can be moved

laterally, independently of any play in the freehub body.

We are occasionally moved to install thin spacers just behind the cassette, in order to ensure a tight fit under the lockring. But you can't be going all ape-shit with this, at the very same time, because an over-tightened lockring will in some cases actually bear down too heavily on the hub bearings, enough perhaps to even slow things down. If the hub spins less freely after the cassette is installed, this would be why.

C. Overhauls

All the hub's individual parts can be cleaned up nicely with thin oil, which breaks down any crusty old grease it may encounter. You may want to *gently* pry off the dust caps, to better swab the hub's

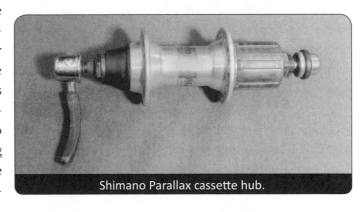
Shimano Parallax cassette hub.

races. Be careful if you do; the old school metal dust caps are bent and dented quite easily. The small flathead screwdriver will suffice to chisel away any old grit featuring on the dust cap's underside. You press it back in place with the side of your wrench, when you are done, to leave the dust cap nice and level across the hub.

Any pitted cones should get recycled, together with the bearings they rolled in with. Once the bearing races are clean, use the grease gun to lay down some nice fat donuts therein. I tend to reuse bearings, because I'm fast enough already, but we always finish overhauls with new bearings at work. They all plop right down into this greasy donut, one by one. Quality bicycle-specific greases such as Rock "N" Roll's white will hold them in place, while you reassemble.

In the great majority of cases, we want to install ten ¼" balls in each side of the rear hub, and nine ³⁄₃₂" bearings in each race up front. Grade 25 steel bearings are fine quality; grade 200 bearings may suffice if they need to. **CERAMIC BEARINGS** have been used in various applications since the 1990s, but they've only crossed over to the bikes in the last few years. They are both lighter and stronger than our conventional steel balls, and can thereby be expected to roll smoother and last somewhat longer, so rest assured you'd pay for the difference. Ceramic bearings can be found in all our favorite sizes, and they require no special care or feeding; the techniques described herein should be universally applicable.

Whatever it is you're playing with, the final bearing adjustment needs to be precise. At the same time, we also need to account for the compression of any quick-release skewers. A well-adjusted hub is tightened *just* enough to avoid any

lateral play with its wheel, when mounted in the frame. It is a pleasantly unambiguous prescription, in the case of bolt-on hubs. We only need to plan ahead a bit when applying it to the quick-release hubs, whose skewers compress the hubs ever so slightly. For this reason, Q/R hubs should be adjusted such that they end up being *slightly* loose.

The cones and locknuts on each side of the hub need to end up supremely tight against each other, in order to maintain any worthy **HUB ADJUSTMENT**. Again, the measure you're looking for rests at an exacting point, midway along the spectrum from loose to tight. However many hubs I've overhauled, I still must pause and reflect every last time I do this. Concentrate, concentrate, concentrate.

Something as simple as a buildup of grease between the bearings and hub surfaces can throw off the adjustment. Seat things in place as best you can in the first place, by spinning a rag across the axle. You will be working in ever-smaller measures, as you tighten down to your finishing point, checking the results after each one. The cone and locknut on one side will be tightened all the way together; the adjustments are made on the other side. Remember that jazz about the control and the experiment, from your grade-school science class? Here it is, at last.

I tend to set the side with the most axle spacers as my control, on old freewheel hubs. This means that the cone and locknut's final positioning is translated across the smallest distance, over on the experimental side, which seems to make things a little easier. The cassette hubs, however, have already made this choice for you: the flats on the drive-side cone disappear inside the freehub body, as it is put back together, so you need to make sure that side is completely tight while it's still out in the daylight.

The axle itself helps us determine whether the cone or lockring is being turned. There will inevitably be some scratch or clump of grit or something on the axle threads, by the time they're ready for their overhauls, and this very thing may be used as a reference point. You can dab on a drop of grease, if nothing else. Keeping an eye on this feature, you should be able to notice whether it is the cone or the locknut that you're turning.

Checking the bearing adjustment will help you to determine just what needs to move: we either back off on the bearing cone to loosen, or bear down with the locknut to tighten. There exists just the slightest bit of play across the axle threads, between the cone and its locknut; our decisions here shove their package toward or away from the bearings. Position your wrenches such that you're clasping them together between your hands, as you finish. This will provide for more leverage.

A cone and locknut might turn simultaneously, for small distances at least. Alas our friend Travis advises that

this method can twist the axle. This said, Campagnolo's technical literature confirms that their some of their recent cassette hub axles are tightened by this very method: we're meant to grip both locknuts at once, so that the cones and locknuts might be made to move simultaneously. One can only imagine that improved designs and materials allow this discretion.

The scientific approach to hub adjustment enlists an axle vise, but to my experience we can almost always get what we need without one. It is hard not to notice when a hub is too loose, when the wheel is mounted in the bike. You can move the rim laterally, in the frame. You set the bike down and it rattles; suddenly everyone knows you need to fix that.

It is more difficult to know if you're riding a hub too tight. The offending wheel becomes less efficient in its duties, but it's not likely you specifically notice this. The wind; that damned pizza; all the beer; so many things may slow us down. Pop the wheel out and check on its axle, if you're worried about it.

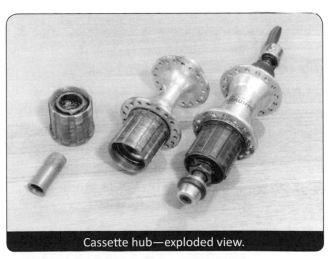

Cassette hub—exploded view.

Bent axles are identified easily enough. They'll bind at some point, when rotated, and the hub's adjustment would be inconsistent: on-again, off-again. The situation becomes all the more obvious, removing the axle and rolling it on a pane of glass. Any replacement axle's thread-

Axle seems bent? Roll it on glass to check.

ing and length would need to match the original—unless you were converting a Q/R hub to use a solid axle, or vice versa.

I cannot afford Campagnolo hubs, but they impress me nonetheless, not least because even the newer ones incorporate grease ports. These were traditionally set at midpoints along the hub body, shielded beneath a rotating band set around the hub's midsection; modern examples ride midway up the freehub splines. Either will open upon only the narrowest of channels, meaning for a pinpoint grease gun.

The bearing adjustment mechanism aboard Campagnolo's newer Record, Chorus, and Daytona hubs is also pretty cool. A solitary 2.5 mm Allen key (or Phillips screwdriver, in the case of Daytona) loosens a collar on the neutral side, which in turn is rotated to tighten or loosen the bearing cones. Said collar

bears a set of 21 mm flats, if you need to do this with the wheel in the frame; we would otherwise just twirl the thing closed with the fingertips.

The hubs themselves are taken apart with a pair of 5 mm Allen screws. Each end of the axle provides for the requisite fittings; the two are simply turned against each other. The freehub is also excused in a distinct fashion. We spy a locknut of the usual style immediately outboard of the freehub body, and this spins off to release it, but this locknut itself will sometimes be secured with a small locking screw of its own— if a diminutive bolt-head features along the locknut's side, it must first be loosened with a 2 mm Allen wrench.

The unique Campagnolo UT-HU080 tool is required to successfully remove and install some Campagnolo freehubs. Everything leaps out and scatters, otherwise. Our mediating device is only a curious loop of wire, which holds the freehub palls and their springs in place as their freehub is lifted away. We clip it into place just as soon as the pall mechanism becomes visible, and it occupies this position until everything (or its replacement) is safely home. Other hubs make their own provisions in this regard, by incorporating a trim wire band around the palls. Do not bend this any more than you would the dainty HU080! You would need to push in on these palls with a small screwdriver or similar, in the latter case, to remount the freehub body aboard its hub.

There are definitely better and worse ways to box a bike for shipment. The wrong approach can easily cause a bike to be damaged or even destroyed in transit, irrespective of how the UPS guy happens to be feeling that day.

Bike boxes are quite large to begin with, but it's only upon leaving the industry that we find the real excesses. Those bicycle boxes I've seen coming from the airlines are just *ridiculously* huge. No wonder they charge so much, passing out boxes like that!

Your bike is more secure if it's not bouncing around the insides of some disposable cavern. The box and bike should sort of brace each other, to make for a more solid whole.

The hard cases will always provide the best protection. Alternately, shops that sell bikes tend to have **BIKE BOXES** kicking around. Tandem-sized boxes are less common; you'd likely have a hunt before you. The recumbents most likely need special recumbent boxes, best obtained from your friendly local 'bent dealer.

You will want to pack a few tools if you plan to reassemble your bike at its destination. The recipe may vary,

Bike packaging.

dependent upon your mount, but in all likelihood you would at least want some Allen wrenches, a pump, and a pedal wrench. You should also figure out if it's possible or necessary to save the box, together with the bits of bike packaging detritus described below.

It might make sense to stow the bike box somewhere, if a local replacement cannot be found. There are not many others that would happen to fit a bicycle. Upright bike boxes are increasingly standardized—one size will probably fit all—but the same cannot be said for recumbent bikes. The 'bents often need one for the frame, and another for the wheels and seat; what we call the

parts box. A set of Rans boxes may be the most universal, last I checked, in that it should fit either long or short wheelbase bikes. I don't think I've ever heard of anyone charging for bike boxes, incidentally—that would strike me as shady.

The front forks on any boxed bike are almost always flipped around backward, to conserve space. The bars also need to come off, with or without the stem— here again, the modern face plate stems simplifies things. The box itself needs to span from the fork to the rear of the back wheel, at the very least. It is also possible to ship a bike with both wheels removed, though it's a bit more complicated as well.

We pull the skewers from any

wheels that are removed, to further save on the space. The axle ends are then capped with **BIKE PACKAGING**, to keep them from gouging the frame or its box. The braces used in the fork dropouts and on both sides of a mounted rear wheel are just as ubiquitous; any shop that sells bikes should be able to set you up.

If you do leave the wheel on, you want to shift into the lowest gear so that the derailleur is moved all the way toward the bike's interior. It will be safest there.

The boxing is really not so complicated, once you have the right box. You remove the front wheel, release the air from each tire and remove the seat and pedals. The fork's dropout brace should be all the way forward, and most likely down on the box's floor. (Some Rans LWB bikes see it resting on a short stack of Styrofoam pillows, to provide for a more fitting angle.)

You do want to keep the box in its original shape. Beware of suspicious bulges; there can be none of that. Imagine there's a wicked machine at the end of the conveyor belt; anything such just gets sheared off. There is only one trick for this, with the upright bikes—with the front wheel removed and the bike kneeling on front fork and rear wheel, slip the front wheel right over the neutral side crank arm. It just slides in between the spokes. You then maneuver the wheel up close to the frame. Be sure to slip a piece of packaging between the front wheel's axle end and the box. There are little round bits designed just for this purpose, for Q/R and bolt-on axles both.

The drop bars can curl around the top tube; the flatter bars may sneak in wherever their controls allow them to fit. Bar ends and aero bars should probably get removed. The stem and bar control levers may be left loose as well, to better go with the flow. You might even release a cable or two—the front brake, for example—to allow the bars to slide into a better spot in the box.

The very last thing is to tie it all together. We use zip ties, but whatever works. Assume everything will rattle around a bit during shipment. Tape cardboard or T-shirts over any paint worth preserving. Do not toss the small parts into the box itself, lest they disappear forever; throw them into a smaller box or bag or something. It will be much easier to find. Be sure to include the complete wheel skewer set, any loose stem parts and any seatpost collar that would be capable of falling off.

If you do have to take the rear wheel out to ship, go ahead and remove the rear derailleur as well. This will better protect the derailleur hanger. Just turn out the hanger bolt; there should be enough slack in the derailleur's cable to set it out of the way, between the chainstays. Tape plastic bags or something all around it, as well as any loose chain, if the paint has any art left to it. Also make sure the frame is not resting on the chainrings—either remove the cranks, or see to it that the frame's bottom bracket shell is balanced atop a smaller, sturdier box within the bike box, so that the chainrings are not bearing the bike's weight.

The first tendency is to overdress; don't. Maybe you want to pack something extra, if your distances are ambitious, but more usually you want to feel a little underprotected as you walk out the door. You're not sitting down with a lift ticket; you're staying active.

The coolest thing about winter riding has to be the clothes you get to wear. To my experience, it seems best to go as kind of a granola bandit. A lot of the technical sports gear is pretty worthwhile, and you really don't want to leave anything exposed. Not on the super cold days, at least. I grew up in Minnesota, so for me the cold sets in at some point below freezing. I would recommend starting out with the black, form-fitting head sock we call the balaclava. The top can get folded so it just covers your ears, on the warmer days, though more often I find myself wearing a cut-off T-shirt sleeve as a headband. The weight is just about right, and it fits under the helmet nicely.

In the snow I would further recommend some kind of dedicated cycling jacket. These are shells, cut to better fit the cycling profile, just loose enough to accommodate layers beneath. The armpit zippers may be the single most useful things about these—they help with climate control, without baring your chest and neck to the icy wind.

As for the hands, the good old-fashioned chopper mitts may still provide us the best choices, or at least the cheapest, for the deep cold anyway. These of course are the traditional two-piece Minnesotan mittens, the same things I used on my paper route when I was a kid.

Following extended experiments, my preference for winter riding footwear has broadened to include any waterproof boots I don't need to polish. (The feet tend to get sprayed with plenty of snow salt in the winter, fenders or no, and this crap really does a number on leather.) As with most other things, the local Goodwill is a great source.

I have never had the slightest interest in the form-fitting booties, meant to cover cycling shoes in the cold. Clipless pedals do not strike me as a good idea at all, over the ice. I think I'd rather walk.

XIII. Winter Riding

For special added effect, come the thaw, you might slap a pair of cross-country skiing gators over the tops of your boots. They keep your feet nice and dry, and raise the practiced eyebrow as well. I'll never forget the reaction I got from a couple punk rockers, decked-out to the nines, up by the local art school: "Watch it, space hero!" I laughed all the way home.

Working as a messenger in Minneapolis, there was at least one day in my first year when an excess of snow forced downtown to shut down. We got to go home early. I recall another day as well, over the third winter, when the frigid cold snapped the palls in my freewheel. I had to walk off the balance of my packages, but I cannot even imagine trading in for some car that may never start.

Freehubs and freewheels both are pretty famous for failure, in the deep cold. The palls either seize in place or simply come apart. It just coasts in either direction, only technically connected to the wheel.

This may be the cross you bear, if you are set on coasting through the winter. An ailing freewheel might be removed and revived with Phil's Tenacious or motor oil, dropped into the seam around its backside, but that's about all we could do. Spin the freewheel in your hands as you do this, to work it in; you will hear the difference the oil makes. Just douse the thing, until the oil begins to leak out the far side.

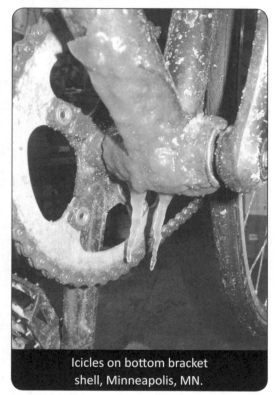

Icicles on bottom bracket shell, Minneapolis, MN.

The same might be done with free-hub bodies, once the hub is taken apart. I imagine the better-quality freehub bodies hold their own somewhat better, as do some of the new high-zoot singlespeed free-wheels, but we're still not in any position to speak of promises.

Derailleurs, too, are vulnerable. They don't actually die; they just stop moving. Irrespective of anything else, a confluence of factors directs us toward the fixed gear bikes in the winter.

Just as the skis open to horizons well beyond the cracked plastic sleds of our childhood, so too the fix takes us past the precarious freewheels. I skied downhill as a kid, and the fix recalls that experience. Where the ski edges are carved into the snow to set a course, the fixed wheel's momentum is momentarily paused to similar effect. The comparison takes a bit of imagination, I realize—we are holding lines against circles—but the reflex itself is in some ways pretty similar.

It gets to the point where you can correct inadvertent skids in motion by pushing back on the pedals. The rear wheel starts sliding out from under you; you press its pedals in the opposite direction. Any kind of freewheel action, you get none of this; all you can do is coast. That back wheel becomes passive and ambivalent; less of a ski and more of a sled.

These things said, a solid case may also be made for wintering aboard the singlespeed mountain bikes. It kind of depends on the weather. The snow tends to be dry, on the days cold enough to threaten the freewheels' integrity, and thus more easily tamed by our thin-wheeled fixed gears. Yet these quiet, crystalline afternoons are bracketed by their opposites, when the heaps of heavy wet snow cannot possibly melt fast enough—the fix's trim pizza-cutters slice like swords, scraping for the bottom of the pan regardless, and we find ourselves quite stuck. These other days, the snow's very softness suggests that the air is not cold enough to shatter the freewheels' palls, and of course the fat knobby tires are more in their element.

Flexibility is key. For quite some time I just *knew* in my heart of hearts that the thinner road tires were the best for riding in the snow, because this was my experience. Where mountain bike tires skidded across the surface, thin tires seemed to cut through the fluff, to better grip the hard-pack beneath. But that was circumstance—I was working as a messenger, and almost all my winter riding was in downtown Minneapolis. The City put much energy toward keeping the streets downtown nearly snow-free through the winter—in part by plowing over any available bike lanes, unfortunately—and so it was that 700 x 20c road tires made good sense in January. It was only years later, ranging further afield and rediscovering the snow banks deep enough for building good snow forts, that I began to see how the knobby tires can do some good, where the plowing is less thorough. For a while anyway, until any serious melting happens—and, of course, assuming you're not in any hurry. The knobby tires will always be slower. But it's the season for it, if ever there was one.

It is best to limit the winter's sore abuses to one unlucky bike, if and when possible, but a case may be made for a pair of them. I know plenty of people who take track bikes without hand brakes through winter after winter, clipless pedals and all; others who swear by singlespeed mountain bikes; at least a couple who dash recumbent delta trikes through the snow. The salient point is that it can be done.

Fresh snow is slower going. It does offer a bit more traction, which may be preferable to dancing around on the compacted cookie-cutter snow. Any surface reflecting any kind of light can cause bigger problems. It is best to avoid the slick spots, where this can be managed, and we are usually able to do so.

If you do find yourself riding on the ice, try not to make and sudden moves. There's no better way to lose it than yanking on the brakes. I do run a front hand brake on my fixed gears, but I barely touch it at all, in the snow. Staying upright is more about controlling the speed, with the legs. Skidding also gets to be a lot easier, even for an oldster like myself.

Winter riding can require additional patience, in traffic. The snow reduces roads to tracks and stripes, just wide enough for solitary lines of cars. Their simple yet relentless momentum can make it feel like you're just supposed to get the fuck out of the way, on the bike in the snow. On a bad day it might even seem that insurance premiums are the only things keeping you from getting flattened. We make it up and more in the summertime, slicing through the gridlock and all that. In the meanwhile, it must be said that winter riding really highlights the everyday relevance of crucial improvements such as the Midtown Greenway in Minneapolis. There are all kinds of things we can say about the whole process of hurry, as it relates to winter. There is nothing remotely natural about trying to rush while the world is frozen around you—to call it "counterintuitive" is already too much effort.

The winter is not a good time for those bikes vain enough to eschew **FENDERS.**

It's hard to miss these elegant creatures—the frame and fork close in right around the tire, clearing the mud's flight path all the way up your backside. The purest track bikes offer the fenders no mounting holes; the sleekest of sidepull brakes likewise deny them any openings. The vaguely enhanced aerodynamics may or may not be worth getting your ass soaked.

Questions around a frame's fender clearance are sometimes resolved with seat-post-mounted fenders, which will fit just about any bike. Suspension forks often lack fender-mounting holes, but we find some to plug right up in their steerer tubes.

The long bolt-on full fender sets provide the best protection. The earliest versions of these were made with hard, brittle plastic. They were famously vulnerable to breakage, especially in the deep cold, but even these were a nice update on the original steel bicycle fenders—lighter, adjustable, rust-free. The better full fender sets now available also use a far more pliable plastic; it takes hits much better.

The full fender set's struts end in little hooks, meant to join eyelets on the frame and fork, by means of short M5 screws. (We might substitute a pair of rack mounting clamps, alternately, for bikes lacking the requisite eyelets.) The far ends of the struts pass through odd little clamp bolts riveted in pairs to the fender's sides. Once attached at the dropouts, the fender is tightened down at appropriate distances from the tire. The arrangements allow us to adjust the fender's position so that it faithfully follows the curve of the wheel, about half an inch out, where it will provide the best protection.

thicker, more adhesive snow that sticks to the tires, and the clip-on sets seem to handle this stuff better. Snow will sometimes build up between the wheels and

Winter brakes.

The clip-on fenders are not encumbered with any struts. Their mounting brackets are bolted on at the fender holes; the rear one also clips on to the base of the seat tube. As the name implies, simple finger-tightened hardware lets us un-clip them in a hurry, in case you and the bike end up going to prom or something. The clip-on fenders are also good for touring, precisely because they can be taken down like this. All the better to put the bike in the box.

The clip-on fenders are sold for maybe half what the full sets go for, but their coverage is not as thorough. During winter, conditions occasionally produce a

the full fender sets, until such a point when it rubs upon the tire, but the clips are pliable enough to bend out of the way and let it pass.

I no longer have much use for the whale-tail seatpost-mount fenders, in part because they're supposed to sit too high to do much good at all, but also because they are continually knocked out of line with the wheels they're meant to watch over. There begets a whole new adjustment to keep track of, the fender's alignment, which is ridiculous—unless you're able to mount the fender down between the chainstays on the seat tube, so that it shoots out between the seatstays.

If this book holds any ambition in particular, it is to help readers avoid the drama and the tedium that can visit with emergency roadside repairs. It is hard to imagine a good time to break down by the side of the road, lucky coincidences notwithstanding, but a life without risk is not one worth leading. Right? The flat tire's abrupt announcement might not be so relevant itself, from the long view. Maybe the issue is with a society which really struggles to realize that shit just happens, sometimes. We need more allowances for *whatever*, and we need them now.

It hurts no one to be ready for roadside repairs, irrespective of whatever the cool kids happen to be doing. A good road kit will have at least something to say in just about any foreseeable circumstance, but there do exist scenarios will find us walking home regardless. These are what we must strive to intercept before leaving, using the techniques outlined in this volume.

The range of roadside repair scenarios is discussed in more detail in the pocket-sized *Roadside Bicycle Repair*. Any worthy road kit should include a pump, spare tube(s) for all those wheel sizes in your care, as well as anything you'd need to remove a wheel. You should be able to find everything you need down at your friendly local bike shop. Note that older bikes may require tools not found in some modern kits, be it a 14 mm socket to tighten up the crank bolts or a 13 mm box wrench for an ancient steel stem.

The ubiquitous Parmesan cheese containers from the supermarket can come in handy for storing road kits, when they're not busy storing the sunglasses. The size is just big enough, it fits nicely in the side pocket of a messenger bag, and best of all nothing is going to accidentally stab the spare tube. Throw a rag up top, under the lid.

Your **FLAT TIRE** is only a pain in the ass if you need to be somewhere. Excluding that small clique of readers with the curious mono-blade forks, you first want to take the wheel off. This will often be easier if you flip the bike upside down. Shift down to the smallest gears, if applicable, if the flat is out back. It's easier to pull the wheel out this way, and

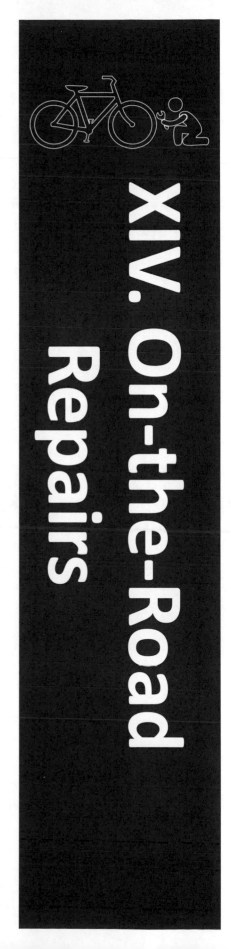

XIV. On-the-Road Repairs

you will also know where to set the chain on the way back in.

Is it raining, or really cold out? Maybe you can go do this inside somewhere, if all you have is the wheel and your bag—campus-type buildings, back entrances, whatever works. You may want to lock the rest of the bike outside, depending.

Do what you can do to get any remaining air out of the tube. You're not creating a vacuum or anything, but the more the tire can move around, the easier it will be removed. The tire may be kind of stuck to the rim, if it has been on there awhile. Trace the tire's bead with your fingertips all the way around the wheel, first one side and then the other. The tire will back off as you do so. It is possible to replace an inner tube without fully removing the tire—you can just leave one bead parked on the rim—but you always want to make sure that you check the tire for any damage or debris.

It is sometimes quite obvious just what made the flat—some nail jabbed into the tire, a gash along its sidewall—but it is more common that you would need to mount a search. Pick a point on the tread, above the tire label for example, and run its full circle through your hands. Let your fingers gingerly sweep the insides for any spikes, with the thumbs doing the same on the outside. It would be best to sweep the whole tire a couple of times, actually. Find anything? Dig debris out with a safety pin, or a big paperclip even; whatever you happen to have. Press the

tiny glass sliver out from the back with a key if you need to.

What about the sides of the tires? See any rips? It does not matter how small; the tube will still try its damnedest to sneak through. Sidewalls are much thinner than the treads, so this does happen sometimes.

Especially ambitious road debris can gouge the tire's sidewall, but the tires would sooner gore themselves on the bike's very own brake pads. Maladjusted pads will carve balding streaks all the way around the tire, like malignant comet tails. Smaller troubles on the sidewalls can be mended with a tire boot, described momentarily, but we can never know where the comets may land. Any tire with balding sidewalls should ideally be replaced, irrespective of how unblemished its tread happens to appear. (Nor would it make sense to try riding such a tire at lowered air pressure, because this in itself would increase the chances of pinch flats.)

Smaller rips and gashes along a tire's sidewall might be mended with a **TIRE BOOT**, which steps in beneath the surface to provide moral support. Tear a silver dollar-sized corner off that last twelve-pack; back it up with a stretch of duct tape. Stick this to a piece of wax paper, or plastic, and throw it in your kit. You might save the scraps from that last roll of Velox, alternately—the nice thick rim tape? Double up a couple pieces, right over the gash. See to it that the booted sidewall is not faced against any generators or dynamos, lest the wee rips tear into chasms.

The oldest and the most doctrinaire road and track bikes sometimes still find use for the **SEW-UP TIRES**, which are glued in place around distinct sew-up rims. A royal pain in the ass they are, though fortunately an increasingly obsolete one as well. The more usual clincher tires are held in place by their beads, which are made of either wire or Kevlar. The one is more usual; the other is more of a lightweight racing thing. Wire beads are not easily bent; Kevlar beads allow for the magical folding tires.

Note that one side of a Kevlar-beaded tire must be mounted on the rim, prior to reinstalling the tube. It would not be possible to seat the tube in the tire before installing the pair together, as we would like to do with the wire-beaded tires. (Kevlar is better known for its protective qualities—against glass; against the bad guys—the beads are more of a side project. "Kevlar belt" indicates a tire with this sort of flat prevention.)

Up at the shop, we like to line up the tube's valve with the tire's logo, to better facilitate flat-spotting the next time it happens. If you are absolutely shocked to find a Vulcan war dart protruding from your tire approximately one-quarter of the way around from its logo, in other words, you would at least have some idea where the hole may be in the tube.

You will have exactly a pair of options, fixing a flat. The spare tube represents the easier one, especially if you're in any kind of a hurry. Inflate the tube until it nestles easily within the tire casing.

The beads found on lower-quality tires often fit their intended wheels only loosely. They'll slip right back in place, without effort. In such cases, it is important to lay the wheel flat on the ground before reinflating the tube. The weight of the wheel itself might be enough to seat the tire off-center on the wheel; laying the wheel flat as you begin inflating the tube leaves the bead installed evenly all the way around.

The guarantees provided by the better tightly fitting tires are more reliable, but as a rule it is always best to avoid using tire levers to reinstall a tire. The tighter things get, the easier it becomes to accidentally pinch a hole in the new tube. Seat one bead all the way around the wheel, then scoot it toward the wheel's midsection. Rims tend to feature shallow valleys down their centers, and parking one bead here loosens things up just enough to make the opposite bead's installation a bit easier. Start the second bead at the valve stem, working outward with the hands in both directions at once.

Patching a tube takes longer. You will of course need to wait for the glue to fully dry, but you'll need to find the hole first. This is not always easy to do, lacking a bucket of water to dunk it in, or the peace and quiet to listen for the hole. You might even need to go find a special place, just for this task. Inflate the tube really big, then run it past your ear and cheek, listening for that tiny rush of air.

Beyond the flat tires, the biggest threat to concern our wheels is that they would be knocked out of true. You packed a spoke wrench, right? Flip the bike upside down and true the wheel as best as possible against the brake pads. You might be inspired to leave the brake's quick-release open for the ride home, depending.

It is sometimes possible to account for a **BROKEN SPOKE** through simple treachery, by over-tightening those spokes featuring to either side. This could be neither righteous nor just, from the wheel's

Pamir Hyper-Cracker on-the-road cassette tool.

perspective, but you'd probably get away with it. The wheel would be left considerably more vulnerable to further troubles, going this route—you would definitely want to take it easy, until you were able to stop and actually replace the spoke—but that's for later, after the bad apple grudgingly rolls you home.

The sad saga of the broken spoke yields yet another reason to tour on the cassette hubs. Their design also happens to simplify spoke replacement. We even have special tools for just such purposes. Recall that we need two levers to remove

the cassettes, one for the lockring and a second for the cogs? The Pamir Hyper-Cracker, the Stein Mini Cassette tool and Unior's diminutive 1669 each enlist the drivetrain itself in the first function, while using the frame for the other.

You slip the Hyper-Cracker on to the lockring and replace the wheel in the frame, with the tool's arm catching on the chainstay. Turning the cranks will pry the lockring loose; turning the wheel forward tightens it back in place. Is that cool or what? The Pamir tool even provides hollows for 14- and 15-gauge spoke nipples, to true up the wheel when you're done.

We find no such luck for the old and tired freewheel hubs. There have already been far too many distinct extraction tools to consider. You would need to pack the freewheel remover specific to your equipment, if you went out touring, because its twin may not be found down at the five-and-dime. You would also need some serious leverage to operate your freewheel's extractor, and this is the bigger issue. It is sometimes possible to remove freewheels by means of a large adjustable wrench, but I wouldn't want to run around with one.

Freewheels can also be removed by means of a bench vise, should you happen to come across one. And you never know, that farmhouse up on the hill may have a vise out in their barn, but it also sounds like they have some dogs . . . Replacing a spoke can become an existential quandary, which is ridiculous given the alternatives.

We carry spare spokes by attaching them to one of the frame tubes. Some of the finer old tour bikes did this quite well, by wearing pairs of diminutive spoke bridges atop the chainstay—over on the drive side, if they're sharp. It was a nice enough detail in its own right, like the old chain hangers or the front derailleur tabs, but the spokes would also protect the chainstay's paint from the chain. They really thought things through, back then. And, as best demonstrated by Surly's lovely Long Haul Trucker, sometimes they still do.

You can tape a few spokes to some quiet and out-of-the-way place, alternately, like inside the neutral chainstay or something. Don't forget the nipples!

The oldsters provide slots for three spokes—the drive pull, drive neutral, and front wheel sizes—but you might just stock up with spokes in the drive-side pull length. These are the most likely to fail, and they can usually fill in for the other sizes.

If your brakes begin to squeak as you're riding, the best thing you can do is to try and ignore it. Seriously. If this is not an option for you, perhaps it is time to upgrade to drum brakes.

So long as the roads are either dusty or wet, as is generally the case, odds are best you can't do anything about noisy disc or rim-mounted brakes in the first place.

The braking surfaces would need a good bath at the least, and the rim brake pads may be due for sound filing. Neither step easily happens on the sidewalk.

The **RUBBING BRAKES** are sooner dealt with. First make sure the offending wheel is properly centered and secured in its dropouts, by sighting down the frame and the tire's center line. This is often the only issue. The road calipers and center-pull brakes are occasionally knocked out of adjustment. Make sure the nuts securing their tail bolts are totally snug.

Most cable-driven braking systems incorporate methods to manually center the brakes; most usually a small screw pointed in laterally toward the wheel. To tighten one of these is to edge the nearest brake pad away from its side of the rim. Work in small increments, and keep an eye on the pads as you work. Some centering arrangements execute quick decisions; others take their time about things. Wiggle any linear pull or caliper brake arms back and forth across their bosses just a bit after each adjustment, to help the new science sink in.

Modern dual pivot sidepulls have centering screws of their own, worn as rank up top on a shoulder. Press hard; the faces will want to strip.

Lacking the appropriate offset brake wrench, the older sorts are best centered manually. Grip both the mounting bolt and its nut, confirm that both are fully tightened and gradually turn the pair of them simultaneously.

Disc brakes typically bear large dials outside the pads, turned with a 5 mm Allen key or the fingers to modify the fixed pad's position.

Are the brakes getting a bit too loose? Every cable-driven braking system should feature at least one barrel adjuster, at some point along its cable. Turning a barrel out increases the cable tension, drawing the pads closer to the rim.

Many barrel adjusters wear knurled collars about their necks, which may be twirled all the way down to their bases, to affirm a given adjustment. But the barrels may also run empty, once they're turned all the way out, in which case it's best to spin them all the way back home. The cable itself can be further tightened down at the component's binder bolt, before fine-tuning the adjustment anew. It is always good to fill the barrel, whenever it runs empty.

The barrel adjusters also provide our best hopes in dealing with the derailleurs, on the road. It is not at all likely that any of the derailleur limit screws have rattled loose. Their diminutive threads hold adjustments well enough. And as I discovered years ago, before beginning my time at the bike shops, any random adjustments to the derailleur screws can be expected to mess things up—the more, the better.

There are only a couple of scenarios in which it may be useful to adjust the limit screws, on the road. We can compensate for the broken link and its shortened chain by dialing the rear derailleur's low limit in a few rotations, just enough to block the derailleur from trying to embrace the largest cog or two. Otherwise, it eagerly stretches itself to death.

We may also use the same screw to account for a bent derailleur hanger, alternately. A bad bend may leave the derailleur's cage riding perilously close to the spokes, in the largest cog, or even hopping right over. Turning the L screw in keeps it back at a safe distance from the spokes. Alternately, slot an Allen wrench into the derailleur's mounting bolt, grasp its extended cage and see if you can't slowly, cautiously lever it back into something like the proper alignment.

As we're riding around, the most common complaint we hear about the drivetrain is that the chain "skips out of gear." This condition most likely descends from one of three conditions: either the drivetrain parts are worn, or the rider is less familiar with the bike's shifting system, or the shift cable has fallen out of adjustment.

Not everyone is taught how to use their shift levers. It's not like there's a test or anything. No big deal; generally easy enough to fix. Some high-end derailleurs are claimed to shift under load, but I can guarantee that none of them actually enjoy it: better to ease up on the pedals and shift before you actually need to. Most levers will require a slight over-shift before falling back to land on the desired gear; just takes practice. This settled, I would next want to check on the cable's tension. The shifting accuracy is more about the shift cable's tension, which is enforced by means of the barrel adjuster. If all of this is as it should be, I might then start to wonder about the implications of worn parts. It is difficult to recognize chain wear by sight, but the toasted hub gears may be more obvious. The teeth on the smaller cogs would be much more pointed. We expect the two conditions to feature together.

Attempts to force the shift levers past their natural stopping points can make for bigger, more intractable problems. Shifters respond poorly to force. It is the easiest way to ruin the plastic ones.

Older or more stubborn bikes may ignore our work with the barrel adjusters if they're hiding rust in the cable housing. Any of this would need to be overhauled or replaced, to resolve the situation. Adding oil to the chain can make shifting smoother—up to a point, at least—but it remedies neither worn parts nor cable problems.

The darkened corners of most bike shops are cluttered with abandoned chain clippings, among other detritus. Most chains are cut to fit individual bikes, and riders very rarely ask after their remainders. Yet these very segments can become singularly useful when repairing broken chains. Modern chains are assembled with master links or special pins, but on tours especially the spare links can be good to have. No big thing; just throw 'em in your bag on the way out. Whether or not current opinion leaders happen to find scavenging hip, ill-advised, or flatly irredeemable is not necessarily relevant to everyday life. It can make a lot of sense a lot of the time, and that's really all we need to know.

The growing numbers of community-oriented bike shops selling used bikes and parts bear testament to this. The art of reuse has carried from strength to strength in recent years, to the point that it is generally possible to skip the dumpster entirely, at the more interesting bike shops at least. Most of what we'd be looking for is on sale inside already, at prices we can deal with.

Not everything can be brought back to life, usefully or otherwise—dead frames, sorely bent forks, physically broken parts—yet this leaves plenty to play with. Any parts taken from department store bikes can safely be considered the worst possible options, and the old French-threaded bikes are perhaps best left alone as well, but beyond that anything may well go. Scavenged parts are the red-headed stepchildren of the bike industry, abandoned to the shadows for capricious reasons, yearning only to show their real worth.

One small topic we might explore here would be the washers. Harvest them. Take a short section of the aforementioned chain remnant completely apart, to start: the rollers, between the links, fit perfectly around our regular M5 bicycle screws. These may lend the screws attaching your rack or fender just enough clearance to avoid dragging on the chain. Keep an eye out; this problem is neither rare nor quiet. Not all the pump harnesses meant to mount beneath the water bottle cages are necessarily compatible with all the cages themselves, to take another example. The chain

XV. Scavenging, Rust, and Security

rollers may prove to be useful in such circumstances as well.

Rear derailleurs will sometimes shift into top gear a little easier if we slide some kind of thin spacer on to the fixing bolt, to rest between the derailleur and the frame's hanger, and it happens that either the larger (rear) chainring bolt spacers or the 10 mm (standard rear) hub spacers fit this bolt just fine. You might need to play with the limit screws and the cable tension a bit to really get this going, but the spacer occasionally makes a positive contribution where other approaches fail—by moving the derailleur slightly further afield, it effectively resets a tired spring's resting position.

Seat falling apart? No spares? Make a cover for it.

When the count is finally made, simple washers will rank well among the unsung heroes of our craft. A new cartridge bottom bracket sometimes leaves the spider crank hanging just slightly too close to the frame—old and new spindles might have been measured differently; the chainrings may suddenly press against the frame—but we just slip a common freewheel spacer betwixt

cartridge and frame shell, to relieve the pressure. We want to keep as many threads anchored inside the frame shell as possible, so it is best to use really thin spacers here as well; I would be especially careful doing this on bikes with aluminum bottom bracket shells. This remedy should be further restricted to those sealed-cartridge bottom brackets employing hollow cups which do *not* feature a lip around the exterior, which would prevent us from fully tightening the hollow against the bearing cartridge. The hollow cup needs to bottom out on the cartridge itself, rather than the frame, in order to keep the cartridge from shifting around under load. But perhaps there would be *another* hollow cup that could work in such a case, if you're already in the habit of saving useful parts. You get the idea.

It is more common to use a stack of the wider, plastic spacers found between cassette cogs to line up a particular cassette cog at a specific point along a freehub body, when switching a bike over to singlespeed. You want to line up the cog with the chainring as best you can; the handful of spacers makes this easy enough.

Older 7-speed Shimano HG cassettes are often built around three tall and narrow screws, which answer to a 4 mm socket. I don't know if anyone actually makes a 4 mm socket, but you can make your own, by locking a couple of nuts against each other over a M5 screw. Our ubiquitous M5 bike screws commonly have 4 mm heads to them; these are essentially upside-down sockets. (More modern 7-, 8-, and 9-speed cassettes are too often built in accordance with a much cheesier plan; pressed together with fancy rivets basically. You can still get at the individual cogs or spacers, but you must drill them free.)

But I shouldn't get started with all this. I'd need to drag all the parts boxes out of the basement, and they're damned heavy. Suffice it to say that the more you get into it, the easier scavenging gets to be.

Salvaged or no, any bike may face the dread specter of **RUST**. There are things we can do to forestall the confrontation, but the days are long, and the simple truth is that a lot of bikes never get the help they need here.

Excluding (perhaps!) the carbon fiber bikes, you want to make sure the frame's seat tube is thoroughly greased. The bottom bracket threads should always be greased, whether poured from concrete or carved from balsa wood. Other, smaller problems sometimes arise, but as the rust concerns our bikes, these two areas will provide for our most pressing concerns.

If something is seized in place, the classic solution with steel bikes is some kind of a torch. Heating the metal expands it, briefly creating an opening we might exploit. But not everybody has access to that kind of firepower, and experience

suggests we rarely ever need it. Massive blasts of heat mess up the paint, and can weaken some frame materials as well.

If you are dealing with a seized bottom bracket, you'll do best to flip the bike upside down on the floor, for even the mightiest repair stands absorb some portion of our energy. You also need some means to make sure the tool does not slip from its target, as well as a Jesus bar, which is a length of pipe just wide enough to accept the handle of the tool in use.

The modern bottom bracket cups have been thinking ahead, in that their arrangements will be much easier to wrangle upon. Current goods from Shimano, Truvativ, and others each feature broader and deeper splines, to better greet their various extraction tools.

We find a few different ways to hold these in place, from purpose-built shop adaptations to the carpenter's ubiquitous EZ-Grip clamps, but the simplest home method incorporates nothing more than a washer or two. Run down to the hardware store, grab a broad flat washer just wide enough to pass the spindle bolt through, and also one to cover the tool's body, and finger-tighten the both of them atop your extraction tool. Go get your wrench, and reef away to your heart's content. Loosen up the spindle bolt once the cup starts to give.

The only trouble comes with the damned plastic cups, as used by Shimano and a few others. You wouldn't think that plastic can rust itself in place, but it manages to. And you ask the cup nicely to step the hell out of the way, with your monster leverage, and sometimes it will simply crack instead. You would need to pry out the remainder with a screwdriver, once the cartridge is removed from the other side.

No handlebar grips? There's always inner tubes . . .

It has been my experience that a torch is more likely to melt the plastic cups in place, rather than start them on fire, but anything's possible. Check on a given cup's composition before you get all heavy; see what a knife or a file does to its edge.

There may be a way around this, fortunately. The good folks at Problem Solvers provide us with the Up-Cup #54, an alloy replacement for the lame plastic neutral cups associated with Shimano UN54 bottom brackets. It is threaded to our favorite English dimensions, in widths to coincide with either 68 mm or 73 mm bottom bracket shells.

A survey of older bottom bracket hardware makes clear how lucky we've been, more recently. There was much less for tools to hold on to back then, over on the neutral side especially. Thus do our excavations being over on the drive side with the fixed cup, with the oldsters. It is often possible to convince a fixed cup wrench such as Park's HCW-4 to stay on top of the job until the mission is complete, but you will need to provide it some guidance.

Where modern bottom bracket extraction tools are able to dig into their splined targets for a useful bite, the clumsy old fixed cup wrench is too easily distracted. It trends off to angles and drops angrily to the floor, left to its own devices. Maintain a slight pressure on the wrench, in plane with the offending cup's threads, in order to prevent this. It is possible to use a Jesus bar with these wide old wrenches, assuming you can find one to fit: hold the face in place on its cup, as you slip the tool's tail up the tube.

You first want to try moving the lockring, over on the adjustable side. This and the adjustable cup simply move together, a lot of the time. If your lockring tool only features one tooth, rather than two or three, make sure you keep this digit pressed firmly into position: it will be only too happy to slip free and strips the lockring, otherwise. The various multi-toothed lockring tools are more useful in this respect, if somewhat more particular as well; a given example may not fit every lockring it meets.

The adjustable cup spins out or at least loosens with the lockring, if you're lucky, but it's at least as likely the fucker won't even budge. The adjustable cups on old ball-and-cup sets answer to either a conspicuously flat wrench, or a wispy little spanner—Park's HCW-11 or the SPA-1, respectively. Either of these would need to be clamped in place with an EZ-Grip, before applying any serious torque, which is why we evacuate the fixed cup first. It is much easier to clamp down flat, once the bottom bracket spindle has been pulled out the far side.

You may want to enlist the help of a couple door hinges as well, or something like them, in order to provide the clamp with useful pressing surfaces. One fits over the empty cavity where the fixed cup once squatted; the other jams the wrench or spanner firmly in place atop the adjustable cup. The omnipotent EZ-Grip then climbs over everything and squeezes it all together into a supremely tight sandwich, which you gradually begin to loosen as soon as the frozen cup moves.

You only need to break the original rust bond; the struggle becomes much easier just after that.

It is unusual that such methods fail to yield results, to my experience. But we may try one last thing, before lighting upon the torch. Do you have access to a die grinder? Open an elongated box into the offending cup; something just big enough to stick with the open end of one of your wrenches. A nice big strong one, like maybe the 15 mm. You just made your own personalized custom spanner! Grip it right up there by the head with a big old crescent wrench, slide the Jesus bar over the end of this and push.

No dice? A simple propane burner is fine; oxy-acetylene is overkill. You heat up the area around the problem a minute or two, then go. See if you can chip anything plastic out of there, prior to beginning, because we could expect it to either melt or burn. Note that the jaws on the EZ-Clamps are vulnerable in this respect as well; you should set them aside and just use the tool's skeleton for this operation.

Seized seatposts are even more fun. The last time I confronted one of these, with a nice old Santana road tandem in the Calhoun Rental fleet, I found myself stripping the bike down to the frame. This allowed me to flip it upside down and clamp the seized post in a vise, whereby I was eventually able to begin swinging the frame back and forth, to finally ease the fucker loose. Just about toppled the workbench, but it worked.

Seatposts really don't provide much for useful surfaces, the old-style straight posts in particular. You might install wrench flats on your own, depending on the situation, using your Jesus bar to wind up the vise, but of course there could be no going back from this. The modern Laprade units provide for a pair of flat surfaces up top, once the mounting hardware is removed; these are easier lined up to our advantage.

Given the time, drip as much penetrating oil into the frame/post interface as possible. Let the thing sit a couple days, if you can, stopping by periodically to dribble in more oil. Once the time comes, begin by trying to rotate the post in the seat tube, to get it moving, while tugging it upward as well. You kind of screw it up, I guess we could say.

Peace Corps bikes, Mauritania, 2008.

The worst thing you can do is to try and chop the post out. An old friend presented me with just such a project, not so long ago—it was a nice old Bridgestone XO-1, unfortunately, and I could not do a thing for it. The only possible hope I could have in such a situation would involve the intervention of a machinist, which would be expensive if it even worked at all.

RUSTED SCREWS are a smaller pain in the ass. They attack anywhere it's not hot and dry, which may suggest to us that they are somewhat passive-aggressive. You don't have to be doing anything at all; eventually they just come around to fuck with you. It sucks.

They are also our Cassandra figures. When we see rust in the screws, it is time to check the rest of the bike for similar problems.

Metal threads are especially vulnerable to rust. It is rare that both a screw and its fitting are born with any intrinsic rustproofing. The microscopic gaps they require to move against each other are just wide enough to slurp up any spare water that comes along, but this is only the beginning.

Rust is in fact taking over, everything and everywhere, because this was always inevitable. The most we may hope to do is rally ourselves for heroic rearguard actions, hoisting our clever opposable digits in defiance and all that, but it's necessarily a touch pathetic. The sum of our skills is still nothing to nature.

As it relates to the bikes, rust is always easier to deal with on a preventative basis. It takes all of a few seconds to dab some grease on the threads. That is all you have to do. Stems and seatposts and steerer tubes, same thing.

There are only a couple exceptions to this. Spoke nipples are discussed on page 206; various recipes are in use. The fixing bolts securing brake components are also traditionally slopped with some kind of thread-locking compound, in place of the grease—this is meant to keep the bolts from loosening, and it also prevents their corrosion. Some manufacturers further apply thread-locker to the bottom bracket fittings, in order to spare the bearings some measure of the compression force associated with the heavier torque their installation would otherwise require. An intriguing idea, perhaps, but I am not sure how much I would trust the thread-lockers to fight the rust. Their interests would seem to converge; I might suspect a conflict of interest.

Suffice to say that it is good to strip everything down for a thorough lubrication, every now and again. Make a ritual of it. But let's get back to that little screw, shall we? The first thing to ascertain is that it has in fact seized. Drop some thin penetrating oil around its base, the T-9 for example, and let this sit for a bit. Holding the tool quite firmly, to prevent slippage, check one last time to see if the screw can be moved at all. It just may turn itself out nice and slow, if you take your time, squeaking ever so slightly through the dust.

Use your best tools, when the time comes to turn it on out, and push down really hard. Worn-down edges on the Allen wrenches in particular are inclined to slip off target. But this may not end the world, even if the poor screw does begin to strip, because it's possible you can modify the situation just enough to earn a second chance. File a pair of parallel flats on the sides, for a wrench, or see if you can cut a new slot for the screwdriver with your hacksaw. Either of these would fill out the aforementioned pathetic rearguard gesture; there could be no guarantees at all.

The bonds of rust will have grown stronger than the screw itself, if you are especially unlucky, and past a certain point its head will simply snap off. Any remainder would need to be drilled out. Is this you? Give the penetrating oil every opportunity to soak in, first. See if you can arrange for the rusted threads to be more or less level and facing up so that gravity helps ooze the oil down where it's most useful. Can you let things sit for a couple days? Even better. You might even build up a small oil reservoir, with pieces of a heavy plastic bag and duct tape, immediately around the affliction we're concerned about.

Flip the project over and do the backside a few times, if applicable, but make sure the bike is very still indeed before you grab the drill—up in a stand, preferably, or at least somewhere it won't get kicked. You will be shooting your smallest drill bit directly down the center of this dead screw; getting bumped and breaking the thing midstream would be vastly counterproductive.

It is kind of a trick, getting started. You just barely push on the drill, only enough to keep it on target, and play with the angle to keep it centered. I encourage you to take your time with this. You aim for dead center; the drill bit gets distracted and wanders off to the side; you angle the drill such that it's back on target. It's as if you're carving out a tiny bowl, scraping its sides only when you need to, always aiming back to the deepening pit.

The purpose of this tedious little exercise is merely to blaze a trail for one of the various easy-out bits, which reverse-thread backward into the stump as means to corkscrew it back out. But the original drilling may well loosen things up by itself, given enough time and good fortune.

Rust has always been a pointed and unrelenting nemesis, for the bikes, and the same could very much be said for the thieves. Locking the bikes, for quite a long time, was a fairly straightforward proposition. The standard-sized cable locks, which can all be cut quite easily, failed to deter even mildly ambitious thieves. The cheaper U-locks were something of an improvement, if not a

solution, because they employ designs wide enough and steel weak enough to fully invite wrenching defeat from car jacks. Thus did we steer people toward Kryptonite's Evolution **LOCKS,** at the least, which bend hardened steel into smaller and more useful profiles.

The trim Evo packages often leave our wheels exposed—unless you pack a spare or something—but various remedies may be applied to the situation. Kryptonite had just introduced an excellent locking skewer system, in fact, when everything suddenly changed. This was 2004. The tubular cylinder key-ways, as used throughout the industry for three decades, were suddenly found to be worthless. Any of them could be defeated quite easily, as it turned out, with the plastic body of a ballpoint pen.

This had previously been discovered in the United Kingdom in 1992, as contemporary articles indicate, but it took the internet and some wingnut in San Francisco to bring the whole charade to its screeching, acrimonious end. Rather than tell those who may have been able to help about his discovery, this petulant narcissist indulged every last juvenile fixation and posted the news to a website. And just like that, all kinds of people began losing their bikes.

The identical but more complex disc cylinder locks, as used with Kryptonite's New York series since 2000, are not afraid of ballpoints or anything else. The company had planned to introduce such equipment with its less expensive locks at the industry's annual trade show a few weeks later, as I understand it, but this loser needed to get his ego fix instead.

Kryptonite's response to the crisis was all we may have hoped for, given the problem's scale and the abruptness of its imposition. The newer laser-cut keys which all reputable manufacturers have since adopted are not known to be vulnerable to any regular household items.

Given these developments, it is surprising to see how many cylinder locks are still in active use. The disc or cylinder lock keys do wear down, over extended use—they'll still work for a while, just not as smoothly.

The manufacturer would need the number etched to the key, to provide replacements for any of them. You should write this down somewhere. Some locksmiths have the means to produce duplicates, alternately, but they need a working original to copy from.

It is best to lock a bike through its frame in well-lit and well-trafficked sorts of places, using posts that can neither move nor be disassembled.

The guarantee is a lock's plume of feathers: the more it covers, and the

less extra you have to pay for it, the better the lock is thought to be. The ⅝″ shackle extending from my huge Kryptonite New York 3000 is rated to resist 5 tons of pull strength. What is that, a tugboat? But still I'm not worried, because the guarantee was free, for up to $3,000 in coverage. The small print invariably suggests you would need the dead lock and receipts for everything, to collect remuneration—we're trusting the thieves to leave us the evidence, presumably—but the package has been able to sneak past all the lock's lawyers regardless, and this is the point of interest. I do not necessarily expect to see any compensation, in the event of troubles, but I do appreciate the gesture. Nobody's really able to do better.

We also need to account for those low enough to rob your bike of its useful parts. If the thieves have any trouble stripping our bikes to scrap, they need only look for the **QUICK-RELEASE SKEWERS**. Our forebears began with legitimate purposes, when first developing

Securing a quick-release lever with a hose clamp.

the technology—they only wanted to save time and frozen finger-fumbling, out racing. Component theft was likely less of a problem, back then.

The Q/R lever's persistent fixation upon the wheel axles suggests an unfortunate choice of emphasis—that compliance with automotive roof-racks is more important than parking a bike securely. Its association with the

be the only ones together enough to pack an Allen wrench.

The reflexive response to this oversight—to just pull the seatpost out and bring it inside—carries consequences of its own. The rain and snow rush right down the seat tube, eagerly rusting the bottom bracket in place. It's the fucking snakes again, chasing the damned mongoose around.

Cyclox locking skewer.

The amazing Pinhead locking skewers—first offered by Kryptonite, and later by On Guard—provide the wheels and seat their best defense. You might wrap hose clamps around the quick-release levers, alternately, binding their handles to the frame and fork. These are undone in

seatposts is fully conspicuous. With the rare exception of rental bikes, I struggle to imagine a scenario in which this feature becomes less than a liability. The seat height is critical to the fit, and thereby to the comfort level; why not stick with what we know? The few seconds' foresight and figuring a seat bolt would cost a thief could easily save us so much in hassles. The clever road bikes already expect such rudimentary cautions, when first they're born; why are their wider-tired kin so consistently dumbed-down? As if the roadies would

minutes, of course, but this may be just long enough to keep your bike whole. The bolt-on skewer sets hold a similar promise, on bikes without disc brakes at least. Note that neither these nor the Pinhead locking skewers should be used with disc brake-equipped wheels, up front in particular (see page 24).

The open bolt heads on wheel skewers or other components may also be paved over with Shoe Goo adhesive, finally, or even crumpled tin foil. Either can be scraped out with a small screwdriver.

The best wheels have always been built by hand. You can find machine-built composite wheels that are lighter and in some ways stronger than their more traditionally bespoken kin, but these tend to be leagues more expensive as well. Their maintenance options can also be very limited; the simplest problems suddenly require specialists. The classic recipe provides for wheels we can build and repair ourselves.

A truly fine wheel begins with double- or triple-butted spokes, to take advantage of their increased resilience and reduced weight. The DB spokes' thinner midsections flex a bit more, and this diffuses much of the stress which visits wheels in use. This makes for a more comfortable ride, and it also helps to protect the more vulnerable elbow bends we usually see up by the hubs. Spokes break quite rarely, but those that do typically fail up at their elbows.

A wheel's mass might be further reduced with alloy spoke nipples: the lighter the stone, the easier to twirl the sling-shot. The regular brass nipples are far more durable. We may even slip tiny brass washers beneath the spoke heads, to account for hub holes that have been drilled a bit wide. Wheel building quickly becomes about as intricate a science as we may have use for. Several books have been dedicated to the subject. Gerd Schraner's *Art of Wheelbuilding* enjoys a solid reputation. In keeping with this book's theme, the contribution I would hope to make concerns building wheels with used parts.

The great majority of modern wheels are assembled by machines, unfortunately, none of which have learnt to read so well. The skills required to build wheels are broadly accessible, but for the present at least the craft generally benefits from a human touch.

A solid wheel build requires a truing stand, and probably a tensiometer as well. Fit a small binder clip to the truing stand somewhere, to use as a bookmark on the spokes if ever someone happens by to ring the doorbell.

Any useful wheel must begin with a worthy hub. Things come together somewhat easier with new spokes and rims,

XVI. Building Your Own Wheels

yet novelty is not necessary to the process. I have built dozens of wheels with used rims and spokes, for my friends and myself and the rental bikes as well. I don't really buy new parts unless I actually need to.

If you are working with used parts, be sure that all the spoke nipples are of the same size. The spoke wrench should fit nice and snug, every last time. Also note that the drive-side spokes on rear wheels are often slightly longer than those over on the neutral side. This is an important discrepancy we will soon explore; suffice it here to say that you should avoid mixing up spokes from the different sides of the wheel.

With rare exception, spokes arrive in multiples of four, as do the holes drilled to hub and rim, and it is important that everything matches. Put a thumb over two spoke holes on a hub, cover the two opposite holes on that same side with your other thumb, and count the holes between your thumbs—seven indicates a thirty-six-hole hub, six means thirty-two, five is twenty-eight, and so on.

The spoke holes on the **HUBS** are offset against each other, across the two flanges. This effectively divides the rim's holes between the two hub flanges, as with even and odd numbers. Any prospective hub would need to enjoy the appropriate axle dimensions for the intended frame or fork, and would also need to align with

the drivetrain. You may not want to do a damned thing with a Suntour cassette hub, for example, because your odds for finding any useful cassettes are not good at all. (They still had a good stack of them at the old Hayes St. Freewheel in San Francisco when I worked there, but that was years ago.)

Counting holes in a hub: this one is a 36.

Alloy rims can represent a substantial improvement over the ancient steel hoops. They are lighter, stronger, and rust-free. Alas it's not so simple. Where reputable manufacturers like Mavic reliably provide us with fine examples, the aluminum rims found with department store bikes have more in common with soda cans. The distinction becomes readily obvious when truing or building a wheel—cheap rims really can't take much of a hit, and they're far too easily swayed by the suggestions of wayward spokes.

The best rims enjoy double-walled construction—the spoke nipples sprout from a distinct terrace, set above the tire bead's ground floor. We may also look for a flawless seam, machined braking surfaces, and stainless steel eyelets around the spoke holes. We earn a marginal weight penalty with these eyelets, but they do spare the rims some stress. The spoke nipples roll their hard shoulders heavily forward as we tighten them toward the truth, executing strenuous circle-dances upon the softer alloy floor; the eyelets fly in and take the edge off. The disc brake-equipped hubs should always be built with eyelet-equipped rims.

Wheels built using the old standard of 36 spokes will take more of a beating, but not everyone is into that, so the 32-hole drilling has really emerged as a standard. Every other spoke hole on a rim may be offset to either side of a central line, but this in itself doesn't really say anything about its quality.

The tired old zinc spokes become ever more brittle, as time goes on, and they are far more inclined to rust to their nipples. But this is old news; even the department store bikes flash stainless smiles these days. DT, Sapim, and Wheelsmith enjoy good reputations for their spokes; their products tend to fail somewhat less than generic offerings. Everything looks quite similar from a distance, but up close the double-butted spokes become easy enough to spot, and eventually one begins to recognize the tiny logo outlines impressed to the spoke heads.

Bicycle spokes have traditionally been harvested in the non-butted "straight" 14-gauge size. The thinner and lighter straight 15 has really been fading out; the 14/15/14 double-butted spokes are more common these days. The straight-pull spokes charge straight out from

their burly straight-pull hubs, but their direct approach is still fairly uncommon. The flattened aero spokes, which often need specially slotted hubs of their own, are about as unlikely. (Some aero spokes are simple hooks, which can be inserted backward into a regular old non-slotted hub. These may make for workable spares, on a tour, but I wouldn't build a whole tour wheel with them.)

There is some chance you may come across the Spline Drive system, which uses bizarre starfish-shaped nipples in order to prevent us from even thinking about stripping things out. These clogged with mud far too easily, unfortunately, and so it was they went extinct.

The round Spokey nipple biscuits make it easier to bring the spokes to higher tensions, by gripping their nipples on all four sizes, but they're rarely necessary to the process. Sapim provides us with curious T-handled 5.5 mm socket wrenches, with which to dial the bases of their elite racing nipples—the long-necked giraffes, among the spoke keys. The hub-mounted nipples featured with Shimano's wheel sets are instead adjusted with miniature flat wrenches, in patient and wholly counterintuitive measures. Try this sometime; you may see what I mean.

Whichever sort of spokes you're working with, exercise caution with any nipples that cannot be made to turn on their own. Grip the spoke with your fourth hand tool right above the nipple, to prevent it from simply winding up (and eventually snapping).

When building a wheel, we also want to install an enlightened intermediary between the spokes and their nipples, to both inhibit rust and forestall their loosening. There exists some debate as to what is best for our purposes here. I caught some flak for advocating the use of blue Loctite, a removable-strength thread-locking compound, in my first repair manual. My recipe came courtesy of this guy Dave, a mechanic of twenty years, but its reception suggests the Loctite thing is a minority view. (I am not sure! I have no survey data.) Blue Loctite easily holds the spokes in place; the concern is that it does so too ambitiously. A spoke compound is no help if it prevents further tensioning and adjustment. I no longer use this method myself, but I'm not necessarily convinced it's a bad idea, because I have never had any real troubles with it—I have not yet seen a wheel built this way that cannot be trued, upon oiling its spoke threads. I may be a freak, but that is my story.

In a professional setting, it is not uncommon to hit the tops of the nipples with a lighter, thinner thread-locker such as the Three-bond, once a wheel has been built—just one little drop each, then spin the wheel for the centrifuge effect. This may be done on one side or both, depending on whom you speak with. It makes the most sense over on the rear wheel's neutral side, where the spoke tension is lesser; the drive-side spokes are more likely to be tight enough to hold their own.

A distinct theory holds that some sort of lubrication is best, for wheel builds.

We soak the nipples in oil, or dab a little grease on the threads, or maybe even both. The effort surely keeps the rust under control, but the real goal is to facilitate the spokes' achievement of a higher tension. Lubrication has that effect; it often convinces metal fittings to go just a little tighter. I know those who swear by this method, but it has always been a minority position among mechanics I know.

Personally? I began experiments with Rock "N" Roll's Nipple Cream spoke compound a few summers ago, on the advice of persons I found reasonably credible, and things seemed to work out well enough. But this is actually too bad, because I'd only recently invested in a couple tiny buckets of Wheelsmith's staid Spoke Prep compound—which, as it turns out, might last an individual mechanic for a really, really long time. The sad thing is that this purchase might *itself* have been twice as stupid, because it wasn't long thereafter that Joel Greenblatt clued me into what may be the classic spoke compound—linseed oil, of all the odd things.

Linseed is very toxic, cheap, and flammable. These others, less so. Any serious excess of the linseed oil will gum up the works, so you want to set up some kind of rationing system such that only the bottom thirds of their threads are dosed. Something like that. Designate a spare spoke as your paintbrush; dip its threads in the goo and slide this across the others.

The Loctite or Nipple Cream arrives within convenient dropper bottles.

Wheelsmith Spoke Prep comes in tiny plastic tins; you barely dip the tips of half the spokes' threads and roll them against their peers. Wheelsmith is also unique in asking us to let their pastel pastes dry thoroughly, before beginning our wheels.

You also want to decide upon a **SPOKE LACING PATTERN**, before getting started. Each pattern requires a particular spoke length, for every distinct hub-and-rim combination. Full-sized wheels may use spoke lengths from about 250 to 310 mm; the smaller recumbent and folding bike wheels make far shorter demands of their own. Shops tend to stock the sizes their bikes use the most; a few may have the brilliant Phil Wood spoke-cutting machine as well.

The **SPOKE LENGTH FORMULA** considers this lacing pattern, the number of spokes and the dimensions of both hub and rim. We used various scientific calculators and curious wall charts to determine spoke length, at the first couple shops I worked for, but in recent years it is far more common to enlist computer programs such as the ubiquitous Bike-alog, which is kept updated with hub and rim manufacturers' specifications, thereby sparing us all the tedium of measuring and entering the data ourselves. Plug in the hub and rim models, hole count and lacing pattern, and

it will spit the answers right back at you. Pretty cool. Working from home, it has become easy enough to find spoke calculators online. Whatever you do, avoid guessing—spokes a couple of millimeters too long or short very rarely work out.

Wheels bearing more than a single cog will often require **WHEEL DISH**. The multiple gears require the axle to extend further toward the drive side than the neutral side, in order to accommodate their greater width, and this in turn means that the rim itself needs to scoot in the same

A 7-speed wheel dish: a healthier number.

direction, in order to remain centered in the frame. Wheel dish. Spoke length programs account for this, as required by hub and rim selections, suggesting sizes that are about 2 mm longer on the neutral side.

You may simply split the difference, alternately—using 299 mm spokes to cover for both the 298 and 300. It is best to use double-walled rims with such projects, lest you find yourself faced with the supremely annoying task of filing down overlong spoke ends. You can get away with leaving a spoke thread or two exposed over on the neutral side, so long as their nipples are formed of

Wheel dish? Suspend one caliper; true each side of wheel in turn.

wholesome brass, but any serious excess beyond this point may well collapse the whole damned cave. I'm thinking of this backyard science experiment of a wheel someone passed me the other day—its neutral spokes were all way the hell too short; a good half-dozen popped free of their nipples as I tried to true the thing.

Spokes braced at greater angles between hub and rim are left in stronger positions. The drive-side spokes on 8/9/10-speed 130 mm road wheels are necessarily more vulnerable than those found on 7-speed 135 mm mountain wheels, simply because of their more extreme dish. The less a wheel needs to be dished, the stronger it will be.

Shops have dedicated dishing tools, which measure a rim's relative position

against the hub's axle ends, but the wheel dish may also be sampled by flipping the wheel back and forth in the truing stand. A given stand's calipers may be less than perfectly centered themselves, but at least one should appear equidistant to the rim in either orientation. I'm in the habit of measuring wheel dish in the frames myself, because I worked as a rental mechanic for a few too many summers. The dishing tool lived eight blocks away at the main store; there was not always time for science.

Singlespeed or fixed cog wheels are not supposed to require any dish at all these days, but this really depends on what you're doing. Prior to the rise of adequately spaced track and flip-flop hubs, singlespeed and fixed gear mountain bike conversions enlisted longer axles and spacers to update or rearrange narrower hubs, and in some cases this left the wheel with a **REVERSE DISH**, with its steeper spokes scaling the neutral side. But this is fine, because reverse dish is a good thing. As a maintenance issue, dish only concerns us when it appears on the drive side. The disc-specific rims don't strike me as nearly universal enough, though I can appreciate the logic of the various off-center rear rims, in that they minimize the wheel dish.

Prior to beginning the wheel build, it is useful to bear in mind the sequence in which the spokes are installed. Those whose heads end up on the outside of the hub flanges—whose lengths extend down from the insides—are installed first. These will compose one half of the spokes required to build the wheel; the rest will be layered atop them.

Excluding one cross, crossed lacing patterns finds each example of this second half of the spokes tracing over at least one of its peers, before passing underneath the last spoke its trajectory encounters before meeting the rim. *Lacing* the spokes. This will require us to flex the spokes just enough to manage. Stainless spokes, as you will notice, have some spring to them— they can deal with this; they'll straighten right back out again. Three cross, the most common lacing pattern, sees each spoke passing over two and under one. Four cross, the burliest lacing pattern we really like to use, goes over three and under one. You can probably guess the two cross, right? Over one, under one?

Radial lacing fills in as the dedicated iconoclast, among the lacing patterns. Its spokes don't even want to touch each other. They only happen to be sharing the same wheel.

Sexy as it is, radial lacing has always been more controversial. This is a function of the radial laced wheels' curious convention, to a large extent: all of the spoke heads are typically set on the outsides of the hub flanges, and this indulgent streamlining upsets the carefully balanced stress loads associated with more conventional lacing patterns, which alternate with every other spoke head ending up on the inside of the flange. Flanges have been known to break right the hell off, across the spoke holes. This happened to me once, many years ago, with a Mavic hub no less. I heard the flange pop off in the middle of the night. Freaked me the hell out, it did.

Many hub manufacturers, including Surly and Campagnolo, discount radial lacing outright. Mavic discourages all-out radial lacing as well, but they also acknowledge a back door of sorts, referring to the use of alternating spokes to build radial wheels. The spokes simply meet the hub flanges as they would on any old cross-laced wheel, with every other spoke head faced to each side of the flange. If you want to build a radially laced wheel, this would be the way to go.

Does the wheel call for two distinct spoke lengths? Lay the ones perpendicular across the others, to avoid mixing things up.

The cross-lacing patterns may appear complex, at first glance, but any of them may be broken down to four groups of spokes. The wheel's right and left sides are known as the drive and neutral sides, and each features what we call the pull and push spokes. The latter distinction considers the wheel's forward momentum: where half its spokes appear to be pulling it along, the rest may be seen to push it from behind. Pull spokes and push spokes.

We always start with the drive-side pull spokes. It does not necessarily matter where on the hub flange the first of these is deposited, but out on the rim we generally begin with the *second* spoke hole clockwise from the valve. A given rim's spoke holes are often angled to accept spokes coming in from the drive or neutral hub flanges—every other hole may be offset, or angled to either side—and we are meant to follow these cues. We also want to consider the cross-laced spokes' trajectories, which together form greater and lesser triangles as they meet the rim. By tracing our first drive-side pull spoke to the second hole from the valve, we establish a pattern with our lacing which will ultimately leave the greatest possible space above the valve, making it that much easier to put air in your tire.

There once was a rim-drilling pattern that contradicted this logic, by drawing the first drive-side pull spokes to the first hole past the valve. But we see these very rarely, in North America. For that matter, the convention of installing with the pull spokes on the insides may be nothing more than that. Will Mackin at the Hub in Minneapolis discerns no particular reason for this habit, suggesting instead that the pull spokes might even do better on the outside, where they could stand instead of merely lift the weight. For purposes of simplicity, the wheel build here described will be based upon what has become the traditional approach, with the pull spokes falling to the interior of the flanges.

The rest of the drive-side pull spokes occupy every other hole on their flange, before descending to fill every fourth hole on the rim. There should be exactly

First spoke installed to the second hole from the valve: note offset.

enough holes, in each case. For the moment, thread the nipples halfway up.

The first set of spokes is in!

Take hold of the rim with one hand and the hub with the other, and twist the hub clockwise. The spokes all draw into the rim; you can imagine this first set of *pull* spokes trying to drag the circle forward. We will make this very twist permanent shortly, when installing the opposing push spokes, but we need to leave things loose for the moment.

The neutral pull spokes—the first half of the slightly longer ones, in the case of the dished wheels—shadow the pioneering drive-side pull spokes all the way around their circle. Peering straight down from the wheel's neutral side, these fall one hole back on the rim, and half a place back on the hub flange.

As with their drive-side peers, the remaining neutral pull spokes follow the same pattern, entering every other hole on the hub and every fourth on the rim. This done, twist the hub again, such that all the spoke nipples sink down through their rim holes. It is common that a few may get kind of hung up on the edges of their spoke holes, as if they're afraid to make the plunge or something. Shake the hub around a bit; they'll go and do their thing.

I'm in the habit of beginning the push spokes where we left off, over on the neutral side, if only to spare the hassle of switching the two piles around. Push spokes begin inside the flange and exit

The second set of spokes shadows
the first, over on the neutral side.

Building 3-cross: over 2 spokes, bending just enough to go under the third.

Everything works better if the spokes all begin with the same advantages.

The elbows atop new spokes are set to 90-degree angles, but when building a wheel the rim will typically ask those on the outsides to bend just more than this, so we **PRE-TENSION THE SPOKES** before continuing. The push spokes spilling off from the outsides of the hub flanges need to be bent in a bit, in order to shoot down to the rim without bowing out. We merely press them flat with the thumbs, right up by the hub. It is a basic task, but an important one. It helps to ensure that all the spokes begin with a similar tension, which as we shall see becomes very useful in the wheel's continuing development.

outward. Excepting radially laced or one-cross wheels, the push spoke crosses over any pull spokes in its path, save for the very last one it encounters. In the case of our three cross, each spoke goes over two others before ducking beneath the third—in a straight line, over two and under one should point to one open hole in particular. The remainder of neutral push spokes follows the very same pattern.

This should leave us with only one last set, the drive-side push spokes. The hub and rim, by fine coincidence, should each have just as many holes available. As with the previous set, be sure to submerge these beneath the last spokes they meet.

Did that work out? Cool. Go all the way around the wheel and tighten each nipple up to the second from the last of the spoke threads. Twist 'em up right to the top, then *stop*.

We next want to take the wheel up to a **WORKING TENSION**, at which point the spokes are tight enough to impact upon the wheel's overall trueness. The spokes

Pre-tensioning a wheel.

Be sure to oil the bases of each spoke nipple before tensioning.

become suspended within their own web; they're no longer rattling loose between hub and rim. This condition typically arrives after five or ten half-turns on all of the spoke nipples; something on that scale at least. Differences across hub flange and rim dimensions necessarily leave this measurement a little vague, but that's fine. The important thing is to be doing the same for each one, to start things off nice and level. Bear in mind that the nascent wheel's tension is gradually increasing, as you continue to tighten the spokes: they will start to feel incrementally tighter, as you continue. Be sure to account for this, whenever deviating from your pattern. Suppose you're adding an even five half-turns of tension to each spoke, for example—you might opt to add an extra two or three half-turns to an exceptionally loose spoke, as you make the adjustment around the rim. The spokes will all be that much tighter toward the end, so by that point even a vaguely loose spoke might get the same bonus treatment. But this suggestion is presented only as

a bit of short-hand to save some time; it is not necessary to the process. Sticking with the even five half-turns will still get you there; it just might take a bit longer. Spokes too loose at the beginning will be sure to present themselves later on, trust me. You will come across spokes that would seem to require a turn or two more to reach the prevailing tension you are establishing around the wheel, or perhaps a turn or two less; go ahead and level things out. We'd like to finish the pre-tensioning with all the spokes at the same kind of tension, just tight enough to avoid rattling against the rim.

Any big problems in reaching this working tension would suggest that the spokes were of the wrong size, or perhaps laced incorrectly. Lengths far off their marks are occasionally, inadvertently redeemed by switching the parts around—maybe they'll work with that one *other* hub.

Once the pre-tensioning is done and a working tension has been reached, it is time to begin tensioning and truing the wheel. You will be using the very same techniques outlined in the treatment on wheel truing, beginning page 51, but you'll be starting with a blank slate. Our adjustments are more universal, to begin, and generally more ambitious as well. A wheel build first sets out to produce a wheel that is as round and true as possible—a feat made much easier by the softer working tension—and only then provides for the much higher spoke tension that will be required to keep the wheel in good shape. Thus we add our tension incrementally, all the way around, in small numbers of half-turns on the nipples, checking both roundness and lateral true after each round.

The working tension is very generous, in that it's soft enough to allow for easier adjustments—something like wet clay, maybe. Once this status has been achieved, true the wheel to a basic level, keeping in mind that we'll find opportunities to become more precise as we finish our work.

At this early stage in the build, our first concern should be with ironing out any hops or flat spots that may appear in the rim. The final rigidity we're working toward presses any hops and flat spots into

place. The softer working tension affords us a unique opportunity to start things out right.

The truer your wheel becomes, the smaller its corrections should need to be. The spoke nipples' benchmark half-turns slim down to quarters; these eventually become less routine and more exceptional. And it is here, with the round and lateral true accomplished, that you want to get more serious about sorting out the wheel dish. Measuring in half or full turns, make the same adjustments all the way around either side of the wheel, tightening the spokes on one side to pull the rim in that direction, or loosening them to do the opposite. Once the wheel dish has been dialed in, any further tensioning should be applied equitably to both sides of the wheel.

The trials a wheel may face venturing out into the world can be far more challeng-

Stressing the spokes.

ing than the patient negotiation which best characterizes our work in the truing stands, so it's always a good idea to **STRESS THE SPOKES** before saddling up and riding away. First grab the spokes in pairs, all the way around each side of the wheel, squeezing each set together with conviction. You may hear a little creaking, as the parts settle into place. Next press the wheel flat to the floor and bear down upon its rim. You may or may not hear the spokes creak again. Rotate and press the rim a few more times, regardless, all the way around. Flip the wheel and get the other side as well.

This last step is best accomplished in dusty basements and the like, lest the wheel's axle grind ungainly divots from the precious hardwood, but its pursuit also presumes for a judicious use of our strength. Especially old and tired zinc spokes may even snap, beneath excessive stress—better in the patient basement than out in the wild world, needless to say. So don't go being a hard ass; think in terms of a nice firm shove.

This stressing will sometimes highlight the distinctions between drive and neutral tensions, with practice, and perhaps among different rims as well. Where the delicate road rim may *barely* begin to buckle beneath a healthy stress, a burly old Sun Rhyno Lite easily remains stern and impassive. But you get the idea.

Set the wheel back in the stand, once you're done, and check things over. There may be a spot or two that has gone slightly out of true, and this would be the point of the exercise.

The spokes together form a carefully balanced collective. The poorly tensioned member is not able to do its job; it secretly fears everyone else may be let down. The sum of the spokes' tension is crucial; their average needs to be pretty high. I used to habitually stop shy of an effective wheel tension, before I learnt better, and I would further venture that this is a common mistake.

We can get a *general* feel for the spoke tension with the hands. I built this way for years, actually—it becomes obvious if some spokes are far tighter or looser than others, at the least, and these appraisals should ideally be confirmed within the truing process. We like to find ourselves tightening the overly loose spokes and loosening the exceptionally tight ones, in other words, bearing the drive side's higher tensioning in mind.

Deviations from this rhythm first suggest some problem with the rim, if it already has some miles on it, but I would also wonder if I wasn't missing some problem with the spoke tension, like an exceptionally tight spoke somewhere.

A useful **FINAL TENSION** is not easily described with mere words. It is best measured with the tensiometer, as described momentarily, but not necessarily so. See if you can track down some wheel of upstanding reputation, which may be relied upon as a reference—a quality hand-built wheel on a good bike, for example. Squeeze its spokes, and transfer this feeling to the ones you're building with. Or pluck the spokes, if you're musical, tuning the new wheel to the original's resonance.

Where either of these tests are preferred to the open voids of space, the tensiometer speaks with real authority. It balances

Using a tensiometer to evaluate a wheel's final tension.

above the truing stand at the old Hayes St. Freewheel, which recommended a tension of 130 to 135 mm of pressure as a good average, for the 14/15/14 gauge double-butted spokes generally used when building nice wheels. This average worked out well enough.

Building a wheel with used parts can be more challenging. All the parts involved may have enjoyed the opportunity to really let their hair down. The spokes might have picked up a few minor bends; their holes in the hubs may have been carved out by various microns; it is possible the rim has scored a flat spot or two.

a pair of dynamic points across a spoke so that a carefully calibrated spring may translate from the wheel's third dimension to our more legible second. The spoke tension is measured out in millimeters of pressure or kilograms of force, dependent on the tool's manufacturer.

Straight and double-butted spokes become tense at slightly different rates. Park Tool's tensiometer arrives with a handy reference chart, outlining the successive tension levels for different spokes. I once relied upon an old and faded note posted

Any of this may make for greater or lesser problems, balanced against your circumstances. To the extent it becomes possible, you should strive to begin with components that are worthwhile, lest their project waste your precious time. The hub, for example, will either spin well or it will not. An overhaul may improve a given situation. It would be a good thing to know either way.

A rim's merits can be more difficult to appraise. A given example's troubles may fill out the distance between numbingly routine maintenance and just riding along, depending. The lateral dents that sometimes afflict older and softer rims may be carefully resolved with a rag and some pliers, for example, but the corresponding flat spot we normally look to see in such situations will only continue to cause problems. My first inclination is to assume the second-hand rims cannot be usefully redeemed, actually.

More than the hub or the spokes, either of which is more amenable to a straight up- or down-vote, the potentially troubled rim bears the burden of proving itself wholesome. Hold any prospect lightly against a new rim of the same dimensions; you will be able to spot any flat spots or lateral deviations.

Older wheels which were over-tensioned early in life will occasionally sprout tiny cracks around the spoke eyelets. These cannot be redeemed. Check out the braking surfaces as well—the brake pads (or worse, their posts) patiently carve widening channels to the sidewalls, and given enough time they may even break on through to the other side.

There exists an odd tool meant to press out a rim's flat spots, by leveraging against the hub, but I have never seen it used. Any rim so crudely realigned would be left with weak spots at the least; nobody could put a warranty on something like that.

Reusing spokes can be controversial. It really depends who you talk to. Some shops offer the service, under certain optimal conditions—when rebuilding with an identical rim, for example—but the default is to build with new spokes.

I reuse spokes all the time. With this at least, what worked for the rental bikes is fine enough for me. Avoid using damaged spokes—those ravaged by tossed chains in particular—but that's probably obvious enough. The zinc spokes begin with disadvantages of their own; I try not to mess with them either. Quality stainless spokes can recover from anything less than sharp bends, and those as well if they really need to. You just ask the box pliers about this; they'll know what the hell's up.

My biggest concern, when reusing spokes, is what the threads look like. They may need to soak a night or two in the straight citrus solvent, to get rid of any dusty grit. If the nipple does feel all gritty against the threads, I tend to let this stand in for any spoke compound. It is the opposite of scientific acumen, to be sure, but that's how it has to be sometimes.

A wheel built with used parts comes together in the same way, in terms of our truing and tensioning techniques, but the truing process will likely highlight greater discrepancies among the spokes' relative tension, mandating a wider range of adjustments.

S tripping down to a single gear may seem counterintuitive, contingent on the perspective, but the trend has grown legs all around the world. Singlespeed was the best and probably the only option for many of the decrepit old bikes we saw in the RIM. Elsewhere it forms the basis for a whole new subculture. I still think of Surly when the talk turns to singlespeeds, because they were among the first manufacturers to take the idea seriously. The 1 x 1, their original benchmark, emerged as kind of an iconic figure, back home in Minneapolis. We even drafted one into service in our rental fleet. To be fair, it was originally far more popular among the staff than with our clients.

The curious reader might check in with the good folks at *Outcast* magazine, as mentioned in the resources section, for the latest and greatest in singlespeed glory. Any decent SS bike features track-style horizontal dropouts and the clearance to run wider tires. The department stores haven't yet picked up on the scent, so for the moment at least we can say the average SS bike is built relatively well; your time isn't so wasted with disposable crap.

Sometimes 180 mm cranks are used, for the sake of their improved leverage, and the frames are starting to have the extra ground clearance these need to spin. Riser bars, slightly wider than regular flat ATB bars, are favored for similar reasons; you want to take full advantage of the available leverage. Up to a point, perhaps. Steve Post, a singlespeeder I know in Minneapolis, habitually called to bar-end extensions "tree hooks." They end up marooned out there pretty far, on the riser bars; the trees probably do find them more interesting.

Chain adjustment is simple enough, on bikes with horizontal drops—you pull the wheel back in its frame, and you tighten it in place. Note that the SS chains should not be quite as tight as fixed-wheel chains; the mechanism that allows for the coasting needs a little breathing room.

Excluding some of those bikes afflicted with rear suspension, it is always possible to convert a working multispeed bike to singlespeed. Any such project makes the bike quite a bit lighter—the singlespeed's diminished mass is central to

XVII. Singlespeeds

its charm. The mass of derailleurs, shift levers, cables, spare chain and chainrings adds up. (You even get some loot to take to the next bike swap!)

Save one of the derailleur cables, if the frame does not have horizontal dropouts, for reasons shortly to be explored.

Singlespeed conversions don't necessarily represent any magical caterpillar-to-butterfly transformations—a nicer geared bike will make for a nicer singlespeed—and this first becomes evident as we strip things down. The lame riveted cranksets associated with crappy mountain bikes, for example, cannot be asked to surrender their extra rings. These often feature aboard bikes bearing multispeed freewheels, rather than cassette hubs, a further concession which erases our best opportunity for enlightening the rear wheel.

The better your resources, the easier an SS conversion becomes. The **SINGLESPEED CASSETTE HUBS** redistribute the rear axle's width just enough to provide for a dish-less rear wheel. These are not wide enough to accommodate multispeed cassettes, but it is usually possible to borrow individual cogs from them.

In terms of the gearing, it is most natural to simply split the difference, pairing the middle cog in back to the middle ring up front. This gives the average hybrid or mountain bike something in the range of 32/16 for gearing. The 2-to-1 ratio is pretty standard for 26″ SS off-road bikes; city-going versions may do better matching a middling cog to the top chainring.

Many gear cassettes are easily disassembled; others will have never been bolted together in the first place. Whatever you happen to find back there, hang on to the spare cogs—and your extra chain links, for that matter—until you're sure about the gearing.

You will find that the chainring bolts featuring aboard a double or triple crankset are too long to properly embrace a solitary ring—an extra chainring may be kept in place, if need be, but a pack of the shorter track/singlespeed bolts should only cost a few bones.

Whichever chainring you end up using, it is important to finish with a good **CHAINLINE**, with the cog in use *directly* behind the ring, such that the chain does not have to bend to the side in order to engage it. This will probably find your ring mounted on the crank's inside shelf. This in turn will occasionally require a bottom bracket spindle of a different length, with some older setups at least. A good chainline is very much worth the trouble, with the fixes and singlespeeds in particular.

The cassette hubs again become particularly useful, when arranging for a singlespeed chainline. A solitary working cog is mounted to the freehub body, between stacks of the ever-more-ubiquitous cassette spacers, and you simply arrange the elements to your advantage. Press a ruler to the chainring up front; see how this lines up in back. Easy.

We've only one important caveat, in fact: you will want to hang on to the top cog the cassette came with. Use it just under the lockring, such that the serrated faces of each line up and groove, just as they're meant to. This will leave your new singlespeed with *two* cogs out back, technically speaking, but it will also keep the lockring nice and snug.

Things were somewhat more arduous, back in the olden days. It was necessary to rearrange a multispeed freewheel hub's spacers and re-dish the rear wheel, in order to align a BMX-style singlespeed freewheel beneath the warm glow of a healthy chainline. The operation makes the wheel marginally sturdier, by moving the dished spokes and the longer axle segment over to the neutral side, but this approach is more time-consuming.

If you do find yourself with such a project, note that a hub's cones will sometimes be particular to the drive and neutral sides, so really it should only be the drive-side spacers themselves which hop over to the neutral side, to trade places with the thin washer you'd find sandwiched betwixt cone and locknut.

This operation also presents an opportune moment for overhauling the hub, or at least shooting some new grease down into the bearings, but all you really need to actually *do* is roll the axle across its cones toward the neutral side. Be sure to finish with the same volume of axle extending from the end of each locknut.

Re-dishing the wheel is an equally straightforward project. All the spokes on the drive side are loosened by a few turns, while those on the neutral side are tightened by a similar measure. But we just discussed wheel dish, on page 54.

Singlespeeds favor the horizontal frame dropouts, but their program does not necessarily require them. The **CHAIN**

Bike in Atar.

TENSIONER, installed to the derailleur tab, allows frames with vertical drops to participate as well. Surly's Singleator was among the first of these—it set a derailleur pulley under strong spring tension, in such a way that it may be aligned at any particular point beneath the freehub body. Where a singlespeed unencumbered by such kit may follow the chain length formula outlined in the final chapter, those so equipped would do better with that used for the derailleur bikes.

Honestly though, all you'd really need is the bike's original rear derailleur. It must only be convinced to sit still, under the one cog. This may simply be done by dialing the high limit screw all the way in,

right there. The adjustment is then tuned with the barrel adjuster.

There is an even simpler way to do this, alternately. White Industries' eccentric ENO flip/flop hub introduces an offset pivot around the hub axle itself, allowing us to fit either a track cog or a freewheel to a frame with vertical dropouts. Better still, it is available in 126, 130, and 135 mm spacing. The wheel slots into the

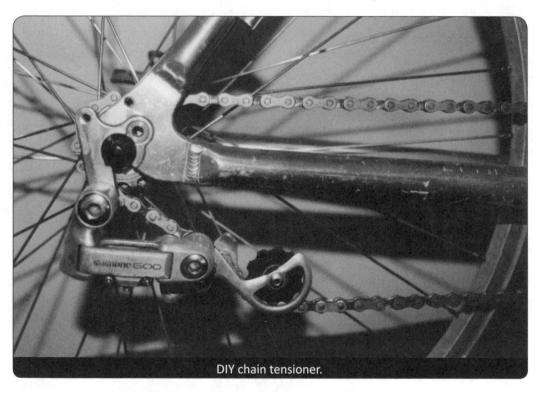
DIY chain tensioner.

if you're really lucky, but odds are you probably can't: limit screws tend to bottom out before their cage arrives upon any useful chainline. Did you save one of the derailleur cables? Shoot it straight into the derailleur, with the cable's head landing where the cable housing would otherwise have ended. Push the cage in, such that its pulleys line up directly beneath the cog, and fix the binder bolt

drops, just like before, but the offset effectively lets it sit a little forward or backward in the frame.

Every singlespeed freewheel I've come across has been installed and removed with the same mighty four-toothed BMX freewheel extractor. In the Park arsenal it is the FR-6.

I f there is a drawback to the bicycle's prevailing design, it is that not everyone finds it to be so comfortable. It follows that if we're serious about getting more bikes on the road, we should be happy that growing numbers of them are recumbents. Everybody knows what I'm talking about, right? The sit-down bikes, with the big comfortable seats and the pedals out in front?

If you've always kind of wondered what those things are about, I must tell you that you're hardly alone. It was in my livelihood to rent recumbent bikes, the first four summers of our millennium, and I can confirm that all kinds of people are just fascinated by them. This was all so many days in the life, at the time; it only became remarkable once I'd moved on. The strange truth is that misunderstandings persist, with regards to the recumbents. *What the hell are those things? Who are those bikes for, anyway?*

My own service to the realm of recumbents ended several years ago, and I can't say that I've really kept an eye on developments therein, but what I learnt while visiting has stayed with me. The 'bents can be very curious machines; their details are not easily forgotten.

The first of their line appeared more than a century ago. The design was already controversial by the 1930s, when the reigning authorities banned the recumbent profile from all serious bicycle racing—its aerodynamic advantages were already becoming clear. Thus denied meaningful opportunities for greatness, the beleaguered 'bents fell into obscurity and took up residence on the margins of things, making way for the endless parade of ungainly and giraffe-like diamond frame bikes that has since risen to the fore. But the secret was already out—recumbents are surely the fastest bikes, and possibly the most comfortable as well, dependent on the perspective.

The recumbent frame, seat, and handlebar are often quite distinct, but the bikes themselves are bound together by the same sorts of components we find elsewhere in the bike world. More so than elsewhere in the bicycle universe, the field of the recumbents is characterized by a nearly relentless innovation. This cuts both ways, but from what I've

XVIII. Recumbents

seen it'd be fair to say that the average has been steadily improving.

The 'bents arrive in a number of distinct formats. Their frames tend to be somewhat longer than those on conventional bikes, necessitating the use of tandem-length control cables, for the rear brakes and derailleur at least. This, in turn, makes cable lubrication more of an issue.

Not every 'bent manufacturer has had the means or the inclination to incorporate finishing details such as cable housing stops, and some have adopted the old department store bike formula, using zip ties to bundle the cables to the frame. This approach handily protects the cables from grit and corrosion, yet the zip ties also compress the housing and add supplementary bends along its length, when tightened enough to stand in as housing stops, and this does no good for the cables' performance. Bike E, once the largest recumbent manufacturer in the United States, was famous for this mistake, among others. Every last Bike E was born with all the cables tightly strangled to their stems; as if the bikes were somehow self-conscious about them.

The solution, as demonstrated by the heroic Rotator Pursuit and its fine friends, is to zip the cables to each other, just tight enough to stay together—they quite naturally form one solitary and graceful arc. Freeing up a Bike E's cables in such a way can only help things along. It got to the point where I would reflexively do this with any Bike Es entering the rental fleet, back when we rented them; it just makes

that much of a difference. Looks cool enough, too; more forthright, less artifice.

Where the upright bikes accommodate us with adjustable seatposts, the recumbents incorporate horizontal solutions. Poor Bike E once again made the wrong call here, providing a seat at fixed angles which merely slid back and forth along their blunt Simple Simon frame beam, dutifully accommodating a range of different-sized riders, but overlooking as well the notion that some of them might develop inclinations to lean *back*. Certain other, more interesting recumbent manufacturers such as Rans, Bacchetta, and Rotator have before and since also considered the seat's angle—which, for longer rides especially, becomes helpful. As with an upright bike, a good fit ends with a very slight bend to the knee, when the legs are at full extension, as measured while pressing all the way back against the seat back.

The alternative is to just leave the seat put and make the pedaling axis move back and forth, and this is actually quite common. The nose cone, known as the **BOOM**, is merely a length of frame tubing fitted with a bottom bracket shell and a short stalk to carry a front derailleur. It is typically attached to the frame with a pair of M6 bolts on the frame's underside.

The advantage to this approach is that it finds all riders sitting in the same relative position, which allows the frame's designers to be more specific with the geometry. The complication comes with the chain, which needs to retain its prescribed length, irrespective of how far the cranks are pulled away from the gears out back. The best solution to this dilemma, as developed by Vision and Inspired Cycle Engineering, among others, incorporates a pair of pulleys: one fits to the frame, while the other hangs from the more transient boom, with the chain slack forming a fluid "Z" between them.

The recumbent canopy shelters number of curious tendencies, but we may at least discern betwixt two established factions, the long wheelbase and short wheelbase bikes (LWB and SWB). The first shoots the front wheel out in front of the feet; the other tucks it in under the knees. **LONG WHEELBASE** recumbents disperse riding vibrations better; longer rides are more comfortable. Their head tubes are set at mellower angles, and this does widen the turning radius, but it also provides for a mellower and more intuitive steering experience. An especially long and slender stem rises from this distant nose; basic steering is accomplished more with leaning.

Vision and Burley both produced LWB bikes with **STEERING LINKAGES**. A steeper head tube is connected to a parallel steering tube, set farther back on the frame. The handling becomes sharper; more like a SWB.

The long frames are usually a bit heavier than the **SHORT WHEELBASE** recumbents. This affords the shorter 'bents some advantages in climbing and accelerating. The head tubes are necessarily steeper, comparing to those we find with the traditional LWB bikes—the long stems would skewer us, otherwise—and the geometry to result lends itself toward city riding. But I've met lots of people who take LWB bikes around town, and plenty more to tour on SWB 'bents. Our acronyms only fulfill the most general of descriptions.

The **COMPACT LONG WHEELBASE** bikes are the grand compromisers among the 'bents. Theirs is the syrup Cannondale and most other upright manufacturers have tried to push, when entering upon the recumbent market. The front wheel is downsized to 16", which allows the fork to be moved back in toward the rider. We're left with an approximation of the more stable LWB handling, in a more convenient SWB-sized package.

Bike E did fairly well with this format, but theirs is not the best example. The company weathered an unfortunate number of warranty

Burley recumbent with steering linkage.

recalls—the failing welds on the seat struts, to take one example, were notorious. Their obsessively timid efforts may have marked the friendly CLWB format in unfortunate ways, but it is still the recumbent profile that most people will find the easiest to get used to.

This gregarious truth is not without consequence, in that the design also takes the easy way out on another of the 'bents' major controversies, the bottom bracket height. The relatively low CLWB pedal height is less foreign, coming in from the world of the upright bikes, and is thereby more adaptable, over those crucial first few minutes' riding time at least. Alas it is also somewhat less efficient. The riding position is almost conspicuously casual; it does not easily provide much for leverage.

Taller bottom brackets are associated with increased speed and performance, among the recumbents. We're better able to push off against the seat back. I've seen some bikes with seriously high-ass bottom brackets—my first home-build, Hellbent, kind of accidentally ended up with one of these—but most are more reasonable. The pedaling axis does not need to be much higher than the seat base, before earning worthy advantages.

A well-fit recumbent leaves the pilot sitting at a comfortable chair's height, with the feet flat upon the ground, and it is fair to say that different 'bent manufacturers have better considered the shorter and taller riders. Your best option is to visit your friendly local recumbent specialist for some test rides.

Where an especially low seat enjoys pressing advantages with the aerodynamics, the taller profiles provide for improved visibility in traffic situations. Most 'bents produced for the American market enjoy relatively high seat heights, while some of the more European-based designs feature distinctly lower seats. It is only a sprinkling of hardened zealots, known as the low racers, that really hug the ground.

Rans has put a lot of energy into expanding their range of semi-recumbent bikes, a category they have usefully renamed as **CRANK FORWARD**. Whichever way they're called, the design rests closer to conventional diamond frame (upright) bikes, but with the frame stretched out like taffy. A distinctly tall head tube rises up front, with the cranks and pedals none too far behind, trailed further back by a wider and low-slung seat. The handlebars are thus made to perch much higher in relation to the seat, and at stoplights the feet easily rest flatly on the ground— a profile, glancing at Rans' website, which seems to have resonated.

The recumbent drivetrains generate questions, together with momentum. The chain is going to be at least twice as long as that driving to an upright bike, and it's likely to run through at least one chain pulley. "Chainline" begins to reference horizontal contours, as well as the lateral alignment—snaking under the seat, or, in the case of SWB bikes, over the fork crown. Those pulleys featuring along the chain's top run need to be considerably stronger than those lifting its lower length, to better accommodate the pedaling force. Cheap pulleys are simple plastic biscuits on metal bushings; better ones mold rubber wheels around sealed bearing cartridges. The pulley should not need teeth, whether mounted above or below; in this context they'd only slow things down and make more noise.

We also have the **MID-DRIVES**, which move the front shifting to the middle of the frame, some distance back from a separate drive crank up in front. The extra-long recumbent chains can make the shifting more sluggish; the mid-drive snaps this problem neatly in half. Though it has featured on a number of production bikes, the technology itself might still be described as somewhat exploratory. None of the reputable component manufacturers has really investigated the idea—the 'bents, comprising mere percentage points of the specialty bicycle market, are too often dismissed as some kind of fringe group. The fanciest mid-drives ever made have thus been cobbled together with whatever was on hand. You lop off the arm on a spider crank, or figure out how to mount some kind of freewheel midway up the bike frame; whatever seems to work.

The mid-drives also introduces a multiplier effect upon the gearing, an attribute which complements the smaller drive wheels we often find with the recumbents. Lacking such, decreases in the drive wheel's size are best answered with commensurate increases in chainring size. The 20″/406 drive wheels found with many recumbents might be matched with chainrings of 42, 52, and 63 teeth to approximate a standard touring crank, for example.

The recumbent **STEMS AND HANDLEBARS** are generally distinct to particular frame designs. Together with the particulars of the stem, the placement of a bike's head tube will tend to favor one style or another. Bacchetta's cool swept-back bars might well look nice anywhere, to take one favorite example, but they really work best with the forward-thinking stems and head tubes we find on their own bikes. Note that some 'bent bars are much lighter than those we'd find on upright bikes—the hands are just sitting there, after all, rather than supporting a portion of our weight—thus they can't be expected to do as well in more demanding settings.

The extra-long LWB stems are sometimes built light enough to allow for a small degree of flex, to further dampen riding vibrations. Your hands only happen to be sitting there, rather than supporting your weight; they get away with it. The SWB stems are expected to be more solid—they are made responsible for more weight and torque, by virtue of their positions—but they are still somewhat dainty, comparing against the stems associated with upright bikes. Many pivot forward, in fact, to allow for easier mounting. These **FLIP-IT STEMS** have become nearly ubiquitous among the SWB bikes.

There should be some provision to move the handlebars up and down, with any of these. SWB stems should also benefit from a set screw, with which to determine the bar's resting position. (LWB flip-its are quite uncommon, but I've put a few together, for purposes of storage and the like.)

The goofy-looking **UNDER-SEAT STEERING** handlebars will more easily catch the eye, but the more pedestrian above-seat handlebars have always been far more popular. ATP Vision's underhanded wingspan dominated the diminutive USS kingdom, in its time: a bow-legged alloy trapeze was fixed to a stem extending from the rear of the fork, and control levers were mounted to its end points. These very features were the first to smash, when the bars ran aground—repair bills tended to be far-reaching. These sorts of USS bars might or might not be safe or comfortable, dependent on whom you speak with. They swing out pretty far, on the corners. This makes for a bumper-height truck lure. I cannot really recommend USS bars for commuting purposes.

Those so inclined may have better luck with **SIDE STICK STEERING**, if only for the sake of this last point. Side stick bars also begin from beneath, but they only shoot out and then straight up, to provide for well-positioned joysticks. The side sticks will not flare out on the turns, however, because they are built around a steering linkage—the handlebar stem is mounted on a second pivot set back from

the fork, with the linkage connecting the two. This allows the axis of motion to be made lengthwise, to better coincide with the bike frame, and this in turn helps you stay out of trouble. The bars still arc out a bit, twirling around their steerer tube, but it's nothing like the mad flailing we might worry about with the USS bars.

Grasping the side sticks, our discussion soon arrives upon the recumbent **TRIKES**, most of which are so equipped. Of the two possible configurations, the forward-thinking tadpole profile makes for better handling and performance. The pilot is installed between the two front wheels, and this approach provides for splendid aerodynamics and a fairly unique vantage on the world.

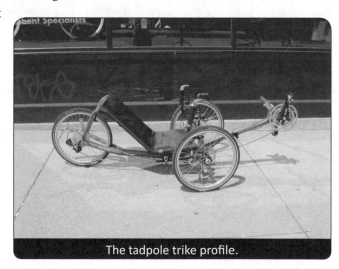
The tadpole trike profile.

The lower and wider a given trike becomes, the more stable it will be. The tadpole design often finds riders seated only inches above the ground—somewhat lower than is the case with most other recumbents. The tadpole's opposite, the utilitarian delta trike, is more usually associated with semi-recumbent designs and cargo platforms.

The trikes, like the regular 'bents, accept just about any bike accessory you'll find use for—fenders, lights, bells, whistles. Every tadpole trike I've worked on has also featured an adjustable boom, to fit different-sized riders. The remarkable Trice has even taken this one step beyond, by incorporating a second boom at the frame's tail end, with which to dial in the seat's angle. But there are so many cool things about the Trice.

I ended up working on the trikes and all the other 'bents quite a bit, while in the employ of a recumbent specialty shop, and it was only after moving on that I realized how odd this experience might have been. I have since met quite a few bike mechanics who prefer to remain resolutely clueless about the 'bents—strange, but true. I suppose it does take all of a minute's figuring to realize how to hoist the

'bents up in the repair stands, and some of their parts are indeed rather unique, and their appearance in some ways could be seen to undermine the successive layers of marketing shrouded around conventional upright bikes. The curious bias against the 'bents is more than a little mystifying, especially within a trade so often cast as independent-minded. If ever friction is encountered while looking into the recumbents, suffice to say that it would be well worth the time to track down a recumbent specialty shop.

I don't ride a recumbent. I may or may not in the future; I have absolutely no idea. Any of it assumes I keep waking up in the morning! Yet I have already met all kinds of people who just love the things, including many who would not or even could not ride conventional diamond-frame bicycles, so of course I'm happy to help as I can. Who would I be to impose an uncomfortable ride on an eager cyclist?

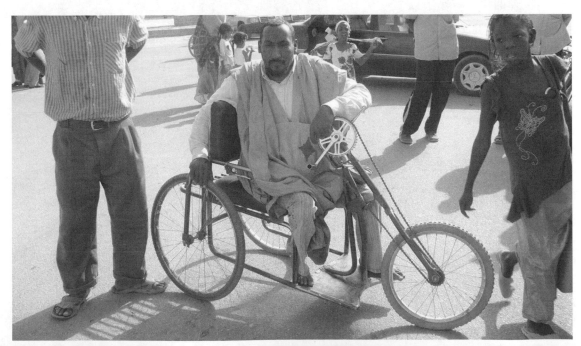

T he **FIXED GEAR** is the original bicycle. A cog is paired to a chain: your legs move faster to accelerate, or slower to do the opposite. There is no coasting; no gears to shift. It is a ripe peach, set against the churning fruit salad.

I want to tell you the fix delivers the best advantages in both speed and control, for this was my first impression, but it's not quite so simple. I find myself riding in city traffic mostly, over distances of a few miles or less, and it is in such circumstances that the fixes really stand out. I've known a few people who've done some touring on fixed gears, but I'd venture most riders would favor geared bikes for such purposes.

Fixed gears have grown enough to become more of a cultural phenomenon, the merits of which sometimes become controversial. Much of the discord is spurious—a self-conscious scrimmage, pitting the white belts and their sympathizers against what might be described as the spandex element, over the best interpretation of cycling tradition or something like that—but bigger questions come into focus as well. Many fixed gear riders see no need for hand brakes, to take the most famous example, which makes various others wonder if they're just fucking nuts.

The brakeless thing traces back to the velodromes, from whence the current fixation originated. The tracks in use at such places are carefully banked wooden ovals, meant to showcase the most elemental form of cycling—hand brakes would only mess up the flow. At some point, it was further discovered that any old bike with horizontal dropouts could become a fixed gear, and out unto the world they went. What once may have been an obscure curiosity has since developed into more of a coherent perspective, one which a number of major bicycle manufacturers have been more than happy to accommodate.

I was told once that the scientific term for all this is "fixed wheel." "Fixed gear," a broader term, can *technically* include singlespeeds as well. Whatever it is we call them, there are plenty of good reasons to ride a fix in the city. The cadence can become something to rely upon—no need

XIX. Fixed Gears

to putz around with any gears, coming up on busy intersections, just move the legs faster or slower, pushing forward or backward—and as mentioned earlier, this formula ends up working out particularly well in the snow. The fixed gear also provides us our closest glimpse of a maintenance-free riding experience.

Downsides? It will scale right the hell up the hills—you'd be made to realize just how much energy is lost, keeping a freewheel under pressure—but fixed gears are much harder to control while descending, lacking a hand brake. I have also heard that the fixes are bad for the knees, but this strikes me as more of a rumor, in that I've never seen the proof: the way the bikes are sometimes used, perhaps, but not the fixed gears in themselves. A good fit is important, as with any other bike in regular use.

In terms of their design, the fixed gears present only one rule: the pedals cannot be allowed to hit the ground, when banking the turns. Think about it: the pedals won't easily stop under speed, and neither will the asphalt be going anywhere—*ka-boom.* Dedicated track bikes set their bottom bracket shells a bit higher off the ground, for just such reasons. Geared bikes come in a little more down to earth, in pursuit of their more generous standover heights, but shorter crank arms may allow for their conversion as well.

The gearing is another important consideration. I learnt this one the hard way originally, beginning with a gear that proved too big for me to comfortably push—it

was my first winter on a fixed gear; the slower cadence had seemed more stable on the snow. For the 700c wheels found on most fixed gears, more reasonable gearing would reflect something like a 3-to-1 ratio, which is to say we'd use a chainring with three times as many teeth as the cog—in that range, anyway. I find 47x17t to be an especially comfortable combination. But gearing is subjective; it really gets down to individual preferences.

A given cog and chainring's particular fortitude may best be described in terms of the **GEAR INCHES**. When everything rolls forward by precisely one rotation, the gear inches describe the distance gained across the floor. Their sum considers the cog, chainring, and wheel sizes, together with the crank arm length. City-going riders may do best between the high sixties and the low seventies, generally speaking.

Dedicated track bikes arrive with a chain, cog and chainring in the wider ⅛″ (BMX) width, but each piece is available in the narrower ³⁄₃₂″ (7/8-speed) as well. The narrower cogs can simplify fixed gear conversions, by accommodating the existing chain and chainring.

The **TRACK COGS** have traditionally threaded on to dedicated **TRACK HUBS**, which in the original recipe incorporate two distinct layers of threads, the upper of which being reverse-threaded to accommodate a matching lockring. The threading dimensions used are indeed the same as those we'd find on the freewheel hubs, so it should be stressed that threaded cogs need to be paired with actual track hubs, because the freewheel hubs will not accept the reverse-threaded track lockrings. Riding fixed inevitably finds us pushing backward on the pedals, if only to control speed, and it is easy to imagine how a hard shove to the rear could start the cog spinning right off a freewheel hub, lacking the reverse-threaded lockring. Then you'd really be screwed, especially if you didn't have a hand brake.

Suzue Junior track hub.

While we're on the topic, bottom bracket lockrings should be ruled out as well. By further coincidence, it happens that the lockrings used with old English, Italian and French bottom bracket sets coincide with the threading found on their respective hubs. This probably made some sense from the production perspective, but that's really all it could be. None of these would be able to fill in for an actual track lockring. Both the BB ring and the cog would be threaded in the same direction, and thus a BB lockring might only make the cog loosen more *slowly*, which would actually be worse. The cog's hard steel threads would grind away at the

hub's softer alloy threads, every last time you pushed the pedals back and forth to stop and go, until it eventually, suddenly gave under pressure—as when dodging a truck, for example. Nor could we find a thread-locking compound strong enough to forestall such an outcome.

We might find ourselves brazing seals across the old freewheels' backsides, once civilization collapses, before thread-locking them aboard regular threaded hubs— such might cautiously approximate a fixed gear, after being pedaled up a big hill a few times—but given the raw luxuries of our passing present, anything less than a proper track hub is conspicuous.

The **TRACK LOCKRINGS** typically provide but a pair of openings, for our lockring tools. It is easy enough to strip these out, so do take your time here. Our professional lockring tools circumvent their tedious old dilemma, by gripping the north and south poles at once, but the single-toothed consumer versions need a finer touch: you need to hold the tool's tooth firmly in place with one hand, while bearing down upon its handle with the other.

Like many of my friends, I began my own fixed gear experiments with the Suzue Junior loose bearing track hubs. They're obscenely cheap; the wholesale cost approximates a night out at the bars. I was always broke, and at first I wasn't sure I would enjoy the ride; the Junior set had seemed like the way to go. The things do work, as we were all to discover, but the cones and dust seals and axles are all crap. Better hubs have since become more available. Most anticipate cogs threaded to the 1.37" x 24tpi English/ISO standard, with lockrings reverse threaded to 1.29" x 24tpi. Note that Campagnolo and Mavic each employ cogs and lockrings threaded to their own distinct standards. You should never feel as if you're forcing any of these parts into position.

Make sure you grease the threads. Some people I met in California use mild thread-locking compounds on the lockring threads, but this does not strike me as a good idea. I grew up riding through the winter road salt, which happily rusts through anything it may touch; helping this along with the thread locker just would not have occurred to me. Whatever it is you find yourself doing, make sure everything is tightened securely.

The cogs beneath are traditionally attached and removed with a chainwhip. Its flail should be ⅛" wide, to better accommodate any wider cogs it may encounter. The more completely the cog is gripped, the more comfortably you can lean on the chainwhip. You might even loop a rubber band around the top of the handle, to better catch the flail's swinging tail.

Christian from Blazing Saddles in Minneapolis once showed me another way to install and remove track cogs, using the very chain that drives the bike. Loosen the wheel and loop the chain around the frame's bottom bracket shell, then double the chain back over itself, such that it wraps twice around the cog,

and spin the wheel to move the cog: forward to install, or backward to remove. The wheel itself becomes a massive lever; you're able to tighten or loosen the cog with less force. (The chainwhip might be augmented with a Jesus bar, alternately, if leverage becomes an issue.)

Sugino, Miche, and White Industries have all introduced proprietary splined track cogs, meant to work with their own special hubs. Whatever; good for them, I guess. The new **BOLT-ON COGS**, by contrast, are fucking brilliant. They ditch the temperamental and easily fouled track hub threading for the widely used ISO 6-bolt pattern found on many disc brake hubs. In so doing, they provide us the freedom to manage outcomes with a tool that fits neatly in the pocket.

A rougher, homemade rendition of the plan, involving a cassette cog and a drill, was described by Jason Millington on the off-road fixed gear site 63xc.com back in 2003. It was later discovered that a Shimano Deore XT M756 front hub might be reborn as a regular 120 mm track hub—the M756 in particular features an M10 axle, narrowed to 9 mm at the ends to fit the intended front dropouts, as well as the standard six-bolt pattern Shimano's disc hubs began with—swap out for a longer solid axle, add 20 mm worth of spacers and we end up with an odd new track hub. Something like a perfect storm.

LeVel Components may have produced the first 120 mm track hub meant for use with the bolt-on cogs; Vallie Components has more recently introduced a sturdily built example as well. Phil Wood makes one now, their ISO Track Hub, and we couldn't ask for a better endorsement than that. One might enlist a frame with horizontal drops spaced to 135 mm, alternately, as when moving a singlespeed mountain bike to fixed gear. Plenty of 135 mm disc brake hubs kicking around, these days.

The tensioned master links supplied with SRAM and ConneX chains are awesome for derailleur-equipped bikes, comparing against the lame Shimano or Campagnolo master pins, but they're not meant for use with the fixed gears. Neither manufacturer provides such connectors with their track-specific chains, actually. The sudden changes in momentum associated with the fixed chains may loosen master links, especially if the chain is already loose.

Loose chains really suck, on the fixed gears. They are always threatening to

fall off; their cogs and rings wear more quickly; the slop that results punctuates your decisions with an unfortunate hesi-

A Surly chain tensioner doing its thing on bike #5.

tance. The track chain is tensioned when you can't get more than an inch of play, pushing up and down upon its length. We accomplish this by walking the hub backward in the dropouts. Begin with the neutral side locknut tightened, and the drive-side locknut loose. Grab a handful of spokes up behind the crank, and pull the front of the wheel toward the drive-side chainstay—the drive-side axle end should edge back into its dropout. Tighten the drive-side locknut down in this new position, as you're holding the wheel taut. This done, loosen the neutral locknut and re-center the wheel within the frame: the chain should have a higher tension.

You might find yourself repeating these two steps a couple times, before arriving upon a good chain tension. The BMX chain tensioners are often helpful in preserving a chain's tension.

A track chain needs to be just long enough. You should not be able to pull the axle all the way back to the end of the dropouts, when the chain is mounted. Were this the case, you would need to remove a link. The axle can only be pulled back to some midpoint along the dropouts' horizon, if things are as we like them to be. Go ahead and tighten down the neutral side axle nut, at this particular point.

I have not yet managed to wear out a fixed drivetrain, but it is at least theoretically possible. Travis tells me the chain's rollers start breaking away, eventually. Grandpa's chain would sooner lose a link, once the wear stretches it all the way back in the drops, but by then it'd probably be best to replace the whole drivetrain. A new chain applied to a toasted old cog grinds and makes lots of noise, until the weary cog at last convinces it to shut the hell up, but by then the eager new chain would be just as burnt and cynical itself.

We expect the bona fide track chainrings to be nice and round, but many of those arriving from multi-speed systems are slightly ovalized instead—the chain's tension is on-again, off-again. This condition is only immediately obvious with gems like Shimano's old Biopace chainrings. or the contemporary Sugino Ovaltech rings, each of which was far less than round. The more common sloppy grins are less easily discerned—you'd need to actually set things up on the bike, to get a sense of the situation.

The vast majority of multispeed chainrings can be made to work fine,

with the fixes. You only need to position them correctly upon their spiders. There tends to be a small degree of play *across* the crank's bolt shelves, when first a chainring is mounted, and this minor oversight may be turned to our advantage. Loosen the chainring bolts to finger-tight. See to it that the chain is properly tensioned, and spin the crank through a few rotations: the chainring will trend toward the most central location. And that's it; bolt the ring down while everything is perfect.

Dedicated track frames are spaced to 120 mm. The hubs can be expanded to meet 130 or 135 mm frames, given a longer axle and some spacers—these last would end up over on the neutral side—but it's more common these days that we would use a **FLIP-FLOP HUB** instead. These can be found in all three common rear hub spacings; the side opposite may feature threading for either a singlespeed BMX freewheel or another track cog. Your gearing choices would need to be of at least roughly similar sizes—within a couple teeth, at least—in order to use the same length of chain.

The classical approach to controlling speed on a fix merely pushes backward on the pedals, to counter the wheels' momentum. This artful exercise may take a second to work, so people sometimes skid as well. As this relates to a crowded urban environment, people talk about threading the needle, or finding the hole, or going for the opening—the actual distances required to stop a skidding bike can be significant.

Any brake mounted to the front wheel is spared a good deal of the ground fire the tail gunners may face, by virtue of its strategic position, and this supreme leisure allows the brake pads to wear more slowly. Front brake cables are also quite a bit shorter, comparing with the others, and thereby subsist with only a minimum of lubrication. Of their pair, physics awards the front brake with something like 80 percent of the stopping power. The sum of these characteristics does lend itself toward simple brakelessness.

That said, it becomes counterintuitive to rely upon a hand brake as the principal means of controlling a fix. Its use gets to be entirely superfluous, in normal conditions. The lever becomes so much lawn furniture, perched atop the handlebars— it might be obligingly pulled out to accommodate serious downhills, or panic stops. All things being equal, we can generally get what we need with the legs, but it is always nice to have a backup plan.

The smaller your gearing choice, the easier it is to stop. You might even learn to skid. This erases the tires, just as it did when we were young, but think about that—skidding a fast bike to a stop! It's as if the butterfly has sprouted wheels. If only we could slip some flint in the tires, to make for a proper comet-tail effect . . . What was it we were talking about?

The easiest way to learn is to start on the snow. For our purposes here, it's best to find a reasonably fresh patch, something compacted but not quite solid. The traction isn't nearly what the outside world

would like it to be, but this very consideration bends handily to our own nefarious purposes—we're more easily able to lock up the knees, at level points in the pedals' rotation, and this is basically all it takes.

You skid just fine on the ice, needless to say, but the odds are good it'll be ass-first. That's what the snow is for; it gives us just enough of a grip on reality. You'd want to enlist straps or toe clips or clipless pedals, as soon as the snow melts, because the abrupt appearance of improved traction forces our return to the boring old rules of physics. The dry pavement seizes upon the passing tire; the locked knees buckle and threaten to give way.

I run a hand brake on my fixed gear, and I prefer the leisure afforded by regular old rat-trap pedals, so I don't skid so much myself. In the summer, at least. The fit just feels good—my feet are left free to scoot around; they gravitate toward the best positions. If this footloose abandon presumes healthy intuition, the professional frame fitting session actually does the math instead. But a good fitting's sublime precision really anticipates the appearance of shift levers and their kit; the jackrabbit pulse of urban fixed gearing may well stretch and fray its careful answers. Whatever it is you do, it's best to find the pedaling axis spinning beneath the balls of the feet—raising the saddle effectively pitches it toward the toes, and the reverse is also true.

The cheap way to get into fixing is to convert an old road bike. Anything with horizontal dropouts may be up for the task, actually—I'm thinking of my friend Jordan's first fix, a born loser of a decrepit old mountain bike whose peeling decals identified it simply as the Mud Slugger. It was one of the earlier fixed wheel conversions to roll out of our old spot down at Calhoun Rentals. Later projects became somewhat more refined. Our friend Xara's bike Detail, once just another dusty and anonymous frameset from the old Bauer warehouse, springs easily to mind. None of these were necessarily meant to be track bikes—we can always tell, spying the derailleur tabs—so all of them needed shorter 165 or 170 mm cranks, to avoid catching a pedal on the turns.

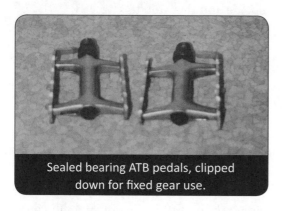

Sealed bearing ATB pedals, clipped down for fixed gear use.

Fixed gear pedals need to be narrower as well, for the same reason, but the dedicated track pedals' tranquil velodrome profiles aren't always ideal in adverse weather conditions. Their cages have no teeth; our wary soles too easily slide off into the void. But many of the clipless pedals are short enough already, and the aluminum cages on better rat-trap mountain bike pedals are trimmed down easily enough with tin snips. Cut their ends flush with the axle's end, and file down the ensuing dog-ears, lest you pop your shins.

The rental shop was a project of Calhoun Cycle, recumbent and folding bike specialists, where flourishes a fair appreciation for advancements in the cycling arts. The owner Luke had arranged a decent arsenal of metalworking equipment in the basement, for just such purposes, and it was downstairs that I got curious about building a fixed gear recumbent. He'd shown me a picture of a fixed long wheelbase from the 1960s somewhere, once I'd ventured my theory, so there even appeared to be a precedent.

I was staying at my friend Christina's house at the time, and her boyfriend Gino had gathered a respectable pile of abandoned bicycles out back in the yard. This might have been where I found an old 24″ chromed BMX frame, which seemed an ideal candidate for my newest ambitions. (BMX is a very traditional platform for the homemade recumbent bikes.) A boom tube was brazed to its snout, once the chrome had been scuffed away, and Hellbent was born. The name honored Christina's wonderful black cat, Hellbat.

I hadn't asked nearly enough questions, prior to beginning my experiments. My principle design prerogative—to the extent that I had any—had been to avoid putzing around with any chain pulleys. And I did get the pure and direct chainline, but the chain still had to leap over the fork crown, and this left the pedals jabbing angrily toward the sky, with the seat nestled in the frame's valley far below. The riding position was left untenable: too much accordion, not enough flute.

The War Bike meant to improve on this. Its own snout extended a good foot forward off the bottom bracket shell, ending in a thick square of sturdy metal, to make for a battering ram. The whole thing was pretty well overbuilt, actually. It did fare better—I rode all the way to Saint Paul and back, at least once—but this fortune only revealed a more damning contradiction. The whole body presses the back wheel to the ground, on a recumbent: this means, in the case of fixed gears, that one cannot simply hoist up the tail and kick a pedal into starting position. It is a small point, and I might have learnt my way better with time, but I found myself tipping over to the side in the interim. This got to be a drag, in traffic especially.

The War Bike was propped menacingly in a corner somewhere, to glare angrily at passers-by so long as it might be useful. I was left with my 20″ fixed gear wheel set, which had begun to seem quite interesting in its own right: the smaller circles are spun and stopped quite a bit easier. This very tendency becomes a famous liability for the small-wheeled folding bikes—they spend their momentum all too easily—but the fixed wheel's centrifuge sooner approximates a metronome. And where all things are equal, the small wheels are stronger and lighter as well.

I went and found another dejected old BMX frame buried within Gino's rusted cornucopia out back, and eventually chanced upon methods to raise the saddle and handlebars to more useful

elevations. Luke had rafters full of cromoly tubing at the shop; a couple pieces happened to fit. And so the airship rose yet again, at which point it became clear the rusty old chassis I'd begun with had been scrapped for good reasons. Luckily my old friend Chuck Cowan was cool enough to provide me with a better BMX frame, upon realizing my dilemma, and the Street Cleaner was born.

This new beast was *fast*. Lovely acceleration; nice handling; the traffic profile of a hungry door mouse. And so a dedicated 20″ fixed frame, bike #3, was pieced together in the basement that fall. The assembly was concluded just in time for winter, whereby I discovered the 20″ front wheel was not really the thing for pushing the snow around; not with the handlebars way up in the air at least. It was like shoveling the sidewalk with a soup spoon.

So I threw together another quick experiment, piecing together tubes from three dead frames—the Yokota, Gitane, and Mongoose decals were all left visible—and this time matched a 700c road front wheel to the 20″ rear fixed wheel. It soon was clear that Patches here was finally what I'd been looking for! But I'd been in quite a hurry, given all the snow, and so wasn't too surprised when the rushed construction failed some weeks later.

The tail section was clipped from another dead road frame, once Patches had been dispatched, and reconfigured to accept a 20″ rear wheel. Unfortunately, the guesswork comprising bike #4's attempts toward frame geometry might have been more carefully considered—the frame's original seatstays, once re-aligned, ended up reaching about mid-points on the original seat tube, and this seemed to generate a reliable creaking, every last time I hit a bump. The ride was also pretty damned harsh. But this is one reason the small-wheeled folding bikes avoid full-sized frame triangles in their designs; their combination pro-vides for a quite literal translation of the pavement below.

Bike #5 might well have been pulled from some grand magic hat, given its willingness to learn from the past. I'd rescued the bat-tered Cannondale Pepperoni moun-tain fork from Patches' tomb, largely for aesthet-ic reasons, but also for its fender holes: they could fit a road caliper brake, which allowed me

to run a 700c road wheel up front. This was a more whimsical decision, to start. The outsized Pepperoni's grip around the wispy thin road wheel suggested boastful cartoon characters more than anything.

The point of the exercise was finally made clear: where the larger front wheel handled and held speed well enough, its smaller companion was positively ideal for urban fixed gearing. I was seated atop

a reasonably flexible pillar, leaning back nearly above the rear wheel, so the trac-tion would be good as well. And at last—that next summer, at least—I had myself a proper *art school* bike. After the hair-style; long in front, short in back?

I did fit the Pepperoni fork with its prop-er knobby mountain bike wheel, come the winter following. My travels began on Oakland Avenue in Minneapolis, at the time, which was not plowed as thor-oughly as uptown or downtown, so this was the natu-ral choice to take. The wheel size also coincided with the fork's original brake bosses, for-tunately enough, allowing its tired old caliper brake to be replaced with a righteous Deore LX cantilever set. Which was cool, because this was about the time I started riding downtown again. Old chum Brad Emery needed someone to cover his shift, on the days he went hunting, and it happened I was looking for employment.

I found myself switching back to a thin-tired fixed gear at some point, but only because the knobby tire was way too slow for courier work. The art school bike did just fine, in every other respect—odd lit-tle beast, but a fast one.

A to B Magazine
40 Manor Road
Dorchester
DT1 2AX, UK
http://www.atob.org.uk

Alliance for Biking and Walking
PO Box 65150
Washington, DC 20035 USA
http://www.peoplepoweredmovement.org

Bicycling Empowerment Network
PO Box 31561
Tokai, 7966
Cape Town, South Africa
http://www.benbikes.org.za

Bicycle Inter-Community Action and Salvage
Bicycle Education and Recycling Center
P.O. Box 1811
Tucson, AZ 85702 USA
http://www.bicas.org

Bicycle Retailer and Industry News
http://bicycleretailer.com

Bicycle Times Magazine
3483 Saxonburg Blvd.
Pittsburgh, PA 15238 USA

BicycleSafe
How to not get hit by cars.
http://www.bicyclesafe.com

Bike! Bike!
Annual Gathering of Community Projects
http://www.bikebike.org

Bikes Belong
Coalition sponsored by the U.S. bicycle industry with the
goal of putting more people on bicycles more often.
http://www.bikesbelong.org

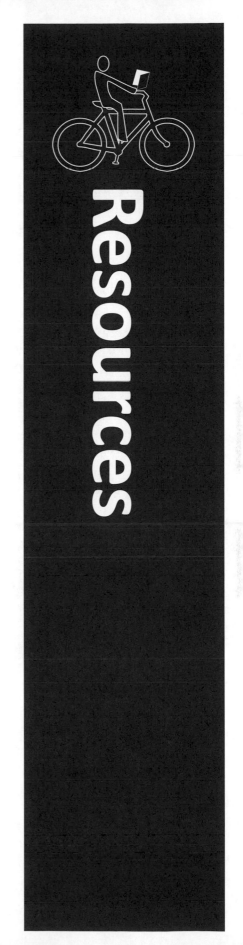

Black Women Bike
http://blackwomenbikedc.tumblr.com/

Busted Carbon
Photos of broken carbon fiber bicycle components.
http://www.bustedcarbon.com

Car Busters Magazine
http://carbusters.org

Cars-R-Coffins
3346 Lyndale Avenue South
Minneapolis, MN 55408 USA
http://www.carsrcoffins.com

Copenhagenize.com
http://www.copenhagenize.com

Hubstripping.com
All you need to know about the planetary gears.
hubstripping.wordpress.com

International Federation of Bike Messenger Associations
http://messengers.org

Momentum Magazine
Suite #214 - 425 Carrall Street
Vancouver, BC
V6B 6E3, Canada
http://momentummag.com

The National Brotherhood of Cyclists, Inc.
PO Box 280931
Nashville, TN 37228-0931
http://thenbc.org

The Outcast 'Zine
http://yesweareontheweb.com

Shockspital Midtown Bike Center
2834 10th Avenue South
Minneapolis, MN 55407
http://shockspital.com

The Stolen Bike Finder
https://racklove.com/stolen-bike-finder/

Surface Transportation Policy Project
1707 L St., NW, Suite 1050
Washington, DC 20036 USA
http://www.transact.org

Urban Velo
PO Box 9040
Pittsburgh, PA 15224 USA
http://urbanvelo.org

Velo Vision Magazine
York Environmental Centre
St. Nicholas Fields
Bull Lane, York
YO10 3EN UK
http://www.velovision.co.uk

Victoria Transport Policy Institute
1250 Rudlin Street
Victoria, BC
V8V 3R7 Canada
http://vtpi.org

World Bicycle Relief
1333 N. Kingsbury, 4th Floor
Chicago, IL 60642 USA
http://www.worldbicyclerelief.org

Worldbike
1078 60th Street
Emeryville, CA 94608 USA
http://worldbike.org

Index

The Guest Book, Minneapolis, 2003.

Allen wrenches 5–6

belt drive 142
bicycle boxes 175–177
bicycle packaging 176–177
bicycle repair stand 3–4
bike sling 4
bottom brackets 149, 157–164
  ball-and-cup sets 162–163
  BB30 161–162
  external 150, 162
  one-piece (American) 158
  sealed-cartridge 158–162, 194
  splined 150, 156
  three-piece 162–164
brakes
  brake bosses 92–93, 98–99
  cantilever 86, 92–97, 100
    automatic toe-in 96
    quick-release 95
    straddle assemblies 94–95
    straddle cables 93
  centerpull 90–91
  disc 101–103
    centerlock interface 101
  hydraulic 92, 102, 105–107
  pads 84–87, 89, 91, 95–97, 98, 99, 101–102
    toe-in 85, 87, 97
  rubbing 189
  sanding rims 84

sidepull 87–90, 189
  brake reach 88
  dual pivot 88, 90, 189
  recessed brake nuts 89
soup spoons 105
squeaking 84–86, 87, 98, 102, 106
U brakes 91, 92
V brakes (linear pull) 85, 86–87, 88,
    98–99, 100
  brake noodles 99

cable cutters 7, 74, 106
cables 71–81
  barrel adjusters 73–74, 75, 190–191
  binder bolts 74, 75, 80
  cable donkeys 79–80
  derailleur 71, 72, 75, 80–81
  ferrules 74
  housing 72–73, 74, 75–81
  housing length 78–79
  housing stops 76–77
  internally routed 77–78
  mountain brake 73
  reuse 74, 75, 81
  road brake 72–73
ceramic bearings 172
chain hook 138
chains 134–142
  chainline 19, 156, 220–221, 226
  Hyperglide chain pins 135
  installing and removing 135–136
  length 140–141
  master links 135
  replacement 136, 139–140
  tight links 139
chain tensioner 221, 235
chain tool 12, 135–136, 138–139, 142
chain whip 12
cone wrenches 9, 89

crank backer 11
crank extractor 10, 155–156
cranks 148–157
  bent cranks 157
  bolt circle diameter 150, 151
  chainring bolts 152–154, 220, 236
  chainrings 151–152
  compact road 119, 151
  cottered 148–149
  crank bolts 154–155
  crank bolts, self-extracting 155
  crank profile 150, 156
  one-piece 148
  removal 153, 154–155
  spider 151
  spiderless 152
  three-piece 149, 150–151
  two-piece 150, 155
crown race hammer 33, 35

derailleurs 110–123
  braze-on front 119, 121
  B-tension screw 116–117
  friction 110–115
  indexing 115–123
  indexing, cable adjustments 122–123
  indexing, front 118–122
  indexing, rear 116–118
  limit screws 111–114
  pulleys 111, 114, 117–118
drivetrains
  cleaning 136–137
dropouts
  BMX 19
  horizontal 19
  sliding 19
  track 19
  vertical 19

extraction tools 11

fenders 182–183
fixed gear 231–240
  cogs 232
    bolt-on 234–235
  gear inches 232
  hubs 232
    flip-flop 236
    lockrings 233
forks 23–25
  rake 24
  steerer tubes 25
fourth hand tools 7–8, 52, 95, 99, 125
frame 17–25
  alignment 21
  asymmetric head tube 28
  creaks 21–23
  replaceable derailleur hangers 21
  tubing decals 17

gearing, planetary 131–134
  adjustment sleeve 132–133
  Clickbox 133
  Dual Drive 133–134
grease gun 15, 32, 172

handlebars 63–68
  bar-end extensions 66
  brake lever diameters 63
  clamp diameter 63
  Grip Shift levers 64
  grip tape 67
  mountain 64–66
  road 67–68
headset 27–35
  crown race 33

integrated 27
internal 27–28
overhaul 32–35
replacement 27–28, 34
stack height 25
threaded 28–30
threadless 30–32
  adjusting cap 32
  centering sleeve 34
  preload bolt 31
  star nut 31
headset press 34, 162
headset wrenches 9
hubs 165–174
  adjustment 172–174
  cassette 169–171
    freehub body 169–171
    singlespeed 220
  freewheels 167–169
  overhauls 171–174
  spacing 166

Jesus bar 25, 146, 195–198, 234

lockring tool 8, 171, 197
locks 200–201

metric caliper 13
multi-tools 13

nylock nuts 16

offset brake wrenches 9
oil dropper 14

pedals 142–148
  clipless 147–148
  installation 144–145
  rat-traps 146
  removal 145–146
  toe clips 146–147
pedal wrench 9, 144–145

Quik Stik 12, 44

recumbents 223–229
  boom 224
  compact long wheelbase 225
  crank forward (semi-recumbent) 226
  long wheelbase 225
  mid-drives 227
  short wheelbase 225
  steering linkage 225
  stems and handlebars 227–229
    flip-it stems 227
    side stick steering 228
    under-seat steering 228
  trikes 228–229
rust 195
  screws 198

seatposts 57–61
  Laprade 60–61
  maximum height line 59–60
  microadjust 60–61
  shims 61
  sizes 58–59
  straight 60
  suspension 61
shift levers 123–131
  bar-end shifters 124, 126–127
  dual control levers (brifters) 126
  trim 123
  twist shifters (Grip Shift) 127–128
spanners 8
spare fingers 8
spokes, broken 50–51
spoke wrenches 12, 51
stems 37–42
  adjustable 41–42
  quill 39
    expander bolt 39
  threadless 40
  top-loading 38

tensiometer 12, 216
tire boot 186
tire levers 43
tires 47–48
  bead diameter 47
  flat 185–188
  sew-up 187
  size 47
  wear 48
    dry-rot 48
torque wrench 13

wheels 43–55
  building 203–217
    final tension 215
    pre-tensioning spokes 212–213
    reverse dish 208
    spoke lacing pattern 207
    spoke length formula 207
    stressing spokes 214–215
    wheel dish 207
    working tension 212
  composite 55
  inner tubes 43–45
    slime sealant 46
  pie plates 49
  quick-release skewers 201–202
  rim strips 45–46
  rim tape 46
  tires 47
    tubeless 45
  truing 48–55
    broken spokes 50
    final tension 54
    wheel dish 54
wheel truing stand 5

Sam Tracy began working as a bike mechanic in 1993, when he cut his teeth at Wheel and Sprocket in Milwaukee. After receiving a BA in political science from the University of Wisconsin, he returned to Minneapolis, where he found work as a bicycle messenger. In 1998 he moved to Arcata, CA, for a position as Managing Editor of the *Auto-Free Times*, a nonprofit quarterly. His first bicycle repair manual, *How to Rock and Roll: A City Rider's Repair Manual*, written during this period, was published by Black Kettle Graphics in 2001.

In 2000 Tracy was hired to manage Calhoun Rentals in Minneapolis, a position he held for four years. Among other tasks he was responsible for maintaining a 70-bike rental fleet, a complex and challenging mission which demanded a commitment to safe and effective low-cost repair techniques. Over the winters he worked as a mechanic at Calhoun Cycles, a recumbent bicycle specialty shop, where he became immersed in the lively and experimental DIY frame-building culture for which the 'bent enthusiasts are known.

After signing on with Speck Press to write *Bicycle! A Repair & Maintenance Manifesto* in 2003, Tracy moved to the cycling mecca of San Francisco, where he worked to further refine his repair skills at the Freewheel, a high-end commuter and road bike shop. He picked up numerous key techniques from the seasoned mechanics that really kept the place going.

After releasing *Bicycle!* in 2006, Speck Press published Tracy's third book, *Roadside Bicycle Repair: A Pocket Manifesto* in 2008. Returning to the non-profit sphere, Tracy spent two years as Office Manager for HomeStart, a non-profit dedicated to ending homelessness in the Boston area. In 2008 he and his wife left to serve with the Peace Corps in the Islamic Republic of Mauritania, which among other things provided exposure to a whole new level of resourcefulness in bicycle repair.

Most recently, in 2010 he worked as a mechanic at the Hub Bicycle Co-op, the Twin Cities' only cooperatively owned bike shop. Tracy's first book is out of print, and his last two are now in second editions. He is currently working on a novel. He and his wife live in Riga, Latvia, where she is posted as a U.S. diplomat.

About PM Press

politics • culture • art • fiction • music • film

PM Press was founded at the end of 2007 by a small collection of folks with decades of publishing, media, and organizing experience. PM Press co-conspirators have published and distributed hundreds of books, pamphlets, CDs, and DVDs. Members of PM have founded enduring book fairs, spearheaded victorious tenant organizing campaigns, and worked closely with bookstores, academic conferences, and even rock bands to deliver political and challenging ideas to all walks of life. We're old enough to know what we're doing and young enough to know what's at stake.

We seek to create radical and stimulating fiction and nonfiction books, pamphlets, t-shirts, visual and audio materials to entertain, educate, and inspire you. We aim to distribute these through every available channel with every available technology, whether that means you are seeing anarchist classics at our bookfair stalls; reading our latest vegan cookbook at the café; downloading geeky fiction e-books; or digging new music and timely videos from our website.

Contact us for direct ordering and questions about all PM Press releases, as well as manuscript submissions, review copy requests, foreign rights sales, author interviews, to book an author for an event, and to have PM Press attend your bookfair:

PM Press • PO Box 23912 • Oakland, CA 94623
510-658-3906 • info@pmpress.org

Buy books and stay on top of what we are doing at:

www.pmpress.org

FOPM

MONTHLY SUBSCRIPTION PROGRAM

These are indisputably momentous times—the financial system is melting down globally and the Empire is stumbling. Now more than ever there is a vital need for radical ideas.

In the five years since its founding—and on a mere shoestring—PM Press has risen to the formidable challenge of publishing and distributing knowledge and entertainment for the struggles ahead. With over 200 releases to date, we have published an impressive and stimulating array of literature, art, music, politics, and culture. Using every available medium, we've succeeded in connecting those hungry for ideas and information to those putting them into practice.

Friends of PM allows you to directly help impact, amplify, and revitalize the discourse and actions of radical writers, filmmakers, and artists. It provides us with a stable foundation from which we can build upon our early successes and provides a much-needed subsidy for the materials that can't necessarily pay their own way. You can help make that happen—and receive every new title automatically delivered to your door once a month—by joining as a Friend of PM Press. And, we'll throw in a free T-Shirt when you sign up.

Here are your options:

- $25 a month: Get all books and pamphlets plus 50% discount on all webstore purchases
- $40 a month: Get all PM Press releases (including CDs and DVDs) plus 50% discount on all webstore purchases
- $100 a month: Superstar—Everything plus PM merchandise, free downloads, and 50% discount on all webstore purchases

For those who can't afford $25 or more a month, we're introducing *Sustainer Rates* at $15, $10 and $5. Sustainers get a free PM Press t-shirt and a 50% discount on all purchases from our website.

Your Visa or Mastercard will be billed once a month, until you tell us to stop. Or until our efforts succeed in bringing the revolution around. Or the financial meltdown of Capital makes plastic redundant. Whichever comes first.